BEST OF
BAKING

Annette Wolter
Christian Teubner

HPBooks

Publisher: Helen Fisher; Editor: Veronica Durie
Art Director: Don Burton; Book Assembly: Ken Heiden
Typography: Cindy Coatsworth, Joanne Nociti, Kris Spitler
Photography: Christian Teubner.

Published by H.P. Books, P.O. Box 5367, Tucson, AZ 85703
602/888-2150
ISBN 0-89586-071-6   ISBN 0-89586-041-4 (cloth)
Library of Congress Catalog Card No. 80-81593
©1980 Fisher Publishing, Inc. Printed in U.S.A.

First published under the title
Back vergnügen wie noch nie
by Gräfe und Unzer GmbH, München, 1978

English edition published by
The Hamlyn Publishing Group Limited, 1979

Contents

ANOTHER BEST-SELLING COOKERY VOLUME FROM
HPBOOKS

Best of Baking introduces over 330 of the best ever baking recipes. Each recipe is illustrated with a beautiful color photograph so you can see how the finished cake, pastry or cookie will look. This is an encouragement and a tremendous time-saver as you can appreciate at a glance all the finer details of decoration and garnish.

While choosing recipes for this book, the following question came up: when do people bake and which recipes do they enjoy making most? The best-known recipes have therefore been selected from the widest range available: old-time favorites, specialty recipes, both traditional and modern, some for everyday and some for more special occasions. Family celebrations, parties and entertaining have been covered, giving you many new and unusual ideas. There is a section on cakes and gâteaux made with fruit, and for the health-conscious the chapter on whole-wheat baking will prove more than satisfying. If you think a cake or gâteau looks too complicated, do not lose heart; start with the simpler recipes, progressing until you have successfully made even the most elaborate ones—do not set an upper limit for yourself. Practice will make you experienced and more confident, and help you develop different ideas. For years to come you will be baking all sorts of delights—cakes, gâteaux, tartlets, pastries, cookies and flans—and you will be surprised how quickly you develop your own ideas and variations.

The section at the beginning of this book on the Art of Baking gives you valuable information on baking techniques and methods. It takes you through the basic recipes in clear and simple stages so you can master these with confidence before moving on to more elaborate cakes and gâteaux. Explanations of some of the unusual ingredients can be found in the Glossary of Baking Ingredients. Finally there is a section called Baking for the Freezer and a comprehensive freezing table. Use this valuable information when you want to bake extra quantities and freeze the surplus.

We wish you much success in baking and pleasure in discovering your own favorite recipes. We hope that you will enjoy baking, as well as the fruits of your labor, as never before.

Annette Wolter and Christian Teubner

Useful Facts & Figures
Notes on Metrication & Sizes

Measurements for ingredients used in the recipes in this book are given in both United States Customary and metric measures. This poses a problem because no standard for conversion has yet been established. To maintain the exact proportions and ensure successful results with these recipes, it is especially important that you follow *either* the United States Customary or metric measures, *never* both.

Spoon measures—All spoon measures given in this book are level unless otherwise stated.

Can and package sizes—At present, cans and packages are marked with the exact metric equivalent of the avoirdupois weight of the contents, so we have followed this practice when giving can and package sizes.

Yield—Many of the recipes in this book make very generous quantities. Some cooks will find it useful to make a large amount and then freeze at least part of it.

Baking Hints

● Baking is an exact art! For the best results measure all necessary ingredients exactly. Unless specified otherwise, the recipes in this book have been tested using a medium-size egg. If you use smaller or larger eggs you may need to adjust the recipe accordingly.

● If the recipe indicates dough should be kneaded, rolled or worked on a floured surface, sprinkle the surface with only a very little flour. Dough absorbs flour readily and too much would alter the recipe proportions.

● When grated lemon or orange peel is called for, thoroughly wash the fruit before grating.

● If the pan or baking sheet is to be greased, sprinkled with breadcrumbs or flour, or lined with waxed paper, do this first. Then when the mixture is ready there will be no delay before baking. This is especially important with cakes.

● Remember always to preheat the oven to the required temperature. Place the oven shelves in the correct position before turning the oven on. As a general rule, yeast mixtures and pastry dishes should be cooked towards the top of the oven, cakes and cookies should be placed in the center of the oven, and meringues should be cooked as low in the oven as possible to prevent browning during slow cooking.

● Place cake pans directly on the oven shelf—not on a baking sheet, unless called for in the recipe.

● If cakes brown too quickly during baking, cover the tops with waxed paper or foil.

● Never open the oven door during the early cooking stage. You can look at small cookies after 5 minutes, but generally the door should not be opened during the first 15 to 20 minutes.

● Test cakes with a wooden pick or skewer at the end of the given baking time. Insert a wooden pick or warmed metal skewer into the center. If it comes out with no uncooked batter clinging to it, the cake is done.

Cook's Tips

● Apples, pears and bananas quickly turn brown when peeled and cut. Use a stainless steel knife to cut the fruit and immediately sprinkle with lemon juice or a mixture of lemon juice and water.

● If pastry or cookie dough is difficult to roll out, place it between two floured sheets of waxed paper, or wrap in plastic wrap and refrigerate for at least 30 minutes before rolling out.

● If you do not wish to bake pastry dough immediately, wrap it firmly in foil or plastic wrap and refrigerate for up to a week.

● Fruit cake with a high dried fruit content will stay fresh and moist after cutting if you wrap it well and store in an airtight container.

● Ground spices will not keep their flavor for much longer than a year and then only if stored in airtight and light-proof containers. It is best to buy spices unground and to mark the purchase date on the container.

● Baking parchment saves time and effort. For all kinds of cookies, line the baking sheet with this paper. The baking sheet need not be greased and will remain clean. When cool, it is easy to remove cookies from the paper. The same paper can be used several times.

● You will find it easier to turn a cake out of the pan onto a wire cooling rack if you place the rack on the pan, hold the pan and rack with a cloth and turn both together.

● Cheesecakes and cream cheese cakes should be left to cool in the oven after baking. Turn off the oven and leave the door open until the temperature inside the oven is the same as that outside. This will prevent the cheesecake from sinking.

● You can collect egg whites for meringues. When you need an egg yolk alone, lightly beat the white and place it in a small screw-top jar or freezer container and freeze it. When thawed, it can be used like fresh egg white.

● When cutting out basic pie or cookie dough with a small cutter, dip the cutter into flour to prevent sticking.

● When baking cookies, it is a good idea to bake one or two trial cookies to see how much they spread during baking. You can then estimate how many cookies to put on each baking sheet.

● If you notice too late that you do not have any powdered sugar to sift over a cake, grind granulated sugar in a coffee grinder or blender and use this instead.

Handling Yeast Correctly

Yeast is living matter composed of tiny cells which, when combined with a liquid and sugar at a suitable temperature, will divide continually. This produces carbon dioxide which forms bubbles in the dough, causing it to rise.

Yeast works most effectively in a warm temperature and should be at room temperature when used. Make sure all baking ingredients are at room temperature in advance. Ingredients such as milk or melted fat should never exceed 100° to 110°F (38° to 43°C). Many recipes say *"cover dough and let rise in a warm place"*. Most kitchens are warm enough for the yeast to act. However, dough should always be covered with a damp cloth or plastic wrap to protect it from drafts which could prevent its rising, and to prevent a skin from forming.

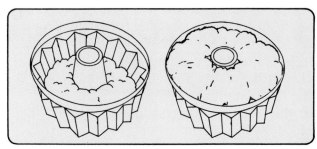

When proving dough, fill pan or mold only half-full, put into oiled plastic bag and let dough rise to top of pan.

Basic Yeast Dough

This is a basic recipe for all types of yeast dough.

Pinch of sugar
1 cup (250 ml) warm milk or water
   (110°F, 43°C)
2 pkgs. active dry yeast
4 cups (500 g) all-purpose flour
1/2 teaspoon salt
4 tablespoons (50 g) butter
1 egg
1 egg yolk, beaten

Make sure all the ingredients are at room temperature and are measured exactly. Bring the liquid to the correct temperature. Grease a 9-1/4x5-1/4-inch (23x13-cm) loaf pan, two 8-1/2x4-1/2-inch (22x11-cm) loaf pans, or a baking sheet.

Stir the sugar into the warm milk or water and sprinkle the yeast over the liquid. Let the mixture stand for about 5 minutes or until the surface is frothy. Stir gently to moisten any dry particles remaining on top. Sift the flour and salt into a large bowl. Melt the butter and let it cool slightly. Lightly beat the butter and whole egg into the yeast mixture. Beat this yeast mixture into the flour mixture using a large wooden spoon. Continue beating until a dough is formed. On a lightly floured surface, knead the dough until it is smooth and elastic, 5 to 10 minutes. If the dough remains too moist and sticks to your fingers, it must be vigorously beaten again. If necessary, you can work in a little more flour. When the dough has been kneaded enough, sprinkle it lightly with flour, cover with a damp cloth and let it rise in a warm place until doubled in bulk. This is called the *first rising*.

Knead the risen dough lightly again and shape it to fit the prepared loaf pan, or form into individual rolls and place on the greased baking sheet.

Before baking, the shaped dough must rise again or *prove*. Put the pan or baking sheet containing the dough inside a large oiled plastic bag. Proving time depends on room temperature but it is usually shorter than the first rising period. When using a pan, fill it only halfway and let the dough rise to the top of the pan. While the dough is proving, preheat the oven to 450°F (230°C).

Brush the yeast dough with beaten egg yolk before baking. Bake a large loaf for 35 to 45 minutes, smaller loaves for 25 to 35 minutes and individual rolls for 15 to 20 minutes. The cooked loaf should be slightly shrunken from the sides of the pan. Loaves and rolls should sound hollow when turned out and tapped on the underside.

Puff Pastry
Cook's Tips

- Let frozen puff pastry dough thaw at room temperature for about 1 hour.
- Roll out puff pastry dough on a lightly floured surface. During rolling, it is important to roll the dough in two directions, from top to bottom and from left to right. If rolled in one direction it will not rise evenly during baking.
- Cut puff pastry dough with a very sharp knife to prevent the edges from sticking together. If using a pastry cutter, dip it in cold water before cutting out the dough.
- When brushing puff pastry dough with egg yolk, avoid the cut edges, or the coating will prevent the pastry from rising evenly during baking.
- Dough trimmings can be laid one on top of the other, pressed firmly together and rolled out again. Use small pieces and strips for decoration.
- Always place puff pastry dough on a baking sheet or in a pan which has been lightly sprinkled with cold water. The steam from the water helps the pastry to rise.
- Refrigerate puff pastry dough for 15 minutes before baking.

Basic Pie Pastry

If you follow the basic rules for making this pastry you can be sure of success. Basic pie pastry is easy and quick to prepare, but you must allow extra time for it to rest in the refrigerator before rolling out. If a sweet pastry is required, sugar is added to the basic ingredients. Sugar adds to the crispness of the pastry. Eggs can be added to give a richer dough. The higher the fat content in relation to the flour, the more crumbly the pastry will be. Following are basic recipes and methods for both sweet and savory pastries.

Sweet Pie Pastry
2-1/2 cups (300 g) all-purpose flour
3/4 cup plus 2 tablespoons (200 g) butter or
** margarine, cut in small pieces**
1/4 cup plus 3 tablespoons (100 g) granulated
** sugar or generous 3/4 cup (100g) powdered**
** sugar, sifted**
1 egg

Measure all the necessary ingredients exactly. Fat for the pastry can be used straight from the refrigerator if it is cut into small pieces. Sift the flour to remove any lumps. Because the pastry contains enough fat of its own, it is not necessary to grease the pan or baking sheet.

Sift the flour into a large bowl. Using a pastry blender or 2 knives, cut in the butter or margarine until it is evenly distributed and the mixture resembles breadcrumbs. With a fork, lightly mix in the granulated or powdered sugar and egg to give a smooth dough. Do not over-work the dough or it will become crumbly and tough. Press the dough into a ball, wrap it in foil or plastic wrap and refrigerate for 2 hours. It is essential to wrap the dough to prevent it from drying out. The higher the fat content in relation to the other ingredients, the longer the pastry dough should be refrigerated. Pastry that is well chilled is much easier to shape.

Preheat the oven to 400°F (205°C). Place oven shelf in correct position. Remove the dough from the refrigerator and knead it gently. Sprinkle the working surface and rolling pin with flour and roll out the dough. Take care that as little flour as possible is mixed into the dough when rolling or shaping it. Too much would alter the proportions and texture of the pastry. If the dough becomes too soft, return it to the refrigerator for 30 minutes.

Flan and tartlet shells are sometimes baked *blind*. For this they are pierced at close intervals with a fork before baking to prevent the pastry rising or bubbles forming. The pastry shell is then lined with foil or waxed paper and filled with dried beans. The pastry is baked for 10 to 15 minutes and the beans are then removed. At this stage, you can either return the pastry shell to the oven to finish cooking for 10 to 15 minutes, or add a filling and then continue cooking.

Freshly baked pastry breaks easily. For this reason always let it cool for a few minutes, then carefully turn it out of the pan or lift it from the baking sheet with a spatula. Do not leave pastry in the baking pan or on the baking sheet until completely cool or the fat from the pastry will set and make it difficult to remove.

Basic pie pastry can also be made by quickly kneading all the ingredients together until a dough is formed.

Savory Pie Pastry

1-3/4 cups (200 g) all-purpose flour
7 tablespoons (100 g) butter or margarine, cut in
   small pieces
1 small egg
Pinch of salt
3 tablespoons ice water
Milk, if required
1 egg yolk, beaten, if required

You can either use the same method as for Sweet Pie Pastry, adding the water with the egg, or use the following method.

Sift the flour into a large bowl and form a well in the center. Place the butter or margarine, 1 egg and salt in the well. Work all the ingredients quickly together with your fingertips, gradually adding the water to make a pastry dough. Press the dough into a ball, wrap in foil or plastic wrap and refrigerate it for 1 to 2 hours.

Preheat the oven to 400°F (205°C). Knead the dough gently and roll out on a lightly floured surface. Line tartlet pans, flan tins or muffin pan cups with dough, adding any filling and covering with a top crust if required. Seal the edges with a little milk. Pierce the top crust several times with a fork or make a small hole to let steam escape during baking. Brush the top with egg yolk or milk and bake for the time required to cook the pastry and filling. The pastry shell can also be baked blind, as for Sweet Pie Pastry, page 9.

Cream Puff Pastry

Cream puff pastry is prepared by a completely different method from other pastries. It is extremely important to measure all the ingredients accurately. Since cream puff pastry is unsweetened, it is very versatile and can be used for both sweet and savory dishes.

Basic Cream Puff Paste

1 cup (150 g) all-purpose flour, sifted
4 tablespoons (60 g) butter
1 cup (250 ml) water
Pinch of salt
4 eggs

Measure the ingredients. Sift the flour onto a double thickness of waxed paper. Grease a large baking sheet. Preheat the oven to 425°F (220°C).

Put the butter, water and salt into a medium saucepan. Stir the mixture over low heat until the butter has melted. Increase heat and quickly bring

Remove pan from heat and pour sifted flour all at once into boiling liquid.

Beat vigorously with a wooden spoon until dough forms a ball which comes away from sides of pan.

to a boil. Remove from the heat and add the flour to the boiling liquid all at once, beating vigorously with a wooden spoon. Return to the heat and cook for 1 minute, stirring until the dough comes away from the sides of the pan. Remove from the heat and allow to cool.

Beat the eggs in a medium bowl. Gradually beat the eggs into the cooled cream puff paste, making sure each addition is thoroughly mixed in before adding the next one. This can be done using an electric mixer or beating by hand with a wooden spoon. When the egg is completely blended in, the cream puff paste should be soft, glistening and golden, and will fall in a thick stream from a spoon.

Place the cream puff paste in a pastry bag fitted with a large plain or fluted nozzle. For cream puffs, pipe small round shapes onto the baking sheet; for éclairs, pipe in 3-inch (7.5-cm) lengths and for tart shells, pipe in circles. If you have no pastry bag, the cream puff paste can be spooned onto the baking sheet. Bake for 20 minutes then remove from the oven and make a small hole in the puffs or éclairs to let steam escape. Cool on a wire rack.

Cook's Tips

● When melting the butter in the water, make sure the butter has melted completely before bringing the mixture quickly to a boil. Remove from the heat immediately to prevent evaporation of the liquid and add the flour all at once.
● Cream puff pastry tends to expand during cooking, so leave enough space on the baking sheet to allow for this.
● Use cream puff pastry on the day it is made because it tends to go soft very quickly.
● Cream puff pastry freezes well, cooked or uncooked. Allow 1 hour to thaw, then crisp in a preheated 425°F (220°C) oven for a few minutes, or bake according to the recipe.

Cake Making

A layer cake contains fat creamed with sugar, whereas a sponge usually has no fat and the eggs are beaten with sugar before folding in the flour.

Basic Layer Cake

8 tablespoons (100 g) butter or margarine, softened
1/2 cup (100 g) sugar
2 eggs
1 cup (100 g) self-rising flour, sifted

Prepare and measure all the ingredients. Grease an 8-inch (20-cm) round cake pan or two 7-inch (18-cm) layer cake pans and line with waxed paper. Grease the waxed paper. Preheat the oven to 325°F (165°C).

Place the butter or margarine and sugar in a large bowl and cream with a wooden spoon until light and fluffy. Beat in the eggs one at a time, adding a little of the flour with the second egg. If the eggs are added all at once or if they are too cold, the fat and sugar mixture can curdle.

If the recipe requires flavorings such as vanilla or grated lemon peel, mix them in before the flour is added.

Finally, fold in the flour with a metal spoon. Spread the batter evenly in the prepared cake pan or pans. Bake for 35 to 40 minutes if baking one large cake, and 25 to 30 minutes if baking two smaller cakes. The cakes are done when a wooden pick inserted in the center comes out clean. If the surface of the cake is browning too quickly, cover it loosely with foil or waxed paper.

Let the cake cool in the pan for about 10 minutes before turning it out onto a wire rack to cool completely.

Cook's Tips

● Sift the flour before using to remove any lumps. If using other dry ingredients such as cornstarch or baking powder, sift these with the flour so all the ingredients are thoroughly and evenly mixed.
● Butter or margarine, eggs and milk must be taken out of the refrigerator in advance so they reach room temperature before you begin baking.
● If the butter or margarine is very hard, soften it before using. Soft margarine in tubs is very good for making cakes.
● If the quantity of flour in the cake is high in proportion to the amount of fat and sugar, baking powder is sometimes added to the mixture.
● Do not over-mix while folding in because essential air can be lost.

Variations

● In some recipes, eggs are separated and added to a mixture separately. The yolks are added to the creamed fat and sugar, then the egg whites are beaten and folded into this mixture.
● Some cake mixtures contain dried fruit. The fruit must be tossed well in the flour before folding into the mixture to prevent it from sinking to the bottom of the cake during baking.
● If you are making a marble cake, add sifted unsweetened cocoa powder to half the cake mixture with a little extra sugar. Place alternate spoonfuls of the plain and chocolate mixtures in the pan and swirl with a skewer to give a marbled effect.

Beaten Sponge Cake

This method of cake making is used for gâteaux, bases for fruit flans, layered cakes and various small cakes. Beaten sponge cakes freeze well.

The eggs and sugar are beaten together until pale and creamy, 5 to 10 minutes with an electric mixer. The flour is then very carefully folded in with the cornstarch, if used. Sometimes a little melted butter is stirred in at the end to add richness. Another method is to separate the eggs and beat the yolks with the sugar until creamy and then to fold in the stiffly beaten egg whites.

4 eggs
1/2 cup (100 g) sugar
1/2 cup (50 g) all-purpose flour
1/2 teaspoon baking powder
2 tablespoons (15 g) ground almonds
2 tablespoons (25 g) butter, melted, if desired

Prepare and measure all the ingredients. Grease an 8-inch (20-cm) springform cake pan and sprinkle with flour or fine breadcrumbs. Preheat the oven to 375°F (190°C).

Beat the eggs with the sugar in a large bowl until pale and creamy, 5 to 10 minutes with an electric mixer. Sift the flour with baking powder then mix with the ground almonds. Fold flour mixture into the egg mixture with melted butter.

The Art of Baking

Turn the batter into the prepared pan, smooth the surface and bake for 35 to 45 minutes. Do not open the oven door during the first few minutes of cooking or the cake will sink. The cake is done when a wooden pick inserted in the center comes out clean.

Let the cake cool in the pan for a few minutes then turn it out onto a wire rack to cool.

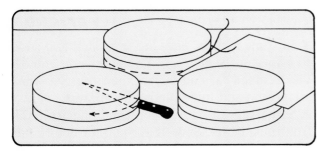

To cut a sponge cake into layers, either cut to the center with a sharp pointed knife and turn cake around until one layer is cut off, or cut through layers with strong thread. It is best to lift off layers with thick paper or thin cardboard.

Chocolate Cake

4 eggs
1/2 cup (100 g) sugar
1/2 cup (50 g) all-purpose flour
1/2 teaspoon baking powder
2 tablespoons (15 g) unsweetened cocoa powder

Follow the method given for Beaten Sponge Cake, page 11, sifting the baking powder and cocoa powder with the flour and leaving out the melted butter.

Jelly Roll

4 eggs, separated, plus 2 egg yolks
1/2 cup (100 g) sugar
3/4 cup (80 g) all-purpose flour
1/2 teaspoon baking powder

Line a 13x9-inch (33x23-cm) cake pan with waxed paper and grease the paper well. Preheat the oven to 425°F (220°C).

Beat the 6 egg yolks with half the sugar in a large bowl until pale and creamy, 5 to 10 minutes with an electric mixer. Beat the egg whites until frothy, slowly sprinkle in the remaining sugar and continue to beat until very stiff. Drop the egg whites onto the egg yolk mixture.

Sift the flour with the baking powder onto the egg whites and fold all into the yolk mixture, blending carefully with a metal spoon. Spread the batter evenly in the prepared cake pan. Bake for 10 to 12 minutes. Cake is done when a wooden pick inserted in center comes out clean.

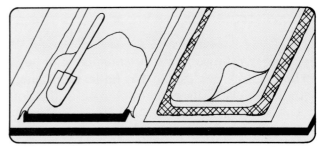

Spread batter evenly over lined cake pan. After baking, turn out cake onto clean waxed paper placed over a damp cloth towel and peel off lining paper.

Place a sheet of waxed paper on a damp cloth towel. Sprinkle the waxed paper with sugar. Turn out the cake onto the sugar-coated paper. Strip off the waxed lining paper and trim the edges of the cake. Fill the cake and roll it up. If the jelly roll is to be filled when cold, place a sheet of clean waxed paper on top and carefully roll it up with the paper inside. Leave the cake until cold then carefully unroll it. Remove the waxed paper, fill as required and roll up again.

Cook's Tips

● A delicate mixture of egg yolks, sugar and egg whites must be made quickly. The beaten egg whites should never be beaten into the yolks, because this would break down the air which has been whisked into the whites and the lightness of the cake would be lost. Sifted flour mixed with cornstarch, cocoa or baking powder, must be carefully folded in using a metal spoon.

● Do not let batter stand for long once it is mixed because it can fall and lose its lightness. Place it in a preheated oven and bake immediately.

Meringues

A meringue mixture is based on egg white and sugar.

6 egg whites
1 cup (225 g) granulated sugar
Scant 3/4 cup (75 g) powdered sugar
1/4 cup (25 g) cornstarch

Line a baking sheet with baking parchment or rice paper. Mark the required shapes on the paper with a pencil.

Beat the egg whites until stiff, preferably using an electric mixer. Slowly sprinkle in the granulated sugar, beating constantly. Sift the powdered sugar and cornstarch onto the egg white mixture and fold in with a metal spoon. Do not beat in.

Fill a pastry bag fitted with a plain or fluted nozzle with the mixture. Pipe the shapes indicated in the recipe onto the baking parchment or rice paper.

Meringues should be baked at a very low temperature, overnight if possible, with the oven door propped slightly open with the handle of a

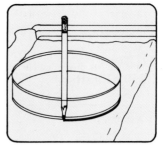 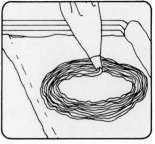

To make a meringue base, draw a circle on the paper using a cake pan as a guide.

Place mixture in a pastry bag and fill drawn circle.

wooden spoon. Alternatively, they can be baked in a 275°F (135°C) oven for 3 to 4 hours.

Cook's Tips

● When beating egg whites, make sure that the bowl and beaters are spotlessly clean and there are no traces of egg yolk. Otherwise the egg whites will not beat properly.
● Make sure the egg whites are thoroughly beaten before adding the sugar. An electric mixer is a valuable piece of equipment to have when making meringues.

Fillings & Frostings

When you have baked a light sponge, or a rich fruit cake, a well-risen Kugelhopf or a sheet of cookies, the next stage begins: completing your *pièce de résistance* with a filling, a frosting or a decoration.

Elaborate Fillings

There are several types of cream filling. Whether the filling is based on eggs or cream, cream cheese or butter, any number of varied combinations will give the desired taste and color. Follow the recommended quantity for the ingredients and use the correct method.

Whipped Cream

Use whipped cream to fill cream slices, cream puffs, layer cakes, sponge cakes and meringues, and to decorate fruit flans and gâteaux.

Butter Cream

Here are two recipes for butter cream: one is a very light butter cream prepared with imported custard powder and the other is French butter

cream which is heavier but has a delightful flavor. Both creams can be used to fill and cover flans, tartlets, slices and gâteaux.

Custard Butter Cream

1 cup (225 g) butter, softened
Generous 1 cup (140 g) powdered sugar, sifted
1-1/2 cups (350 ml) milk
1/4 cup (25 g) imported custard powder
2 egg yolks

In a large bowl, cream the butter and powdered sugar until light and fluffy.

In a medium bowl, blend 1/3 cup (100 ml) milk, custard powder and egg yolks. Bring the remaining milk to a boil in a medium saucepan. Stir the hot milk into the custard mixture. Return the mixture to the saucepan and bring to a boil again, stirring constantly. Remove the custard from the heat and let it cool, stirring frequently to prevent a skin forming. A skin can also be avoided by placing a sheet of dampened waxed paper over the custard.

When the custard has cooled to the temperature of the butter mixture, beat it gradually into the butter mixture with a wooden spoon.

French Butter Cream

1 cup plus 2 tablespoons (250 g) butter
4 eggs
Generous pinch of salt
3/4 cup (160 g) sugar
Few drops of vanilla extract

In a large bowl, beat the butter until pale and fluffy. Beat the eggs, salt and sugar in a medium bowl set over a saucepan of hot water until quite warm. Remove the egg mixture from the heat and beat until cool. Gradually beat the cooled egg mixture into the butter, using a wooden spoon. Beat in vanilla.

Variations

● To make Chocolate Butter Cream, stir 1/4 cup plus 1 tablespoon (40 g) sifted unsweetened cocoa powder and 3 tablespoons (20 g) powdered sugar into the French Butter Cream.
● Butter cream can also be enriched with ground nuts, melted marshmallows, liqueurs, grated peel and juice of citrus fruits, or pureed fruit. Be careful to mix fruit, fruit juices and liqueurs slowly into the butter cream to prevent curdling.

Frostings

Frosting gives a festive appearance to every kind of cake and also helps to prevent cakes from drying out too quickly. When making a frosting, always add the liquid gradually until you reach the required consistency. If you require a shiny frosting, spread apricot jelly on the cake first. To obtain apricot jelly, bring apricot jam to a boil with a little water, stirring constantly. Press the jam through a strainer to separate the jelly. While the cake is warm, spread on the warm jelly. Let the jelly dry a short time before frosting the cake. Spread the frosting over the flat surface of cakes with a spatula which has been dipped in hot water.

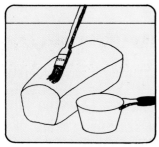

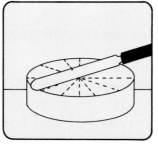

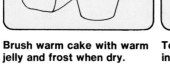

Brush warm cake with warm jelly and frost when dry.

To decorate cake portions individually, divide into equal portions in advance with a spatula or long knife.

Glacé Frosting

2 cups (250 g) powdered sugar
3 to 5 tablespoons (50 to 75 ml) hot water

Sift the powdered sugar into a medium bowl and gradually beat in the hot water until the frosting reaches a coating consistency.

Variations

● Instead of water, you can also make the frosting with milk, fruit juice, wine or spirits, according to the type of cake. You can color the frosting with a few drops of food coloring and flavor it by adding flavorings such as almond extract, rose water or vanilla extract.

Royal Frosting

2 egg whites
3-1/2 cups (450 g) powdered sugar, sifted
1 teaspoon glycerine

In a large bowl, beat the egg whites very lightly until frothy. Using a wooden spoon or an electric mixer on the lowest speed, gradually beat in half the powdered sugar. If using a wooden spoon, continue beating the mixture until it becomes light and fluffy, 5 to 10 minutes. If using an electric mixer, increase the speed and beat for 5 to 8 minutes. Use a wooden spoon to beat in the remaining powdered sugar and glycerine a little at a time. The frosting is ready when it will stand up in peaks.

Variations

● Like Glacé Frosting, Royal Frosting can be changed in both color and flavor by adding food colorings and flavorings. If you add extra liquid, remember to compensate by adding a little more powdered sugar until the correct consistency is reached.

The illustrations which accompany the recipes in this book offer many ideas on how to decorate cakes, tarts, cookies and buns. Most are highly effective, yet easy—you only need to learn the right techniques.

Sifting & Sprinkling

Powdered sugar, instant chocolate drink powder and unsweetened cocoa powder are all suitable for sifting. Place a small quantity in a small strainer and sift over the cake by moving the strainer steadily to and fro.

Whether you buy doilies or make patterns yourself for sifting, this is a quick and effective way to decorate gâteaux, cakes and tarts for every occasion.

Use doilies to make a decorative pattern over a cake or tart. When removing doilies you must be especially careful not to smudge the pattern. With a little skill you can make your own paper patterns, such as stars, a fir tree for Christmas, small birds, flowers or even letters.

For sprinkling, use chocolate sprinkles, sliced or slivered almonds, shredded coconut, other nuts or finely chopped candied fruit. In many recipes you will be instructed to sprinkle the sides of the cake with a decoration such as chopped nuts. The best way to do this is to press the chosen decoration onto the sides with a rubber spatula or plastic pie server. You can even roll the cake in the chopped nuts or other decoration to coat the sides evenly.

Rosettes & Garlands

You can pipe rosettes or garlands with whipped cream or butter cream. You will need a pastry bag fitted with a fluted or plain nozzle. Both fluted and plain nozzles come in various sizes; the smaller the nozzle the more delicate the decoration will be.

If you wish to avoid washing a fabric or plastic pastry bag each time after using it, make your own pastry bags from baking parchment, page 16. Fill the pastry bag no more than half-full with cream so the open end is easy to hold. If you are inexperienced at using a pastry bag, pipe the planned design first onto foil. This does not waste the cream because you can remove it from the foil with a knife and return it to the pastry bag.

To pipe rosettes, squeeze equal peaks from a pastry bag fitted with a fluted nozzle. A large rosette can be topped with a candied cherry, candied coffee bean or segment of fruit. Pipe several small peaks in a circle with a larger rosette in the center to make a flower pattern. Garlands piped with a fluted nozzle can be made to radiate from the center to the edge of each slice of gâteau or tart, ending in a rosette. Garlands can also be piped to form a border around the edge of the cake, or into a heart shape or any other shape which suits the occasion.

You can pipe your favorite variations of rosettes and garlands using a pastry bag fitted with a fluted nozzle. Rosettes are often topped with small segments of fruit.

Writing & Figures

For more delicate decoration, such as writing or figures, use Royal Frosting, page 14.

Crushed Praline

Praline is often used to sprinkle onto cakes and gâteaux. It can be made in advance and stored in an airtight jar.

3/4 cup (175 g) sugar
3/4 cup (75 g) coarsely chopped almonds

Heat the sugar and almonds in a medium saucepan over low heat. When the sugar has dissolved, boil it slowly until golden. Pour the mixture onto an oiled baking sheet and leave it until set. When cold, crush the praline with a rolling pin and use as required.

Chocolate Curls

To make chocolate curls, spread melted chocolate onto a large plastic or ceramic chopping board. Leave it until just set. Using a sharp knife, scrape the chocolate into long curls. For a quicker method, scrape a vegetable peeler along the flat edge of a bar of chocolate, shaving the chocolate off into curls.

Nougat

Nougat is sometimes melted to use in cake fillings and frostings. If you are unable to obtain a very good quality nougat, substitute marshmallows which will give excellent results.

Preparing the Pastry Bag

Fold a large square piece of baking parchment diagonally and cut down the fold to give two triangles. Each triangle can be used for a different colored frosting. Roll the triangles to make cone shapes. Fold over the top edge of the seam side twice so the cone keeps its shape. Cut off the point with scissors. It is important to cut it straight because only in this way will you obtain an even 'thread'. The higher you cut the point, the thicker the thread will be.

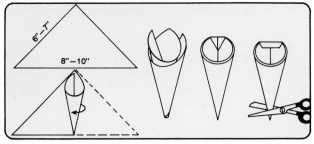

To make a pastry bag, cut a triangle out of baking parchment, roll into a cone and fold the edge over twice at the seam. Cut straight across point to size of 'thread' required.

Practice piping onto waxed paper or foil first. Take care not to hold the tube too near the surface being frosted. The frosting must flow freely so you can control it. Use a pin to mark the desired shapes on the writing surface. You can then frost over the shapes with ease.

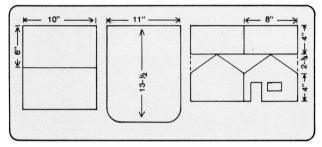

Pattern for Gingerbread House on page 118.

Deep-Frying

When frying foods coated with batter or pastry, the shortening or oil must be at the correct temperature, 350° to 360°F (175°to 180°C). Use shortening which contains absolutely no water and which will not smoke or burn at high temperatures, or choose a good quality oil. A generous amount of shortening or oil is necessary so the food can float in it. Never fill the pan more than two-thirds full or the shortening or oil may spill over the top when the food is added .

If frying in an ordinary saucepan, the shortening or oil must be heated on top of the stove. The temperature can be controlled best with a frying thermometer. If you do not have one, try the wooden spoon test: dip the handle of a wooden spoon into the hot fat—if bubbles immediately form around the handle, the fat has reached deep-frying temperature.

Fry small quantities at a time, allowing the shortening or oil to reach the required temperature between each addition of food. Drain all fried food on paper towels. Immediately after draining, toss the fried food in salt or spices or sprinkle with sugar, as required.

Cook's Tips

● For small items to be fried in batter, use a frying basket.
● Small pieces of fruit dipped in batter, some yeast doughs and cream puff pastries are delicious deep-fried.
● Cooled shortening or oil should be strained through filter paper or cheesecloth and poured back into the bottle or other container until needed again.

Dip the handle of a wooden spoon into hot fat—if bubbles immediately form around it, fat is hot enough.

Fry small items in a frying basket. It is easier to remove them from fat and they can drain well in basket over pan.

Preparation of Baking Pans

Cake, Pastry or Bread	Pan Preparation
Sponge cake mixture Layer cake mixture	Grease pans and sprinkle with flour. If necessary, line with greased waxed paper.
Jelly roll mixture	Grease pan and line with greased waxed paper.
Meringue mixture Macaroon mixture	Line baking sheet with baking parchment or rice paper.
Basic pie pastry	Do not grease baking sheet or pan unless pastry contains only a little fat.
Puff pastry	Sprinkle baking sheet with a little cold water.
Cream puff pastry	Grease pans.
Yeast dough	Grease pans or baking sheets unless making brioches or croissants which contain large amounts of fat.

The decision to grease a pan or baking sheet, to sprinkle it with flour or breadcrumbs, or to line it with waxed paper or foil, does not depend only on the type of mixture or pastry, but also on the pan. Several of the non-stick baking pans need no preparation before the mixture is added. Use butter or margarine for greasing.

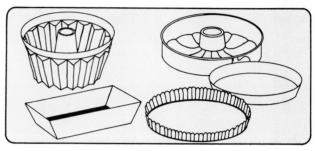

Top row, left to right. Kugelhopf mold, springform with savarin funnel. Bottom row, loaf pan, fluted flan tin, cake pan.

Glossary of Baking Ingredients from A to Z

Many of the ingredients required for the recipes in this book are everyday basics to be found in any kitchen. These ingredients are sometimes used in a different way for baking and for this reason several of them have been included in the following list.

Angelica—Dried and candied stem of the angelica plant which has a slightly bitter, aromatic flavor. Used mainly to decorate cakes and gâteaux.

Aniseed—Spice from the fruit of a Mediterranean plant. This wonderful baking spice is rich in natural oils. You can buy aniseed whole, crushed or ground. It is best to grind whole aniseeds yourself as you need them.

Arrack—Rice brandy. Arrack is a prized flavoring for baking, but it should be used sparingly. Frosting flavored with arrack is delicious.

Buttermilk—Milk which is left after churning butter.

Candied Coffee Beans—Coffee-flavored chocolate shaped into coffee beans, used to decorate cakes and gâteaux.

Candied Fruit—Fruits soaked in a thick sugar syrup and then dried, used mainly to decorate cakes. When finely chopped they can also be mixed into cake batters or form part of a filling.

Candied Orange or Lemon Peel—Candied peel of oranges or lemons which is used finely chopped for cakes, yeast doughs and cookies.

Caraway Seed—Spice from the fruit of the caraway plant. Savory flans, breads and rolls are often sprinkled with caraway seeds. They are also used in some cakes and cookies.

Cardamom—Sharply flavored spice used in some yeast and cookie doughs.

Cinnamon—Spice from the dried bark of the cinnamon tree. Ground cinnamon is light brown in color and has a mildly aromatic smell. It should be stored in an airtight container because it easily loses its aroma. Cinnamon sticks are mostly soaked in milk for fillings and flavorings.

Cloves—Spice from the dried buds of the clove tree, gathered before they flower. Cloves are sold as whole buds or ground. They taste good in apple and plum tarts but should be used sparingly.

Cocoa—Cocoa bean is the raw material for all cocoa products. Cocoa butter, an aromatic and easily melted ingredient of chocolate, and cocoa powder are obtained from it. If unsweetened cocoa powder is used for chocolate cakes you should add a little extra sugar to avoid a bitter taste. Larger quantities of cocoa should be sifted so that no lumps can form.

Coriander—Spice from the dried fruit of the coriander, sold whole or ground.

Evaporated Milk—This can be used in baking as a substitute for fresh milk, but should be diluted with water according to the instructions on the can. It is not recommended that you use it in creams or custards.

Filberts—See Hazelnuts.

Fondant—Basically a sugar frosting made with lump sugar, water and glucose.

Frying Oil—For frying, a pure vegetable oil such as corn, sunflower or safflower oil, is suitable. The frying temperature should be somewhere from 350° to 360°F (175° to 180°C), according to the type of food you are cooking.

Ginger—Spice from the dried root of the ginger plant, sold whole or ground, or preserved in syrup as stem ginger. Ginger has a very strong flavor and should be used sparingly. Crystallized ginger is used as a decoration or can be chopped and added to cake mixtures.

Hazelnuts—Also known as filberts. For cake and cookie mixtures, hazelnuts are often better left unpeeled as their skins are full of flavor.

Mace—Dried shell of the nutmeg which is sometimes sold ground for particular types of baking.

Margarine—Soft margarine in tubs is especially useful for all cake making, whereas a firmer margarine is more suitable for pastry making.

Milk—Every available type of milk is suitable for baking as long as the correct quantity for the recipe is added. Instead of fresh milk you can use reconstituted powdered milk, thinned evaporated milk, thinned half-and-half or thinned whipping cream. Buttermilk or soured milk can also be used if suitable. It is important in every recipe to take note of the method of adding the milk and the required temperature.

Nougat—Mixture consisting of finely ground toasted hazelnuts or almonds combined with sugar and sometimes cocoa. Nougat is usually melted and added to cake fillings or used to join cookies together.

Nutmeg—Spice from the seed of the nutmeg plant. Nutmeg is sold either whole or ground and adds a subtle flavor to spiced cakes, cookies, fruit flans and yeast doughs.

Orange-Flower Water—Made from the concentrated extract of distilled bitter orange flowers, it is a valuable flavoring and aromatic agent used in baking and desserts.

Peanuts—Use unsalted peanuts in baking like other nuts; they make a less expensive substitute when you are not baking a cake which needs a particular kind of nut.

Pine Nuts—Nut-like seed kernel of the pine, used ground in cake mixtures instead of almonds and whole for decorating cakes.

Pistachio Nuts—Fruit of the pistachio tree. They are always used shelled for baking, and are light green in color. Add finely chopped to cake mixtures or use as decoration.

Poppy Seeds—Seeds of the poppy plant which are used ground as an ingredient for fillings or doughs. You can grind poppy seeds yourself in a blender or coffee grinder. Whole poppy seeds can be sprinkled on savory bread rolls.

Rice Paper—Used as a base for macaroons, meringues, gingerbread and candies and is wholly edible. It can be purchased in stores specializing in Oriental goods.

Saffron—Spice from the dried stamens of the saffron or cultivated crocus. This slightly bitter spice is used mainly because of its yellow color; use it in baking wherever an intense yellow color is required.

Sesame Seeds—Small flat seed kernels of the sesame plant. They contain valuable oils and are used crushed as a cake and cookie ingredient, or whole to sprinkle on cakes and bread.

Shredded Coconut—Finely grated flesh of the coconut, sold packed in airtight bags. Once the package is opened it should be used quickly. Fresh coconut which you have grated yourself tastes even better.

Vanilla—Can be used either in its original form as a pod, or as an extract. The dark leathery pods can be cut open lengthwise and then left to steep in boiling milk to obtain the full flavor.

Vanilla Sugar—Sugar flavored with vanilla which is especially useful for baking. The vanilla pod is placed in a jar of granulated sugar to infuse its aromatic flavoring into the sugar. The jar should be sealed and set aside for at least a week before using.

Baking for the Freezer

Anyone who enjoys baking and possesses a freezer can have a wide selection of food available with little extra effort. Cakes, pastries, cookies, bread and rolls can be baked from double or triple the given quantities and frozen. Food mixers really come into their own when you are making large quantities, saving a lot of time and effort. Energy bills are also reduced by baking large quantities at the same time. It is sometimes advisable to freeze large cakes already sliced, interleaving with waxed paper, so you can thaw small quantities as required. A freezing table at the end of this chapter gives useful hints on how to freeze, pack and thaw various foods, with recommended storage times.

Correct Packaging

The quality of frozen foods depends upon correct packaging. Use containers that are moisture-vapor proof. Many years of experience have shown that packaging material for frozen foods should have the following qualities:
- It must be genuine food wrapping able to resist extreme cold and heat.
- It should have no inherent taste or smell which could taint the food.
- It must withstand fat and acidity, as both are present in food.

Special material for packing frozen foods can be bought in supermarkets and department stores. Make sure the material you buy is intended for freezing, as some aluminum foil, plastic bags and containers are only suitable for keeping food in the refrigerator.

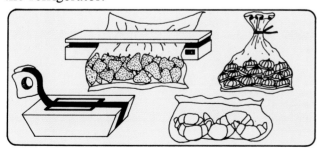

For sealing, ties or plastic clips or freezer tape which will resist frost are suitable, also the heat-sealing device for bags.

Freezing Hints

- *Open-freezing* is the most suitable method for freezing various items of food. These include fragile gâteaux and foods that will be used in their

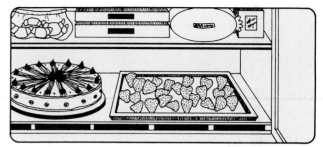

Open-freeze foods that will be used in their frozen state such as soft fruits and fragile gâteaux. Pack carefully once frozen.

frozen state such as strawberries or raspberries and piped rosettes of whipped cream. This method involves placing the items in the freezer without any packaging until frozen. When they are frozen, they can be packaged appropriately and returned to the freezer.
- It is best to open-freeze small cakes, tarts and buns on baking sheets. When frozen, carefully pack them into rigid plastic containers with waxed paper or foil between the layers.
- Baked cakes which have been frozen and thawed should not be refrozen. This will spoil their quality.
- Wrap food to be frozen carefully and only in packaging intended for freezer use. Secure tightly, excluding all air.
- Place the food in the coldest part of the freezer, or on the *fast-freeze* shelf if your freezer has one.
- Do not bring food newly placed in the freezer into contact with food which is already frozen.
- Do not freeze too much food at any one time.
- Always read the manufacturer's instructions for your freezer carefully.

Packaging Materials Available

Foil—This can be molded or shaped around the food to be frozen, making it completely airtight. It comes in two thicknesses, domestic and heavy duty, the latter being suitable for freezing. Cakes which are thawed in their foil wrapping are at the same time protected against drying out.
Foil Containers—These are best suited for cakes, particularly uncooked cake mixtures, as they can be frozen and cooked in the same container. They are sold in various sizes and shapes.
Plastic Bags—These fulfill almost all the requirements of an ideal freezer wrapper. With careful handling they can be used several times. For freezer use, plastic bags must be of thick gauge to be moisture proof. The thinner bags are only

suitable for keeping food fresh. If using bags for freezing several times, test by filling with water before reusing to ensure there are no holes in the bag. After use, wash in detergent, rinse several times in hot water and hang up to dry. This material should be sealed with a heat-sealing device, rubber bands, plastic or metal clips or sealing tape.

Plastic Containers—These must be able to withstand sub-zero temperatures without cracking or warping. The seal must be airtight. Make sure that you buy containers made by reputable manufacturers as less expensive containers will not last for very long. Containers should not be filled to the brim because the contents will expand during freezing.

Sheet Wrapping—This comes in the form of plastic-coated freezer paper or plastic wrap. Freezer paper requires sealing with freezer tape, whereas plastic wrap will cling to itself. Plastic wrap usually comes in two thicknesses, one for short-term freezing and the other for long-term storage. It is used for wrapping irregular shapes and makes frozen food easily recognizable.

Other Packagings—Yogurt, dairy sour cream, cottage cheese and margarine containers can be used for freezing when cleaned thoroughly. They are suitable for cookie crumbs, cake batter, egg whites or whipped cream. Be careful not to fill these containers to the brim as the contents will expand during freezing.

Sealing—Depending on the type of packaging, rubber bands, ties or plastic clips or freezer tape which will resist frost, are all suitable. You can purchase a heat-sealing device which gives plastic bags an airtight seal.

Labeling—Every container, no matter how small, should be labeled. On the label you must note the contents, freezing date and any special characteristics such as *halved fruit* or *whole fruit*. Use self-sticking labels which withstand cold, or sealing tape which you can write on. Write with a ball-point or felt-tip pen. There are also marker pens which will write directly on foil or plastic.

Whichever packaging material you choose, it is important that the air is expelled before sealing and that the material is pulled tight. The only exception is yeast dough which expands slightly in the freezer, so the wrapping should be loosely sealed. With foil, expel the air by pressing firmly and folding the edges over double. Use foil only once for freezing, then use it for covering or keeping food fresh in the refrigerator. After each use, small, barely visible tears occur. If used again in the freezer, torn foil would cause the food to dry out. When using plastic bags, suck the air out with a straw. Never fill boxes or jars too full as the food will expand slightly as it freezes. Leave 1 inch (2.5 cm) clear at the top. If necessary, secure lids with freezer tape. Boxes without lids should be covered with foil folded double and fastened firmly with freezer tape or a rubber band.

Food Freezing Table

Food	Storage Time	Hints on Packaging	Thawing Hints
Yeast Doughs			
Small yeast cakes e.g. doughnuts and croissants	Up to 4 months	Freeze cooked or uncooked.	Thaw cooked food at room temperature, wrap in foil to prevent drying out and reheat in a 325° to 350°F (165° to 175°C) oven.
		If freezing raw dough, place in an oiled plastic bag, leaving enough space for expansion.	Thaw raw dough at room temperature and shape as required.
Large yeast cakes e.g. kugelhopfs	Up to 4 months	Wrap in a plastic bag or plastic wrap.	Thaw at room temperature, wrap in foil and reheat in a 325° to 350°F (165° to 175°C) oven.
Pizza	Up to 3 months	Freeze shaped raw dough bases with a sheet of waxed paper between each one and pack in a plastic bag.	Top frozen dough with filling and bake immediately in a 425° to 450°F (220° to 230°C) oven.
		Can be frozen baked.	Thaw baked pizza at room temperature and reheat wrapped in foil in a 375° to 400°F (190° to 205°C) oven.

Food Freezing Table

Food	Storage Time	Hints on Packaging	Thawing Hints
Bread rolls	Up to 3 months	Pack in plastic bags.	Wrap frozen rolls in aluminum foil and place in a 375° to 400°F (190° to 205°C) oven. Reheat until thawed thoroughly.
Pastries			
Puff pastry (uncooked)	3 months	Wrap in plastic wrap and place in a plastic bag.	Thaw in refrigerator overnight or at room temperature. Use as required.
Puff pastry (cooked)	4 to 6 months	Open-freeze and store in a rigid plastic container.	Thaw at room temperature and reheat in a 325° to 350°F (165° to 175°C) oven.
Basic pie pastry (uncooked)	3 months	Pack in usable quantities in plastic wrap and place in a plastic bag.	Thaw in refrigerator overnight or at room temperature. Use as required.
Basic pie pastry (cooked)	4 to 6 months	Open-freeze and pack in rigid plastic containers. Flan and tartlet shells are better frozen baked but unfilled.	Thaw at room temperature.
Sweet or savory filled and baked flans	Up to 3 months	Wrap in plastic wrap and place in a rigid plastic container. Individual slices can be wrapped in plastic wrap and frozen as above.	Thaw in refrigerator overnight and crisp in a 375° to 400°F (190° to 205°C) oven if to be served hot.
Cream puff pastry	4 to 6 months	a. Uncooked paste—pack in a rigid plastic container.	Thaw in refrigerator overnight.
		b. Uncooked paste—pipe onto waxed paper and open-freeze, then pack into rigid plastic containers.	Thaw in refrigerator overnight or at room temperature then bake according to recipe.
		c. Baked but unfilled—slightly undercook, open-freeze and pack in rigid plastic containers.	Thaw at room temperature and crisp in a 375° to 400°F (190° to 205°C) oven.
Cakes & Cookies			
Beaten sponge cake	Up to 3 months	Interleave sponge layers with waxed paper, pack in plastic bag.	Thaw at room temperature, fill and decorate as desired.
		Can be frozen filled and decorated; open-freeze and pack in a rigid plastic container.	Thaw at room temperature.
Jelly roll	Up to 3 months	Freeze filled, wrapped in plastic wrap or a plastic bag.	Thaw at room temperature.
Meringues (unfilled)	4 to 6 months	Open-freeze, then pack in rigid plastic containers.	Thaw at room temperature and fill as required.
Basic layer cake	Up to 3 months	See Beaten sponge cake.	Thaw at room temperature.
Cheesecake	Up to 3 months	Freeze whole or in slices. Wrap individual slices in plastic wrap.	Thaw in refrigerator overnight.
Cookies (unbaked)	4 to 6 months	Wrap dough in plastic wrap.	Thaw at room temperature, then bake according to recipe.
Cookies (baked)	Up to 3 months	Wrap in plastic bags.	Thaw at room temperature.
Fillings & Frostings			
Whipping cream, whipped	Up to 6 months	Add a little powdered sugar to act as a stabilizer. Store in a rigid plastic container.	Thaw in refrigerator overnight.
		Or, pipe onto waxed paper and open-freeze before packing in a rigid plastic container.	Use almost immediately.
Custard butter cream	Up to 3 months	Store in a rigid plastic container.	Thaw at room temperature.
French butter cream	Up to 3 months	Store in a rigid plastic container.	Thaw at room temperature.

Blackberry Meringue Pie

Pastry:
1-3/4 cups (200 g) all-purpose flour
Pinch of salt
7 tablespoons (100 g) butter, cut in small pieces
2 tablespoons (25 g) sugar
1 egg
About 3 tablespoons ice water

Filling:
2-1/2 cups (350 g) blackberries
1/4 cup plus 2 tablespoons (75 g) sugar
2 teaspoons cornstarch
1 tablespoon water
1/4 cup (75 g) gooseberry jam

Meringue:
3 egg whites
Scant 1 cup (100 g) powdered sugar, sifted

To make pastry, sift flour and salt into a large bowl. Using a pastry blender or 2 knives, cut in butter until mixture resembles breadcrumbs. With a fork, mix in sugar, egg and enough water to make a dough. Wrap in foil and refrigerate 2 hours.
To make filling, sprinkle blackberries with sugar and drain over a saucepan. Warm berry juice. Combine cornstarch and water; stir into berry juice. Bring to a boil, stirring constantly. Reduce heat and simmer; stir until thickened. Add blackberries; cool. Preheat oven to 325°F (165°C). On a floured surface, roll out dough to fit an 8-inch (20-cm) flan tin with a removable bottom. Place dough in tin. Bake blind, page 9, 15 minutes or until golden; cool. Raise oven temperature to 350°F (175°C). Spread jam over pastry shell. Add blackberry mixture.
To make meringue, beat egg whites until stiff. Beat in powdered sugar. Place in a pastry bag fitted with a fluted nozzle. Pipe a lattice over blackberry filling. Bake 15 minutes at 350°F (175°C). Cool slightly in tin. Cool completely on a rack.

Fresh Plum Tart

Pastry:
2-1/2 cups (300 g) all-purpose flour
3/4 cup plus 2 tablespoons (200 g) butter, cut in small pieces
1/4 cup plus 3 tablespoons (100 g) sugar
1 egg

Filling:
3 lbs. (1.5 kg) plums
6 tablespoons sugar crystals
Whipped cream, if desired

To make pastry, sift flour into a large bowl. Using a pastry blender or 2 knives, cut in butter until evenly distributed and mixture resembles breadcrumbs. With a fork, lightly mix in sugar and egg to make a dough. Press into a ball and wrap in foil or plastic wrap. Refrigerate 2 hours.
To make filling, wash and halve plums; remove pits. Cut fruit into quarters. Preheat oven to 400°F (205°C).

On a floured surface, roll out dough to fit a 10-inch (25-cm) flan tin with a removable bottom. Place dough in tin without stretching. Pierce sides and bottom of pastry shell all over with a fork. Arrange plums in a rosette pattern to fill pastry shell. Sprinkle with half the sugar crystals. Bake 30 to 35 minutes; cover with foil if pastry is becoming too brown. Cool slightly in tin. Remove from tin and sprinkle with remaining sugar crystals. Serve with whipped cream, if desired.

Farmhouse Plum Flan

Pastry:
2-1/2 cups (300 g) all-purpose flour
3/4 cup plus 2 tablespoons (200 g) butter, cut in small pieces
1/4 cup plus 3 tablespoons (100 g) sugar
1 egg

Filling & Decoration:
2 lbs. (1 kg) plums
1/2 cup (100 g) sugar
6 tablespoons (150 ml) water
2 envelopes unflavored gelatin
1/4 cup (25 g) cornstarch
Cold water
3 tablespoons coarsely ground walnuts
2/3 cup (150 ml) whipping cream
12 walnut halves

To make pastry, sift flour into a large bowl. Using a pastry blender or 2 knives, cut in butter evenly. With a fork, lightly mix in sugar and egg to make a dough. Press into a ball and wrap in foil or plastic wrap. Refrigerate 2 hours.

Preheat oven to 400°F (205°C). On a floured surface, roll out dough to fit a 10-inch (25-cm) flan tin with a removable bottom. Place dough in tin without stretching. Bake blind, page 9, 20 to 25 minutes or until golden. Cool slightly in tin then transfer to a rack to cool completely.

To make filling and decoration, wash and pit plums. Simmer with sugar and 3 tablespoons water in a medium saucepan over low heat until soft. Dissolve gelatin in 3 tablespoons water over low heat. Mix cornstarch with a little cold water. Add to plums. Bring plum mixture to a boil, stirring constantly. Stir in walnuts. Mix dissolved gelatin with plum mixture and pour into pre-baked pastry shell. Refrigerate until set.

Whip cream until stiff; put into a pastry bag fitted with a fluted nozzle. Mark flan into 12 portions. Decorate with piped whipped cream and walnut halves.

Apricot Slice

Yeast Dough:
1 tablespoon sugar
Scant 1/2 cup (100 ml) warm milk (110°F, 43°C)
1 pkg. active dry yeast
2 cups (225 g) all-purpose flour
Pinch of salt
3 tablespoons (40 g) butter
1/2 beaten egg

Topping:
1-1/2 lbs. (675 g) apricots or 2 (1-lb., 456-g) cans apricot halves
1-1/2 cups (350 g) small-curd cottage cheese
2 eggs, beaten
2 tablespoons (15 g) cornstarch
Grated peel and juice of 1/2 lemon
3 tablespoons (40 g) sugar
2 tablespoons (15 g) sliced almonds

To make yeast dough, stir a pinch of sugar into warm milk and sprinkle with yeast. Let stand 5 minutes or until the surface is frothy. Stir gently to moisten any dry particles remaining on top. Sift flour, remaining sugar and salt into a large bowl. Melt butter; cool slightly. Lightly beat butter and egg into yeast mixture. Pour into flour mixture, combining to make a dough. Knead dough 5 minutes on a lightly floured surface. Cover and let rise in a warm place 30 minutes.

To make topping, wash, halve and pit fresh apricots or drain canned apricots. Press cottage cheese through a strainer into a medium bowl. Mix in eggs, cornstarch, lemon peel and juice and sugar.

Grease a 13x9-inch (33x23-cm) cake pan. Preheat oven to 425°F (220°C). On a floured surface, roll out risen dough to fit bottom of pan. Place dough in greased pan. Spread cheese mixture over dough and arrange prepared apricots cut-side down on top. Sprinkle with almonds. Bake 25 to 30 minutes. Cool slightly then slice and remove from pan.

Blueberry Flan

Pastry:
1-3/4 cups (200 g) all-purpose flour
7 tablespoons (100 g) butter, cut in small pieces
1/4 cup (50 g) sugar
1 egg, beaten
About 3 tablespoons ice water

Filling:
3 cups (500 g) blueberries
3 eggs, separated
1/2 cup (125 g) granulated sugar
1 cup (125 g) ground almonds
Powdered sugar

To make pastry, sift flour into a large bowl. Using a pastry blender or 2 knives, cut in butter until evenly distributed and mixture resembles breadcrumbs. With a fork, lightly mix in sugar, egg and enough ice water to make a dough. Press into a ball and wrap in foil or plastic wrap. Refrigerate 2 hours.
To make filling, wash blueberries and dry on paper towels. Put egg yolks and half the granulated sugar into a large bowl. Beat until pale and creamy, 5 to 10 minutes with an electric mixer. Mix in almonds. Beat egg whites until stiff. Beat in remaining granulated sugar; fold into egg yolk mixture. Stir in blueberries.

Preheat oven to 375°F (190°C). On a floured surface, roll out dough to fit an 8-inch (20-cm) flan tin with a removable bottom. Place dough in tin without stretching. Pierce bottom of pastry shell all over with a fork; spread evenly with filling. Bake 40 minutes. Cool 5 minutes in tin then transfer to a rack. When completely cooled, sift powdered sugar over top.

Cherry Cake

8 oz. (225 g) cherries
5 eggs, separated
3/4 cup plus 2 tablespoons (180 g) granulated sugar
6 tablespoons (80 g) butter or margarine
1-3/4 cups (180 g) all-purpose flour
1/2 teaspoon baking powder
Powdered sugar

Remove stems from cherries; wash, pit and pat dry with paper towels. Grease and flour a 9-inch (23-cm) cake pan. Preheat oven to 375°F (190°C).

Put egg yolks and half the granulated sugar into a large bowl. Beat until pale and creamy, 5 to 10 minutes with an electric mixer. Melt butter or margarine; cool slightly. Beat butter or margarine into egg yolk mixture. Sift flour with baking powder. Fold into egg yolk mixture. Beat egg whites until stiff. Add remaining granulated sugar. Beat again until stiff; fold into egg yolk mixture. Turn batter into prepared pan. Scatter cherries over cake, pressing each one into batter with the handle of a wooden spoon. Cherries will sink into batter while baking. Bake 50 to 60 minutes or until a wooden pick or skewer inserted in center comes out clean. Turn cake out onto a rack to cool.

Sift powdered sugar over cooled cake.

Cook's Tip

Substitute 1/2 cup (100 g) candied cherries for the fresh cherries. Halve cherries and toss with enough flour to coat before pressing into cake batter.

Rhubarb Meringue Tart

Pastry:
2-1/2 cups (300 g) all-purpose flour
3/4 cup plus 2 tablespoons (200 g) butter or margarine,
   cut in small pieces
1/4 cup plus 3 tablespoons (100 g) sugar
1 egg

Filling:
2 lbs. (1 kg) rhubarb
Sugar

Meringue:
3 egg whites
2/3 cup (150 g) sugar

To make pastry, sift flour into a large bowl. Using a pastry blender or 2 knives, cut in butter or margarine until evenly distributed and mixture resembles breadcrumbs. With a fork, lightly mix in sugar and egg to make a dough. Press into a ball and wrap in foil or plastic wrap. Refrigerate 2 hours.

To make filling, wash rhubarb and dry on paper towels. Pull away thin outer skin from top downwards. Cut fruit into 3-inch (7.5-cm) lengths.

Preheat oven to 400°F (205°C). On a floured surface, roll out dough to a rectangle about 10x8 inches (25x20 cm). Carefully lift rectangle onto a baking sheet and pierce all over with a fork.

Arrange rhubarb pieces neatly on dough rectangle; sprinkle with a little sugar to taste. Bake 30 minutes; cool slightly. Do not turn off oven.

To make meringue, beat egg whites in a medium bowl until stiff. Beat in a little sugar then fold in the rest. Put meringue mixture into a pastry bag fitted with a fluted nozzle. Pipe a diagonal lattice over top of tart.

Bake 10 minutes or until meringue is lightly browned. Let cool slightly on baking sheet before cutting into even slices. Cool completely on a rack.

Cook's Tip

If piping is too time-consuming, spread the meringue over the rhubarb with a spatula. The tart won't look quite as distinguished, but it will taste just as good.

Dutch Apple Cake

Pastry:
2-3/4 cups (300 g) all-purpose flour
Pinch of salt
1/2 cup plus 3 tablespoons (150 g) butter, cut in small pieces
2/3 cup plus 1 tablespoon (150 g) sugar
2 egg yolks

Filling:
1 lb. (500 g) cooking apples
1/4 cup plus 2 tablespoons (75 g) sugar
Juice of 1 lemon
Pinch of ground cinnamon
1/3 cup (50 g) raisins
1/2 cup (50 g) ground almonds
1/2 cup (50 g) ground hazelnuts
Water

Frosting:
3 tablespoons apricot jam
Scant 1/2 cup (50 g) powdered sugar
3 tablespoons kirsch or cherry brandy

To make pastry, sift flour and salt into a large bowl. Using a pastry blender or 2 knives, cut in butter evenly. With a fork, mix in sugar and egg yolks to make a dough. Wrap in foil and refrigerate 2 hours. Preheat oven to 400°F (205°C). On a floured surface, roll out just over half the dough to fit a 10-inch (25-cm) removable-bottomed flan tin. Place dough in tin without stretching. Bake blind, page 9, 15 minutes or until golden.
To make filling, peel, core and slice apples. In a medium bowl, mix apple slices, sugar, lemon juice, cinnamon, raisins and ground nuts. Moisten with a little water to blend. Spoon into pastry shell.

Roll out remaining dough to cover filling. Place over filling; seal edges well. Bake 30 minutes. Cool in tin overnight.
To make frosting, warm jam and brush over top of cake. Blend powdered sugar and kirsch or brandy. Spread frosting over jam.

Apple Custard Flan

Pastry:
2-1/2 cups (300 g) all-purpose flour
3/4 cup plus 2 tablespoons (200 g) butter, cut in small pieces
1/4 cup plus 3 tablespoons (100 g) sugar
1 egg
Grated peel of 1 lemon

Filling:
2 lbs. (1 kg) cooking apples
Juice of 1 lemon
1/3 cup (50 g) raisins
1/4 cup (50 g) sugar
1/2 teaspoon ground cinnamon

Custard:
1 tablespoon cornstarch
Scant 1/4 cup (100 ml) milk
2 eggs
1 tablespoon sugar
1/2 teaspoon vanilla extract

To make pastry, sift flour into a bowl. Using a pastry blender or 2 knives, cut in butter evenly. Mix in sugar, egg and lemon peel to make a dough. Wrap in foil; refrigerate 2 hours.
To make filling, peel, core and slice apples. In a large bowl, mix sliced apples, lemon juice, raisins, sugar and cinnamon.

Preheat oven to 400°F (205°C). On a floured surface, roll out three-fourths of dough to fit a 9-inch (23-cm) flan tin with a removable bottom. Place dough in tin without stretching. Pierce pastry shell all over with a fork. Spoon in apple mixture.
To make custard, blend cornstarch with a little milk in a medium bowl. Beat in eggs, remaining milk, sugar and vanilla. Pour over apple mixture.

Roll out reserved dough; cut into thin strips and arrange on top of flan in a lattice pattern. Bake flan 50 to 60 minutes, covering with foil if it becomes too brown. Let flan cool slightly in tin. Remove from tin and cool completely on a rack.

Alsace Apple Tart

Pastry:
1-3/4 cups (200 g) all-purpose flour
Pinch of salt
7 tablespoons (100 g) butter or margarine, cut in small pieces
2 tablespoons (25 g) sugar
1 egg yolk
About 3 tablespoons ice water

Filling:
2 lbs. (1 kg) cooking apples
3 tablespoons lemon juice
3 eggs
1/2 cup (100 g) sugar
1/2 cup (125 ml) whipping cream
1/2 teaspoon vanilla extract

To make pastry, sift flour and salt into a large bowl. Using a pastry blender or 2 knives, cut in butter or margarine until evenly distributed and mixture resembles breadcrumbs. With a fork, lightly mix in sugar, egg yolk and enough ice water to make a dough. Press into a ball and wrap in foil or plastic wrap. Refrigerate 2 hours.

On a floured surface, roll out dough to fit a 9-inch (23-cm) flan tin with a removable bottom. Place dough in tin without stretching. Pierce bottom of pastry shell all over with a fork. Preheat oven to 400°F (205°C).

To make filling, peel, quarter and core apples. Thinly slice each quarter several times without cutting all the way through. Sprinkle with lemon juice. Arrange sliced apple quarters in pastry shell. In a medium bowl, beat eggs and sugar until pale and creamy. Add cream and vanilla. Pour egg mixture over apples. Bake 20 minutes then reduce heat to 350°F (175°C) and bake 25 minutes longer or until custard filling is firm. Cool slightly in tin then transfer to a rack to cool completely.

Apple Lattice Flan

Pastry:
4 cups (450 g) all-purpose flour
1/2 teaspoon salt
1/2 cup plus 2 tablespoons (150 g) margarine, cut in small pieces
2 tablespoons (25 g) sugar
About 2/3 cup (150 ml) ice water

Filling:
2 lbs. (1 kg) cooking apples
Grated peel and juice of 1 lemon
1/2 cup (120 g) sugar
1 teaspoon ground cinnamon
2/3 cup (100 g) raisins
1 cup (100 g) chopped hazelnuts
1 egg yolk, beaten

Glaze:
1/3 cup (100 g) apricot jam
Scant 1 cup (100 g) powdered sugar, sifted
2 tablespoons lemon juice

To make pastry, sift flour and salt into a large bowl. Using a pastry blender or 2 knives, cut in margarine evenly. Lightly mix in sugar and enough ice water to make a dough. Press into a ball and wrap in foil or plastic wrap. Refrigerate 1 hour.
To make filling, peel and core apples. Chop apples coarsely; place in a large bowl. Mix in lemon peel and juice, sugar, cinnamon, raisins and hazelnuts.

Preheat oven to 400°F (205°C). On a floured surface, roll out three-fourths of dough to fit a 15-1/2x10-1/2-inch (39x27-cm) cake pan. Place dough in pan without stretching. Spread apple mixture over pastry shell. Roll out remaining dough, cut into thin strips and arrange over flan in a lattice pattern. Brush with egg yolk. Bake 30 to 40 minutes. Cool in pan.
To make glaze, warm jam; brush over warm pastry. Blend powdered sugar and lemon juice. Drizzle glaze over lattice.

Strawberry Ring

Filling:
3 cups (500 g) strawberries
2 teaspoons vanilla sugar, page 18
Scant 2 cups (450 ml) whipping cream

Cream Puff Paste:
4 tablespoons (60 g) butter
Pinch of salt
Grated peel of 1/2 lemon
1 cup (250 ml) water
1 cup (150 g) all-purpose flour, sifted
4 eggs, beaten

Wash and hull strawberries. Reserve 6 large strawberries and mix the rest with vanilla sugar in a medium bowl. Set aside until sugar has dissolved. Whip cream until stiff; refrigerate. Lightly grease and flour a baking sheet. Preheat oven to 425°F (220°C).
To make cream puff paste, melt butter with salt, lemon peel and water in a heavy medium saucepan over low heat. When butter has melted, increase heat and bring quickly to a boil. Remove from heat and add flour all at once. Beat with a wooden spoon until mixture comes away from sides of pan. Return to heat 1 minute, stirring constantly. Cool slightly then add eggs a little at a time, beating well between each addition.

Put paste into a pastry bag fitted with a large fluted nozzle. Pipe 11 rosettes in a 10-inch (25-cm) ring on prepared baking sheet. After baking, they will be joined together forming a circle. Bake 20 to 25 minutes or until golden and crisp. While still warm, split ring horizontally; let cool.
To make filling, puree strawberry mixture in a blender. Put 3 tablespoons whipped cream into a clean pastry bag fitted with a large fluted nozzle. Combine remaining cream with strawberry puree. Fill cooled cream puff ring with strawberry mixture.

Decorate with piped rosettes of whipped cream and reserved whole strawberries cut in quarters.

Strawberry Cheesecake

Pastry:
2-1/4 cups (250 g) all-purpose flour
1/2 cup plus 1 tablespoon (125 g) butter, cut in small pieces
1/2 cup (100 g) sugar
2 egg yolks

Filling:
1 cup (225 g) small-curd cottage cheese
1/2 cup (100 g) sugar
1 tablespoon cornstarch
Grated peel of 1 lemon
4 eggs
Scant 2 cups (450 ml) whipping cream
1-2/3 cups (225 g) strawberries
1/2 cup (150 g) strawberry jelly

To make pastry, sift flour into a large bowl. Add butter, sugar and egg yolks. Knead to make a dough. Press into a ball and wrap in foil or plastic wrap. Refrigerate 2 hours.

Preheat oven to 400°F (205°C). On a floured surface, roll out dough to fit an 11-inch (28-cm) springform cake pan. Place dough in pan without stretching. Bake blind, page 9, 10 to 15 minutes or until golden brown. Reduce oven temperature to 350°F (175°C).
To make filling, press cottage cheese through a strainer into a large bowl. Add sugar, cornstarch, lemon peel and eggs; beat well. Whip cream until stiff. Fold into cottage cheese mixture. Turn into pastry shell. Bake 50 to 60 minutes. Cool slightly in pan before transferring to a rack to cool completely.

Wash and hull strawberries; dry on paper towels. Halve each strawberry and arrange over cheesecake. Warm jelly in a small saucepan. Drizzle warm jelly over strawberries to glaze.

Gooseberry Meringue Pie

Pastry:
2-1/4 cups (250 g) all-purpose flour
1/2 cup plus 1 tablespoon (125 g) butter, cut in small pieces
2 tablespoons (25 g) sugar
1 egg

Filling:
1 lb. (500 g) gooseberries, washed and stemmed
Scant 2 cups (450 ml) water
1/4 cup (50 g) sugar
Scant 2 cups (450 ml) milk
2 egg yolks
3 tablespoons (20 g) cornstarch

Meringue:
3 egg whites
Generous 1 cup (150 g) powdered sugar, sifted

To make pastry, sift flour into a large bowl. Using a pastry blender or 2 knives, cut in butter evenly. Lightly mix in sugar and egg to make a dough. Wrap in foil and refrigerate 2 hours. Preheat oven to 400°F (205°C). On a floured surface, roll out dough to fit a 9-inch (23-cm) springform cake pan. Place dough in pan. Bake blind, page 9, 20 minutes or until golden. Increase oven temperature to 425°F (220°C).
To make filling, simmer gooseberries, water and 2 tablespoons (25 g) sugar in a large saucepan until soft. Cool in a strainer over a bowl. In a medium bowl, beat remaining sugar, 1/4 cup (50 ml) milk, yolks and cornstarch. Bring remaining milk to a boil in a medium saucepan. Stir hot milk into cornstarch mixture. Return mixture to heat; bring to a boil, stirring until thickened. Pour into pastry shell. Top with gooseberries.
To make meringue, beat egg whites until stiff. Add powdered sugar and beat again. Spread meringue over gooseberries. Bake 5 to 10 minutes or until meringue is lightly browned. Cool slightly in pan, transfer to a rack to cool completely.

Raspberry Meringue Nest

Meringue:
6 egg whites
3/4 cup (175 g) granulated sugar
Generous 1 cup (150 g) powdered sugar
1/4 cup (30 g) cornstarch

Filling:
1 cup (250 ml) whipping cream
1 tablespoon brandy
2-1/2 cups (350 g) raspberries

Line a baking sheet with baking parchment or brown paper. Preheat oven to 225°F (105°C).
To make meringue, beat egg whites until stiff. Gradually beat in granulated sugar. Sift together powdered sugar and cornstarch. Fold into egg white mixture. Fill a pastry bag fitted with a large plain nozzle with meringue mixture. Pipe in a spiral onto prepared baking sheet to make an 8- to 9-inch (20- to 23-cm) round. Form sides of meringue nest by piping rosettes around the edge. Dry out in oven 12 hours, with oven door slightly open. Cool on a rack.
To make filling, whip cream with brandy until stiff. Spread cream evenly in meringue nest and cover with raspberries.

Exotic Fruit Gâteaux

French Orange Flan

Pastry:
8 tablespoons (100 g) butter, softened
Scant 1/2 cup (50 g) powdered sugar, sifted
1 egg yolk
1-1/2 cups (150 g) all-purpose flour

Filling:
1/3 cup (100 g) orange jelly or marmalade
1 cup (250 ml) whipping cream
1/2 cup (100 g) sugar
6 eggs
Grated peel of 3 lemons

Decoration:
1 orange
1/4 cup (50 g) sugar
3 tablespoons water
4 cherries

To make pastry, knead together butter, powdered sugar and egg yolk in a medium bowl. Sift flour over mixture; work in quickly with fingertips to make a dough. Press into a ball and wrap in foil or plastic wrap. Refrigerate 2 hours.

Preheat oven to 400°F (205°C). On a floured surface, roll out dough to fit a 9-inch (23-cm) pie pan or two 6-inch (15-cm) flan dishes. Place dough in pie pan without stretching.
To make filling, spread bottom of pastry shell with orange jelly or marmalade. In a large bowl, beat cream, sugar, eggs and lemon peel until frothy. Pour into pastry shell. Bake 45 to 50 minutes or until filling is firm.
To make decoration, peel orange carefully, removing all pith. Slice thinly. In a small saucepan, dissolve sugar in water over low heat, stirring constantly. Place orange slices in hot sugar syrup 3 minutes; drain. Repeat with cherries. Arrange orange slices on flan and top with cherries.

Kiwi Fruit Cream Tart

3/4 (17-1/4-oz., 489-g) pkg. frozen puff pastry, thawed
1 egg yolk, beaten

Filling:
1 cup (250 ml) whipping cream
3 tablespoons (40 g) sugar
1 tablespoon rum
1-1/2 teaspoons unflavored gelatin
Scant 1/4 cup (50 ml) hot water
6 kiwi fruit
1-1/2 teaspoons arrowroot
2/3 cup (150 ml) cold water

On a floured surface, roll out pastry dough 1/8 inch (3 mm) thick. Cut out an 8-inch (20-cm) round from center of dough. Using a 2-inch (5-cm) round cutter, cut out 12 half-moon shapes from surrounding dough. Sprinkle a baking sheet with cold water. Place round of dough on baking sheet and brush with egg yolk. Pierce dough all over with a fork. Place half-moon shapes around edge of dough. Brush with egg yolk. Refrigerate 15 minutes. Preheat oven to 425°F (220°C). Bake 15 minutes or until pastry is puffed and golden. Cool on a rack.
To make filling, whip cream and sugar in a medium bowl until stiff. Stir in rum. In a small saucepan, dissolve gelatin in hot water over low heat. Cool. Add to cream mixture. When half-set, spread cream mixture over prebaked pastry, mounding in the center. Refrigerate until firm.

Peel and slice kiwi fruit. Arrange in overlapping rings on filling. Blend arrowroot in a small saucepan with a little cold water. Add remaining cold water and bring to a boil, stirring constantly. Set aside until barely warm, then pour over fruit to glaze.

Coconut Mango Cake

Cake:
2 eggs, separated, plus 2 egg yolks
1/4 cup (50 g) sugar
1/4 cup plus 2 tablespoons (40 g) all-purpose flour
2 tablespoons (15 g) cornstarch
3 tablespoons (20 g) unsweetened cocoa powder

Filling:
2 mangoes peeled, or 2 (1-lb., 456-g) cans mangoes, drained
Scant 1/4 cup (50 ml) white wine
2 egg yolks
1/2 cup (100 g) sugar
1 envelope unflavored gelatin
3 tablespoons water
1 cup (225 ml) whipping cream

Topping:
1 cup (225 ml) whipping cream
1 tablespoon powdered sugar
2/3 cup (50 g) shredded coconut
Additional whipping cream

Grease and flour a 9-inch (23-cm) cake pan. Preheat oven to 425°F (220°C).
To make cake, beat 4 yolks and half the sugar in a bowl until thick. Beat whites until stiff; fold in remaining sugar. Fold into yolk mixture. Sift flour, cornstarch and cocoa powder. Fold into mixture. Bake 15 minutes or until a wooden pick inserted in center comes out clean. Cool on rack. Cut into 2 layers.
To make filling, dice mangoes. Mix wine, yolks and sugar in a double boiler on medium heat; stir until thickened. Do not boil. Remove from heat; transfer to a bowl. Dissolve gelatin in water over low heat. Add to wine mixture with most of mangoes. Cool. Whip cream; fold into mixture. Use to fill cake. Let set.
To make topping, whip 1 cup (225 ml) cream with powdered sugar. Spread over cake. Decorate with coconut, additional whipped cream and reserved mangoes.

Tropical Fruit Gâteau

Pastry:
1-1/4 cups (150 g) all-purpose flour
Pinch of salt
7 tablespoons (95 g) butter, cut in small pieces
3 tablespoons (45 g) sugar
1/2 beaten egg

Filling:
3 tablespoons apricot jam
1 (8-inch, 20-cm) Basic Layer Cake, page 11
1 (4-oz., 113-g) carton non-dairy whipped topping

Topping:
4 pineapple rings
2 kiwi fruit
1 mango
5 maraschino cherries
3 tablespoons pineapple juice
1/2 cup (50 g) toasted sliced almonds, page 47

To make pastry, sift flour and salt into a medium bowl. Using a pastry blender or 2 knives, cut in butter until evenly distributed and mixture resembles breadcrumbs. With a fork, lightly mix in sugar and egg to make a dough. Press into a ball and wrap in foil or plastic wrap. Refrigerate 2 hours.
Preheat oven to 425°F (220°C). On a floured surface, roll out dough to fit inside bottom of an 8-inch (20-cm) flan tin with a removable bottom. Place dough in tin without stretching. Pierce dough all over with a fork. Bake 20 to 30 minutes or until golden. Cool completely in tin, then transfer to a serving dish.
To assemble gâteau, warm jam and brush over prebaked pastry round. Place cooled cake on top of pastry base. Spread non-dairy whipped topping over top and sides of gâteau. Cut pineapple rings into pieces. Peel and slice kiwi fruit and mango. Halve cherries. Arrange fruit over gâteau; sprinkle with pineapple juice. Press toasted sliced almonds onto sides of gâteau.

Sweet Pecan Pie

Pastry:
2-1/4 cups (250 g) all-purpose flour
Pinch of salt
3/4 cup (180 g) butter, cut in small pieces
About 1/3 cup (100 ml) ice water

Filling:
3 eggs
1/3 cup (100 g) molasses
3 tablespoons (50 g) light corn syrup
4 tablespoons (60 g) butter
1/4 cup plus 2 tablespoons (40 g) all-purpose flour, sifted
1/2 teaspoon vanilla extract
Pinch of salt
2-1/4 cups (250 g) pecan halves

To make pastry, sift flour and salt into a large bowl. Using a pastry blender or 2 knives, cut in butter until evenly distributed and mixture resembles breadcrumbs. With a fork, lightly mix in enough ice water to make a dough. Press into a ball and wrap in foil or plastic wrap. Refrigerate 2 hours.

Preheat oven to 400°F (205°C). On a floured surface, roll out dough to fit a 10-inch (25-cm) flan tin with a removable bottom. Place dough in tin without stretching. Do not pierce pastry shell. Bake blind, page 9, 10 to 12 minutes or until golden. Do not turn off oven.

To make filling, beat eggs lightly in a medium bowl. Add molasses and syrup; beat well. Melt butter; cool slightly. Stir flour and butter into egg mixture. Fold in vanilla, salt and nuts. Pour nut filling into pastry shell. Bake 25 to 30 minutes. Cool slightly in tin before transferring to a rack to cool completely.

Cook's Tip

Try making this pie with walnuts or Brazil nuts instead of pecans.

Chocolate Almond Roll

Cake:
5 eggs, separated
3/4 cup (180 g) sugar
Pinch of salt
Pinch of ground cinnamon
1/2 teaspoon vanilla extract
Grated peel of 1/2 lemon
4 tablespoons (50 g) butter
3-1/2 oz. (90 g) unsweetened chocolate, grated
1 cup (100 g) all-purpose flour, sifted
1 cup (100 g) ground almonds

Frosting:
4 oz. (100 g) semisweet chocolate
1/2 cup (50 g) toasted sliced almonds, page 47

Grease a Balmoral pan or a 9-1/4x5-1/4-inch (23x13-cm) loaf pan and sprinkle pan with fine breadcrumbs. Preheat oven to 375°F (190°C).

To make cake, put egg yolks, half the sugar, salt, cinnamon, vanilla and lemon peel into a large bowl. Beat until pale and creamy, 5 to 10 minutes with an electric mixer. Melt butter; cool slightly. Beat egg whites until stiff; fold in remaining sugar. Fold a fourth of egg white mixture into egg yolk mixture. Fold in chocolate, flour, almonds and remaining egg white mixture. Fold in butter. Turn batter into prepared pan; smooth the surface. Bake 40 to 50 minutes or until a wooden pick or skewer inserted in center comes out clean. Cool cake on a rack.

To make frosting, melt chocolate in a double boiler over low heat. Spread chocolate over cake. Sprinkle with almonds. Let stand until chocolate is firm.

Daisy Cake

Cake:
1-1/2 cups (300 g) butter, softened
1 cup (100 g) ground almonds
6 eggs, separated
Grated peel of 1 lemon
1 teaspoon vanilla extract
2/3 cup (140 g) sugar
1 cup plus 2 tablespoons (120 g)
  all-purpose flour
Scant 3/4 cup (80 g) cornstarch

Frosting:
1/2 cup (150 g) apricot jam
1-2/3 cups (200 g) powdered sugar, sifted
1 tablespoon lemon juice
1 tablespoon water

Grease a 9-inch (23-cm) fluted cake pan; sprinkle with fine breadcrumbs. Preheat oven to 375°F (190°C).

To make cake, beat butter and ground almonds in a large bowl. Stir in egg yolks, lemon peel and vanilla. Beat egg whites until stiff; carefully fold in sugar. Fold egg white mixture into butter mixture. Sift flour and cornstarch together. Fold into mixture. Turn batter into prepared cake pan; smooth the surface. Bake 50 to 60 minutes or until a wooden pick or skewer inserted in center comes out clean. Remove cake from pan; cool slightly on a rack.

To make frosting, warm apricot jam and press through a strainer to obtain jelly. Brush apricot jelly over warm cake. Let stand 30 minutes. Combine powdered sugar, lemon juice and water in a small bowl. Spread frosting over cake.

Hazelnut Loaf Cake

1 cup plus 2 tablespoons (250 g) soft margarine
3/4 cup plus 2 tablespoons (200 g) granulated sugar
2 tablespoons (25 g) vanilla sugar, page 18
4 eggs
2-1/4 cups (250 g) ground hazelnuts
2-1/4 cups (250 g) self-rising flour
1 teaspoon baking powder
1 tablespoon brandy
Powdered sugar

Grease a 9-1/4x5-1/4-inch (23x13-cm) loaf pan. Preheat oven to 350°F (175°C).

In a large bowl, beat margarine, unflavored sugar and vanilla sugar until light and fluffy. Beat in eggs one at a time. Add hazelnuts. Sift flour and baking powder together. Fold into mixture, combining thoroughly. Stir in brandy. Turn batter into greased loaf pan. Bake 1 to 1-1/4 hours or until a wooden pick or skewer inserted in center comes out clean. Remove from pan; cool on rack. Sift powdered sugar over cooled cake.

Cook's Tip

For deep cakes, test for doneness with a warmed metal skewer. Towards the end of cooking time, insert the warmed skewer into the middle of the cake and then withdraw it. If it comes out clean the cake is cooked.

Crumb Cake

3/4 cup plus 2 tablespoons (200 g) soft margarine
3/4 cup plus 2 tablespoons (200 g) granulated sugar
1 egg
Grated peel of 1 lemon
4-1/2 cups (500 g) all-purpose flour
1 teaspoon baking powder
1 (1-lb., 456-g) jar cherry jam
1/2 cup (50 g) ground almonds
Powdered sugar

Grease a 10-inch (25-cm) springform cake pan. Preheat oven to 425°F (220°C).

In a large bowl, beat margarine and granulated sugar until creamy. Stir in egg and lemon peel. Sift flour and baking powder together. Fold a few tablespoons into mixture. Add remaining flour mixture. With fingertips, work mixture quickly into crumbs. Place half the crumbs in prepared cake pan. Spread with jam. Mix remaining crumbs with almonds and scatter over jam. Bake 50 to 60 minutes or until top is browned. Remove cake from pan; cool on a rack.

Sift powdered sugar over cooled cake.

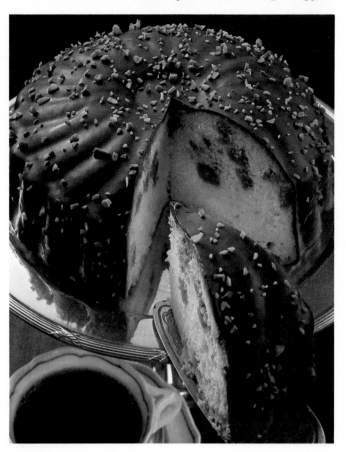

Frosted Orange Loaf Cake

Cake:
1 cup plus 2 tablespoons (250 g) soft margarine
1 cup plus 2 tablespoons (250 g) sugar
3 eggs plus 4 egg yolks
1 cup (100 g) self-rising flour
Pinch of salt
1 tablespoon orange-flavored liqueur
Grated peel of 2 oranges
Grated peel of 1 lemon
3 tablespoons orange juice
1 tablespoon lemon juice
Scant 1 cup (100 g) cornstarch
1 cup (100 g) ground almonds
1/2 cup (75 g) finely chopped candied orange peel

Frosting:
3 tablespoons orange jelly or marmalade
1-2/3 cups (200 g) powdered sugar, sifted
3 tablespoons orange juice
3 tablespoons (25 g) finely chopped candied orange peel

Grease a 9-1/4x5-1/4-inch (23x13-cm) loaf pan and sprinkle with fine breadcrumbs. Preheat oven to 350°F (175°C).
To make cake, beat margarine and sugar in a medium bowl until light and fluffy. Beat in eggs and egg yolks one at a time with a few tablespoons of flour. Mix in salt, liqueur, orange and lemon peel and juices. Sift remaining flour with cornstarch. Fold into cake mixture with almonds and candied peel. Turn batter into prepared pan. Bake 1-1/4 hours or until a wooden pick or skewer inserted in center comes out clean. Remove from pan; cool on a wire rack.
To make frosting, warm orange jelly or marmalade and spread over top of cooled cake. Combine powdered sugar and orange juice in a small bowl. Spread frosting over cake. Sprinkle with candied peel while frosting is soft.

Marzipan Cake

Marzipan:
4-1/2 oz. (120 g) almond paste
1 cup (100 g) grated pistachio nuts or almonds
1 tablespoon liqueur such as arrack or ouzo

Cake:
1 cup plus 2 tablespoons (250 g) soft margarine
1 cup plus 1 tablespoon (240 g) sugar
5 eggs, separated
Pinch of salt
1 tablespoon liqueur such as arrack or ouzo
1 teaspoon vanilla extract
2 cups (230 g) all-purpose flour
Scant 3/4 cup (85 g) cornstarch
1 teaspoon baking powder

Frosting:
6 oz. (175 g) semisweet chocolate
1/4 cup (25 g) chopped pistachio nuts

Grease an 8- to 9-inch (20- to 23-cm) round fluted cake pan; sprinkle with breadcrumbs. Preheat oven to 375°F (190°C).
To make marzipan, knead almond paste with pistachios or almonds and arrack or ouzo. On a surface dusted lightly with powdered sugar, roll out marzipan 1/2 inch (1 cm) thick. Cut into 1/2-inch (1-cm) cubes.
To make cake, beat margarine, half the sugar, egg yolks, salt, arrack or ouzo and vanilla in a large bowl until thoroughly mixed. Beat egg whites until stiff; beat in remaining sugar. Fold into egg yolk mixture. Sift together flour, cornstarch and baking powder. Stir in marzipan cubes. Fold flour-marzipan mixture into egg mixture. Turn batter into prepared pan. Bake 1-1/4 to 1-1/2 hours or until a skewer inserted in center comes out clean. Remove from pan; cool on a rack.
To make frosting, melt chocolate in a double boiler over low heat. Spread over cooled cake and decorate with pistachios.

Fresh Strawberry Savarin

Savarin Dough:
3 tablespoons sugar
1 cup (250 ml) warm milk (110°F, 43°C)
1-1/2 pkgs. active dry yeast
3 cups (350 g) all-purpose flour
1/2 cup plus 2 tablespoons butter or margarine
4 eggs
1 tablespoon vanilla sugar, page 18
1/2 teaspoon salt

Syrup:
1/3 cup (100 ml) rum
1/2 cup (125 ml) white wine
1 cup (250 ml) water
2/3 cup (150 g) sugar

Filling:
1-2/3 cups (225 g) strawberries
2/3 cup (150 ml) whipping cream
1/4 cup (50 g) sugar
1 teaspoon chopped pistachio nuts

To make savarin dough, stir 1 teaspoon unflavored sugar into warm milk and sprinkle with yeast. Let stand 5 minutes or until the surface is frothy. Stir gently to moisten any dry particles remaining on top. Sift flour into a large bowl. Melt butter or margarine; cool slightly. Beat eggs with remaining unflavored sugar in a medium bowl until frothy. Mix in vanilla sugar, salt and butter or margarine. Stir egg mixture into yeast mixture. Pour into flour, mixing well to almost pouring consistency. Cover and let rise in a warm place 10 minutes. Grease and flour a 9-inch (23-cm) savarin pan.

Beat mixture with a wooden spoon and pour into prepared savarin pan. Cover and set aside until mixture has risen almost to top of pan. Preheat oven to 425°F (220°C). Bake savarin 40 minutes or until golden. Turn out onto a rack.

To make syrup, stir rum, white wine, water and sugar in a small saucepan over medium heat until sugar has dissolved. Reduce heat and simmer 5 minutes. Place a baking sheet under cooling rack to catch syrup. Pour syrup slowly over warm savarin until absorbed. Cool. Place cooled savarin on a cake platter.

To make filling, wash, hull and halve strawberries. Whip cream with sugar until stiff. Put whipped cream mixture into a pastry bag fitted with a fluted nozzle. Place most of strawberries in center of savarin and pipe cream over them. Garnish with remaining strawberries and pistachios.

Cook's Tip:

This well-known French dessert can also be served in the following classic ways:

Savarin Chantilly: Steep savarin in sugar syrup made with kirsch instead of rum, brush with warm apricot jam and fill with whipped cream.

Savarin with Raspberries: Steep savarin in sugar syrup made with raspberry-flavored liqueur instead of rum then fill with whipped cream and raspberries.

Marzipan Twist

Yeast Dough:
1/4 cup (50 g) sugar
1/2 cup (125 ml) warm milk (110°F, 43°C)
1 pkg. active dry yeast
2-1/3 cups (350 g) all-purpose flour
Pinch of salt
4 tablespoons (50 g) butter
Grated peel of 1/2 lemon
1 egg, beaten

Filling:
2 cups (225 g) ground almonds
2 egg whites
1/4 cup (50 g) sugar
3 tablespoons rum

Glaze:
1/4 cup (25 g) powdered sugar, sifted
1 tablespoon lemon juice
3 tablespoons water

To make yeast dough, stir 1 teaspoon sugar into milk and sprinkle with yeast. Let stand 5 minutes or until frothy. Stir gently to moisten any dry particles. Sift flour, remaining sugar and salt into a large bowl. Melt butter; stir into yeast mixture with lemon peel. Pour into flour mixture with egg, combining to make a dough. Knead on a floured surface until smooth. Let rise in a warm place 30 to 40 minutes. Grease a baking sheet.
To make filling, combine almonds, egg whites, sugar and rum.

On a floured surface, roll out risen dough to an 18x12-inch (45x30-cm) rectangle. Spread with filling. Roll up lengthwise. Cut roll into 2 equal lengths and wind both pieces around each other to make a single twist. Place on greased baking sheet. Cover and let rise in a warm place 15 minutes. Preheat oven to 375°F (190°C). Bake 35 minutes or until twist is golden brown.
To make glaze, combine powdered sugar, lemon juice and water in a small bowl. Spoon glaze over warm twist.

Surprise Almond Braid

Yeast Dough:
1/4 cup (50 g) sugar
1/2 cup (125 ml) warm milk (110°F, 43°C)
1 pkg. active dry yeast
2-1/3 cups (350 g) all-purpose flour
1/2 teaspoon salt
4 tablespoons (50 g) butter
2 eggs

Filling & Glaze:
1/2 cup (50 g) ground almonds
1/3 cup (100 g) apricot jam
1/3 cup (50 g) raisins
1/2 cup (50 g) chopped almonds
1 egg yolk, beaten
1 tablespoon sugar
1 tablespoon water

To make yeast dough, stir 1 teaspoon sugar into milk and sprinkle with yeast. Let stand 5 minutes. Stir gently. Sift flour, remaining sugar and salt into a large bowl. Melt butter; cool slightly. Lightly beat butter and eggs into yeast mixture. Add to flour mixture, combining to make a dough. Knead dough 5 minutes on a floured surface. Cover and let rise in a warm place 30 to 40 minutes. Grease a baking sheet. On a floured surface, roll out dough to an 18x12-inch (45x30-cm) rectangle. Starting 3/4 inch (2 cm) from 1 end, mark into 3 equal strips lengthwise.
To make filling and glaze, mix ground almonds with apricot jam and spread over middle strip of dough. Sprinkle with raisins and chopped almonds. Cut the 2 outside strips into 3/4-inch (1.5-cm) wide slanting strips; crisscross strips over filling. Place on greased baking sheet. Cover and let rise in a warm place 15 minutes. Preheat oven to 425°F (220°C). Brush braid with egg yolk. Bake 10 minutes. Reduce heat to 375°F (190°C) and bake 10 minutes more or until golden brown. Mix sugar and water. Brush glaze over warm braid.

Berlin Specialty Cake

Yeast Dough:
1/2 cup (100 g) sugar
Scant 1/2 cup (100 ml) warm milk (110°F, 43°C)
1 pkg. active dry yeast
2-3/4 cups (300 g) all-purpose flour
Pinch of salt
3/4 cup (175 g) butter
3 eggs
Grated peel of 1 lemon
Generous 1 cup (200 g) dried currants

Frosting:
4 to 6 oz. (100 to 150 g) semisweet chocolate
1 tablespoon pine nuts

To make yeast dough, stir 1 teaspoon sugar into warm milk and sprinkle with yeast. Let stand 5 minutes or until the surface is frothy. Stir gently to moisten any dry particles remaining on top. Sift flour, remaining sugar and salt into a large bowl. Melt butter; cool slightly. Lightly beat butter, eggs and lemon peel into yeast mixture. Pour into flour mixture, combining to make a dough. Beat dough until it bubbles. Cover and let rise in a warm place 30 to 40 minutes. Grease an 8- to 9-inch (20- to 23-cm) kugelhopf pan and sprinkle with fine breadcrumbs. Preheat oven to 350°F (180°C).

On a lightly floured surface, knead currants into dough. Place dough in prepared pan. Bake 50 to 60 minutes or until a skewer inserted near center comes out clean. Remove from pan; cool on a rack.

To make frosting, melt chocolate in a double boiler on low heat. Pour over cake to cover it completely. Sprinkle with pine nuts while chocolate is soft. Let stand until chocolate is firm.

Viennese Kugelhopf

2/3 cup (150 g) granulated sugar
1/2 cup plus 1 tablespoon (150 ml) warm milk (110°F, 43°C)
2 pkgs. active dry yeast
4-1/2 cups (500 g) all-purpose flour
1/2 cup plus 2 tablespoons (150 g) butter
5 eggs, separated
Pinch of salt
1/2 cup (125 ml) whipping cream
1/2 cup (75 g) seedless golden raisins
3 tablespoons rum
Grated peel of 1 lemon
Powdered sugar

Viennese kugelhopf is particularly small; if possible bake the given quantity of dough in three 6-1/2-inch (16-cm) kugelhopf pans. Grease pans.

Stir 1 teaspoon granulated sugar into warm milk and sprinkle with yeast. Let stand 5 minutes or until the surface is frothy. Stir gently to moisten any dry particles remaining on top. Sift flour into a large bowl. Melt butter; cool slightly. Beat butter, remaining granulated sugar, egg yolks, salt and cream in a medium bowl until frothy. Stir in yeast mixture with seedless golden raisins, rum and lemon peel. Pour into flour mixture, combining to make a dough. Beat egg whites until stiff. Fold into dough. Beat mixture until it bubbles. Turn into greased pans, filling each two-thirds full. Cover and let rise in a warm place 15 minutes. Preheat oven to 400°F (205°C). Bake 40 to 60 minutes or until a skewer inserted in center comes out clean. Turn out cakes onto racks to cool.

Sift powdered sugar over cooled cakes.

Poppy Seed Garland

Yeast Dough:
1/2 cup (100 g) sugar
1 cup (250 ml) warm milk (110°F, 43°C)
3 pkgs. active dry yeast
4-1/2 cups (500 g) all-purpose flour
Pinch of salt
1/2 cup plus 1 tablespoon (125 g) butter
2 eggs
Grated peel and juice of 1 lemon

Filling:
1 cup (175 g) raisins
1 (12-oz.) can poppy seed filling
Pinch of salt
Pinch of ground cinnamon
1 egg yolk, beaten

Frosting:
1/4 cup (25 g) powdered sugar, sifted
1 teaspoon lemon juice
1 tablespoon water
4 candied cherries

To make yeast dough, stir 1 teaspoon sugar into a warm milk and sprinkle with yeast. Let stand 5 minutes or until the surface is frothy. Stir gently to moisten any dry particles remaining on top. Sift flour, remaining sugar and salt into a large bowl. Melt butter; cool slightly. Lightly beat butter, eggs, lemon peel and juice into yeast mixture. Pour into flour mixture, combining to make a dough. Cover and let rise in a warm place 20 minutes. Grease a 9-inch (23-cm) tube pan.

To make filling, wash raisins in hot water; dry well on paper towels. Finely chop raisins. In a medium bowl, combine chopped raisins, poppy seed filling, salt and cinnamon. Preheat oven to 400°F (205°C).

On a floured surface, roll out risen dough to a 20x10-inch (50x25-cm) rectangle. Sprinkle poppy seed mixture over top. Roll up dough from the longest edge, making sure the ends are as thick as the center. Brush edges and ends with egg yolk and press to seal. Place roll in greased tube pan with seam on top. Press ends together firmly so filling does not escape. Bake 50 to 60 minutes or until golden brown. Remove cake from pan; cool on a rack.

To make frosting, combine powdered sugar, lemon juice and water in a small bowl. Spoon frosting over cooled cake. Decorate with halved candied cherries while frosting is soft.

Cook's Tip

Yeast mixtures rise more quickly in a warm room. However, if it is more convenient, the dough may be covered and left overnight in the refrigerator to rise. The next day, the dough should stand at room temperature for about 1 hour before proceeding.

Pear Cheesecake

Pastry:
1-1/4 cups (150 g) all-purpose flour
Pinch of salt
7 tablespoons (95 g) butter, cut in small pieces
3 tablespoons (45 g) sugar
Few drops of vanilla extract
1/2 beaten egg

Filling & Topping:
1 (1-lb., 456-g) can pear halves, undrained
1/4 cup (150 ml) kirsch
9 oz. (250 g) cream cheese
1/2 cup plus 2 tablespoons (140 g) sugar
Juice of 1 lemon
1 envelope unflavored gelatin
1 cup (250 ml) whipping cream
4 tablespoons Crushed Praline, page 15
1/3 cup (100 g) red currant jelly

To make pastry, sift flour and salt into a medium bowl. Using a pastry blender, cut in butter evenly. Mix in sugar, vanilla and egg to make a dough. Wrap in foil or plastic wrap. Refrigerate 2 hours. Preheat oven to 400°F (205°C). On a floured surface, roll out dough to fit an 8-inch (20-cm) flan tin with a removable bottom. Place dough in tin. Bake blind, page 9, 30 minutes or until golden. Cool on a rack.
To make filling and topping, drain pears; reserve 3 tablespoons juice. Moisten pears with a little kirsch. Beat cream cheese, 1/2 cup (120 g) sugar, lemon juice and remaining kirsch in a medium bowl. Dissolve gelatin in reserved pear juice over low heat. Cool slightly. Stir into cheese mixture. Place pears in pastry shell. Fill with cheese mixture. Refrigerate. Whip cream with remaining sugar. Mix two-thirds of cream, 3 tablespoons praline and half the red currant jelly. Spread over cheesecake. Decorate with piped rosettes using remaining cream mixture. Garnish with remaining jelly and praline.

Grape Cheesecake

Cake:
4 eggs, separated
3 tablespoons lukewarm water
2/3 cup (140 g) sugar
1 cup (120 g) all-purpose flour
Scant 1/2 cup (60 g) cornstarch
1 teaspoon baking powder

Filling & Topping:
1 lb. (450 g) cream cheese
2 egg yolks
2/3 cup (150 g) sugar
Juice of 1 lemon
1 envelope unflavored gelatin
2 tablespoons water
1 cup (250 ml) whipping cream
4 oz. (100 g) green grapes
8 oz. (225 g) black grapes
1/2 cup (150 g) grape jelly
1 cup (100 g) toasted sliced almonds, page 47

Grease the inside bottom of a 9-inch (23-cm) springform cake pan. Preheat oven to 375°F (190°C).
To make cake, beat egg yolks, water and half the sugar in a large bowl until pale and creamy. Beat egg whites until stiff; fold in remaining sugar. Fold into egg yolk mixture. Sift flour with cornstarch and baking powder. Fold into egg mixture. Pour into greased cake pan. Bake 40 minutes or until a wooden pick inserted in center comes out clean. Cool on a rack 2 hours.
To make filling and topping, beat cream cheese, egg yolks, sugar and lemon juice. Dissolve gelatin in water over low heat. Cool slightly. Whip cream until stiff. Fold into cheese mixture with gelatin. Cut cake into 2 layers. Fill with half the cheese mixture. Spread remainder over top and sides of cake. Arrange grapes on top as illustrated. Warm jelly; drizzle warm jelly over black grapes. Press almonds onto sides of cake.

Rich Cream Cheesecake

Shortbread:
1-3/4 cups (200 g) all-purpose flour
8 tablespoons (120 g) butter, cut in small pieces
1/4 cup plus 1 tablespoon (70 g) sugar
1 egg yolk
Pinch of salt
Grated peel of 1/2 lemon

Filling:
1 cup (250 ml) milk
3/4 cup plus 2 tablespoons (200 g) granulated sugar
Pinch of salt
Grated peel of 1 lemon
4 egg yolks
2 envelopes unflavored gelatin
3 tablespoons water
Scant 2 cups (450 ml) whipping cream
1 lb. (450 g) cream cheese
Powdered sugar

To make shortbread, sift flour onto a clean working surface or into a large bowl. Dot with butter. Make a well in the center and add sugar, egg yolk, salt and lemon peel. Working from the center outwards, quickly knead all ingredients to a smooth dough. Press into a ball and wrap in foil or plastic wrap. Refrigerate 2 hours.

Preheat oven to 375°F (190°C). Grease 2 baking sheets. Line sides of a 10-inch (25-cm) springform cake pan with a strip of waxed paper. On a floured surface, roll out dough to make two 10-inch (25-cm) rounds. Place on greased baking sheets. Pierce 1 round all over with a fork to prevent it from rising unevenly during cooking. Bake 8 to 10 minutes or until golden brown. While still warm, cut round which was pierced with a fork into 12 equal portions. Cool on a rack with other round.

To make filling, put milk, sugar, salt, lemon peel and egg yolks into a double boiler. Heat gently, stirring constantly until smooth and slightly thickened. Remove lemon custard from heat and transfer to a medium bowl. In a small saucepan, dissolve gelatin in water over low heat. Stir into lemon custard; cool. Whip cream until stiff. Beat cream cheese to soften. When custard begins to set, stir in beaten cream cheese. Put mixture into a blender and process until smooth. Return to bowl and carefully fold in whipped cream.

Place uncut shortbread round in prepared springform pan. Spoon in cream cheese filling; smooth the surface. Arrange cut shortbread on top to form a round. Refrigerate until set.

When completely set, remove cheesecake from pan and carefully peel away waxed paper. Sift powdered sugar over cake.

Cook's Tip

If desired, add fresh or frozen strawberries, raspberries or blueberries to the cream cheese mixture. Frozen fruit should be thawed, drained and sweetened to taste. If fresh fruit is used, wash, pat dry with paper towels and sprinkle with sugar. Let stand for a few minutes before adding to the mixture.

Pineapple Cream Gâteau

Cake:
6 eggs, separated
2/3 cup (150 g) sugar
1 cup (100 g) all-purpose flour
1 teaspoon baking powder
Scant 1/2 cup (50 g) unsweetened cocoa powder
1/2 cup (50 g) ground almonds
4 tablespoons (50 g) butter

Filling & Topping:
1/4 cup (25 g) cornstarch
2/3 cup plus 1 tablespoon (160 g) sugar
2 cups plus 2 tablespoons (500 ml) milk
1 cup plus 2 tablespoons (250 g) butter
1 tablespoon rum
7 slices canned pineapple
3/4 cup (80 g) toasted sliced almonds, page 47
7 candied cherries, halved

Grease a 10-inch (25-cm) springform cake pan. Preheat oven to 375°F (190°C).

To make cake, put egg yolks and a third of the sugar into a large bowl. Beat until thick and creamy, 5 to 10 minutes with an electric mixer. Beat egg whites until stiff. Gradually add remaining sugar and fold in well. Sift flour with baking powder and cocoa powder. Mix in ground almonds. Fold egg white mixture into egg yolk mixture. Carefully fold in flour mixture. Melt butter;

cool slightly. Stir butter into batter. Turn into greased pan. Bake 35 to 45 minutes or until a wooden pick inserted in center comes out clean. Cool a few minutes in pan. Turn out onto a rack to cool completely.

To make filling and topping, blend cornstarch and sugar with a little milk in a medium bowl. Heat remaining milk in a medium saucepan. Stir hot milk into cornstarch mixture. Return to saucepan and bring to a boil, stirring constantly. Cook a few minutes until thickened. Return mixture to bowl and cool, stirring frequently. Beat butter and rum in a medium bowl until pale and creamy. Gradually add butter mixture to cooled cornstarch sauce beating well after each addition.

Cut cooled cake horizontally into 3 layers. Cut pineapple slices into small cubes and reserve 14 for decoration. Spread bottom cake layer with some butter cream. Arrange pineapple cubes on top and cover with a little more butter cream. Place second cake layer on top; spread with butter cream and top with third cake layer. Spread top and sides of cake thinly with butter cream. Put remaining butter cream into a pastry bag fitted with a fluted nozzle. Cover gâteau with almonds. Pipe 14 rosettes of butter cream around top of gâteau. Place a pineapple cube and a halved candied cherry on each rosette.

Cook's Tip

When beating egg yolks and sugar together for an extra light cake, it is quicker to use an electric mixer. If you do not have an electric mixer, set the bowl over a saucepan of hot water and use a rotary or balloon whisk. The mixture is ready when it falls from the whisk in a continuous stream.

Gooseberry Meringue Gâteau

Cake:
6 eggs, separated
2/3 cup (150 g) sugar
1 cup (120 g) all-purpose flour
1 teaspoon baking powder
1/2 cup (50 g) ground almonds
4 tablespoons (50 g) butter

Filling:
1-1/4 cups (150 g) ground almonds
Scant 1/4 cup (50 ml) rum
3 tablespoons powdered sugar
Scant 1/4 cup (50 ml) water

Topping:
1 lb. (500 g) gooseberries
1 cup (225 g) sugar
1/2 cup (125 ml) water
4 egg whites
1/2 teaspoon vanilla extract
1 cup (100 g) toasted sliced almonds, page 47

Grease a 10-inch (25-cm) springform cake pan. Preheat oven to 375°F (190°C).
To make cake, put egg yolks and a third of the sugar into a large bowl. Beat until pale and creamy, 5 to 10 minutes with an electric mixer. Beat egg whites until stiff. Gradually fold in remaining sugar. Sift flour with baking powder. Mix in ground almonds.

Fold egg white mixture into egg yolk mixture. Fold in flour mixture. Melt butter; cool slightly. Stir butter into batter. Turn into greased pan. Bake 35 to 40 minutes or until a wooden pick inserted in center comes out clean. Cool on a rack 2 hours.
To make filling, combine almonds, rum, powdered sugar and water in a medium bowl to make a smooth paste. Cut cooled cake horizontally into 2 layers. Join cake layers with almond filling. Preheat oven to 450°F (230°C).
To make topping, wash and stem gooseberries. Combine 1/4 cup (50 g) sugar and water in a medium saucepan. Bring to a boil and add gooseberries. Simmer over low heat about 10 minutes until gooseberries are soft but not disintegrating. Drain thoroughly. Beat egg whites until stiff; beat in remaining sugar. Fold in vanilla.

Arrange drained gooseberries over cake, reserving 14 whole gooseberries for decoration. Spread about two-thirds of the meringue mixture thickly over top and sides of cake. Place remaining meringue mixture in a pastry bag fitted with a fluted nozzle. Pipe 14 meringue garlands on top of cake, working from center outwards and ending each in a rosette. Bake 1 minute or until meringue is light golden brown on top. Decorate center and sides of gateau with almonds. Top each meringue rosette with a reserved gooseberry.

Cook's Tip

To achieve a light cake, use a large metal spoon to fold in ingredients and work quickly and lightly. Cake batter must be put into a preheated oven without delay.

Caribbean Coconut Cake

Cake:
4 eggs, separated
3 tablespoons lukewarm water
1/2 cup plus 1 tablespoon (140 g) sugar
Grated peel of 1/2 lemon
1 cup (120 g) all-purpose flour
1 teaspoon baking powder

Filling & Topping:
1 coconut or 2-2/3 cups (225 g) shredded coconut
1-1/4 cups (300 ml) boiling water, if using shredded coconut
1 cup (225 g) sugar
1 tablespoon dark rum
1/4 cup (25 g) cornstarch
1-1/4 cups (300 ml) milk
3 eggs, separated
1/2 teaspoon vanilla extract
16 candied cherries

Grease the inside bottom of an 8-inch (20-cm) springform cake pan. Preheat oven to 375°F (190°C).

To make cake, put egg yolks, water, half the sugar and lemon peel into a large bowl. Beat until pale and creamy, 5 to 10 minutes with an electric mixer. Beat egg whites until stiff; fold in remaining sugar. Carefully fold into egg yolk mixture. Sift flour with baking powder. Fold into egg mixture. Turn batter into greased pan; smooth the surface. Bake 35 to 40 minutes or until a wooden pick inserted in center comes out clean. Cool slightly in pan then turn out onto a rack to cool completely. Let stand overnight if possible.

To make filling and topping, pierce coconut twice at thinnest part of shell. Pour off milk and reserve. Cut coconut in half and scoop out flesh. Cover and reserve. In a small saucepan, boil 3 tablespoons coconut milk with 1/4 cup (50 g) sugar until sugar has completely dissolved. Add rum and let cool.

If using shredded coconut, soak 1-1/3 cups (100 g) in boiling water overnight, then strain and reserve liquid. Use reserved liquid in place of fresh coconut milk.

Blend cornstarch, 4 tablespoons milk and egg yolks in a medium bowl. Heat remaining milk and 6 tablespoons (75 g) sugar in a medium saucepan until almost boiling. Stir hot milk into cornstarch mixture. Return to saucepan and bring to a boil, stirring constantly. Remove from heat and stir in vanilla. Cool slightly. Beat egg whites until stiff. Carefully fold in remaining sugar. Fold into cornstarch mixture. Cool a little longer.

Cut cooled cake horizontally into 3 layers. Spread filling thickly over bottom layer. Place second layer on top, sprinkle with half the coconut milk mixture and let soak in. Spread with a layer of filling then top with third cake layer. Sprinkle with remaining coconut milk mixture and let soak in. Spread top and sides of cake with remaining vanilla cream. Finely grate coconut flesh and use to cover cake, or use remaining shredded coconut. Arrange candied cherries around edge of cake.

Austrian Hazelnut Cake

8 tablespoons (100 g) butter, softened
1/2 cup (100 g) granulated sugar
4 eggs, separated
1 cup (100 g) ground hazelnuts
3 tablespoons (30 g) finely chopped candied lemon peel
Powdered sugar

Grease a 10-inch (25-cm) layer cake pan and line the bottom with waxed paper. Grease waxed paper and sprinkle with fine breadcrumbs. Preheat oven to 350°F (175°C).

In a medium bowl, cream butter and sugar until light and fluffy. Beat in egg yolks, two at a time. Add hazelnuts and lemon peel. Beat egg whites until very stiff; fold into egg yolk mixture. Turn batter into prepared pan; smooth the surface. Bake 40 minutes or until a wooden pick inserted in center comes out clean. Turn out cake onto a rack to cool.

Place a paper doily on cooled cake and sift powdered sugar over doily. Remove doily carefully, leaving a pretty design.

Walnut Cream Pie

Pastry:
1/2 cup plus 3 tablespoons (160 g) butter, softened
2/3 cup (150 g) sugar
Pinch of salt
1 egg
2-3/4 cups (300 g) all-purpose flour

Filling:
1-1/2 tablespoons butter
1-1/4 cups plus 2 tablespoons (300 g) sugar
2-1/4 cups (250 g) coarsely chopped walnuts
1 cup (250 ml) whipping cream
1 egg yolk, beaten

To make pastry, beat butter, sugar, salt and egg in a large bowl. Sift in flour. Knead ingredients to make a soft dough. Press into a ball and wrap in foil or plastic wrap. Refrigerate 2 hours.

On a lightly floured surface, roll out two-thirds of dough to fit a 9-inch (23-cm) removable-bottomed flan tin, with 1-inch (2.5-cm) of dough overlapping around top of tin. Place dough in tin without stretching. Preheat oven to 400°F (205°C).
To make filling, melt butter in a small saucepan. Add sugar. Cook, stirring constantly until mixture caramelizes to a light golden brown. Add walnuts and cream. Heat to just below boiling. Cool. Spread cooled filling over pastry shell.

Roll out remaining dough into a circle to cover pie. Place over walnut filling. Brush overlapping sides with egg yolk and press onto pie top to seal. Brush top of pie with egg yolk. Pierce several times with a fork. Bake 30 to 40 minutes or until pastry is a rich golden brown. Cool slightly in tin then transfer to a rack to cool completely.

Swedish Almond Flan

Pastry:
1/2 cup plus 2 tablespoons (150 g) butter or margarine, softened
3 tablespoons (40 g) sugar
1/2 teaspoon vanilla extract
Pinch of salt
2 egg yolks
1-3/4 cups (200 g) all-purpose flour

Filling:
1/2 cup plus 1 tablespoon (125 g) butter, softened
1 cup (125 g) powdered sugar
2 eggs
Generous 1 cup (125 g) ground almonds
Grated peel of 1 lemon
3 tablespoons (20 g) all-purpose flour

To make pastry, beat butter or margarine, sugar, vanilla, salt and egg yolks in a large bowl. Sift in flour. Knead ingredients to make a soft dough. Press into a ball and wrap in foil or plastic wrap. Refrigerate 2 hours.

Preheat oven to 350°F (175°C).
To make filling, beat butter, powdered sugar and eggs in a medium bowl until creamy. Stir in ground almonds, lemon peel and flour.

On a floured surface, roll out dough to fit an 8-inch (20-cm) flan tin with a removable bottom. Place dough in tin without stretching. Spread filling over pastry shell. Bake 45 minutes or until filling is light golden brown. Cool in tin.

Spanish Vanilla Cake

Cake:
Generous 2 cups (250 g) ground almonds
2/3 cup (150 g) sugar
1/4 teaspoon vanilla extract
Pinch of salt
1 whole egg plus 6 eggs, separated
1 cup (100 g) all-purpose flour
1 teaspoon baking powder
1/3 cup (60 g) semisweet chocolate pieces

Frosting:
7 oz. (200 g) semisweet chocolate
2 to 3 tablespoons chopped pistachio nuts

Grease a 9-inch (23-cm) petal-patterned cake pan. Preheat oven to 375°F (190°C).
To make cake, mix almonds, half the sugar, vanilla, salt, whole egg and 6 egg yolks in a large bowl. Beat until creamy. Beat egg whites until stiff; fold in remaining sugar. Fold egg white mixture into egg yolk mixture. Sift flour and baking powder over mixture and fold in carefully. Fold in chocolate pieces. Turn batter into greased cake pan; smooth the surface. Bake 45 to 50 minutes or until a wooden pick inserted in center comes out clean. Cool cake slightly in cake pan then transfer to a rack to cool completely.
To make frosting, melt chocolate in a double boiler over low heat. Spread over top and sides of cooled cake. Sprinkle with pistachios while chocolate is soft.

Viennese Cherry Cake

Pastry:
8 tablespoons (100 g) butter, softened
1/4 cup (60 g) sugar
1-1/2 cups (150 g) all-purpose flour
1-1/2 to 3 tablespoons ice water

Cake:
1-1/4 cups plus 2 tablespoons (300 g) butter, softened
1-1/4 cups plus 2 tablespoons (300 g) granulated sugar
6 eggs, separated
Grated peel of 1 lemon
Pinch of salt
1-1/4 cups plus 2 tablespoons (150 g) all-purpose flour
1-1/4 cups (150 g) cornstarch
1 lb. (450 g) fresh pitted cherries or 1 cup (225 g) candied cherries
Powdered sugar

To make pastry, cream butter and sugar in a large bowl. Sift in flour. Knead well, adding enough ice water to make a soft dough. Press into a ball and wrap in foil or plastic wrap. Refrigerate 2 hours.

Preheat oven to 425°F (220°C). On a floured surface, roll out dough to fit the bottom of a 9-inch (23-cm) cake pan. Place dough in pan without stretching. Bake blind, page 9, 15 minutes or until golden. Reduce heat to 375°F (190°C).
To make cake, beat butter, half the sugar, egg yolks, lemon peel and salt in a large bowl until pale and fluffy. Beat egg whites until stiff; fold in remaining sugar. Carefully fold egg white mixture into egg yolk mixture. Sift flour and cornstarch over mixture and fold in. Pour cake batter over pastry; scatter cherries over top. If using candied cherries, toss lightly in enough flour to coat before adding to batter. Bake 1 to 1-1/4 hours or until a wooden pick inserted in center comes out clean. Cover with foil if cake becomes too brown. Turn out cake onto a rack to cool.

Sift powdered sugar over cooled cake.

Orange Almond Cake

Cake:
7 eggs, separated
1-1/4 cups (280 g) sugar
Grated peel and juice of 2 oranges
1/4 cup (30 g) all-purpose flour
1-1/2 cups (80 g) cake crumbs
2-1/2 cups (280 g) ground almonds

Topping:
2/3 cup (200 g) orange jelly or marmalade
1 cup (100 g) toasted sliced almonds, page 47
14 candied orange segments

Grease a 9-inch (23-cm) springform cake pan and sprinkle with fine breadcrumbs. Preheat oven to 400°F (205°C).
To make cake, put egg yolks and half the sugar into a large bowl. Beat until pale and creamy, 5 to 10 minutes with an electric mixer. Beat in orange peel and juice. Beat egg whites until stiff; fold in remaining sugar. Carefully fold egg white mixture into egg yolk mixture. Sift in flour. Fold into mixture with cake crumbs and almonds. Turn batter into prepared pan; smooth the surface. Bake 30 to 40 minutes or until a wooden pick inserted in center comes out clean. Remove cake from pan and cool slightly on a rack.
To make topping, warm orange jelly or marmalade; press through a strainer to obtain jelly. Brush jelly over top and sides of warm cake. Cover with almonds. Decorate with candied orange segments.

Cook's Tip

Toasted almonds give a professional touch to many recipes. Toast them on a baking sheet in a preheated 300°F (150°C) oven for 10 to 15 minutes. They should be stirred once or twice for even toasting.

Festive Chocolate Gâteau

Cake:
3/4 cup plus 2 tablespoons (200 g) sugar
4 eggs, separated
Scant 1/4 cup (50 ml) hot water
Pinch of salt
1-3/4 cups (200 g) all-purpose flour
1 teaspoon baking powder

Filling & Topping:
1 cup plus 2 tablespoons (250 g) butter
1-3/4 cups (225 g) powdered sugar
2 tablespoons (15 g) unsweetened cocoa powder
4 egg yolks
1/2 cup (150 g) orange jelly or marmalade
1 tablespoon Cointreau
7 candied orange segments
14 candied cherries
1/2 cup (50 g) chocolate sprinkles or chopped chocolate

Line a 9-inch (23-cm) springform cake pan with waxed paper; grease paper. Preheat oven to 425°F (220°C).
To make cake, reserve 1/4 cup (50 g) sugar and put remaining sugar, egg yolks and hot water into a large bowl. Beat until pale and creamy, 5 to 10 minutes with an electric mixer. Beat egg whites and salt until stiff; fold in reserved sugar. Drop egg white mixture onto egg yolk mixture. Sift flour and baking powder onto egg white mixture; fold in. Turn batter into prepared pan;

smooth the surface. Bake 30 minutes or until a wooden pick inserted in center comes out clean. Turn out cake onto a rack to cool. When cake has cooled completely, remove waxed paper.
To make filling and topping, beat butter in a large bowl until pale and creamy. Sift powdered sugar with cocoa powder. Beat egg yolks in a medium bowl. Mix in powdered sugar and cocoa powder. Add egg mixture a little at a time to butter, beating well after each addition. Combine orange jelly or marmalade and Cointreau in a small bowl.

Cut cooled cake horizontally into 4 layers. Spread 3 layers thinly with orange jelly or marmalade mixture and a little chocolate butter cream. Stack layers. Spread top and sides with about two-thirds of remaining chocolate butter cream. Place remaining chocolate butter cream in a pastry bag fitted with a fluted nozzle. With a sharp knife, mark cake into 14 portions. Decorate each portion with a swirl of piped chocolate butter cream ending in a rosette. Halve candied orange segments and place 1 half on each rosette. Top with candied cherries. Decorate sides with chocolate sprinkles or chopped chocolate.

Cook's Tip

When freezing elaborate cream gâteaux, place sheets of waxed paper between slices. This way you can take as few slices from the freezer as you want at one time.

Coffee Layer Gâteau

Cake:
1/2 cup plus 2 tablespoons (130 g) butter, softened
3/4 cup plus 2 tablespoons (200 g) sugar
Pinch each of salt, ground cinnamon and grated lemon peel
6 eggs, separated
5 oz. (130 g) semisweet chocolate
1-1/4 cups (130 g) all-purpose flour, sifted

Filling & Topping:
1-1/4 cups (300 ml) milk
1/4 cup (25 g) cornstarch
1 tablespoon instant coffee powder
2/3 cup (150 g) sugar
1 cup plus 2 tablespoons (250 g) butter
15 candied coffee beans
1/2 cup (50 g) toasted sliced almonds, page 47

Grease the inside bottom of a 9-inch (23-cm) springform cake pan. Preheat oven to 375°F (190°C).
To make cake, beat butter, half the sugar, salt, cinnamon and lemon peel in a large bowl until light and fluffy. Add egg yolks one at a time. Melt chocolate in a double boiler over low heat. Stir into butter mixture. Beat egg whites until stiff; beat in remaining sugar. Fold into chocolate mixture followed by flour. Turn batter into greased pan; smooth the surface. Bake 50 to 60 minutes or until a wooden pick inserted in center comes out clean. Turn out cake onto a rack to cool.

To make filling and topping, combine 1/3 cup (100 ml) milk and cornstarch in a small bowl. In a small saucepan, bring remaining milk to a boil with instant coffee and sugar. Stir hot milk mixture into cornstarch mixture. Return to saucepan and bring to a boil, stirring constantly until smooth and thickened. Remove from heat and cool completely, stirring frequently. In a large bowl, beat butter until light and fluffy. Gradually add cooled coffee cream to butter, beating well with each addition.

Cut cooled cake horizontally into 4 layers. Spread 3 cake layers with coffee cream. Stack 4 layers one on top of the other. Spread top and sides of gâteau with about two-thirds of remaining coffee cream. Mark top of gâteau into 14 portions with a sharp knife. Put remaining coffee cream into a pastry bag fitted with a fluted nozzle. Decorate each portion with a piped swirl of coffee cream ending in a rosette. Pipe a double rosette in the center of the gâteau. Top each rosette with a candied coffee bean. Sprinkle center and sides of gâteau with sliced almonds.

Cook's Tip

To cut a cream gâteau, dip the longest and sharpest knife you possess into warm water before making each cut.

Fruit Layer Gâteau

Cake:
4 eggs, separated
3 tablespoons lukewarm water
2/3 cup (140 g) sugar
Grated peel of 1/2 lemon
1 cup (120 g) all-purpose flour
1 teaspoon baking powder

Filling:
4 oz. (100 g) nougat
1 cup (100 g) ground almonds
1-1/2 to 3 tablespoons kirsch
3 tablespoons water
1 tablespoon powdered sugar, sifted

Topping:
1/3 cup (100 g) apricot jam
3/4 cup (75 g) toasted sliced almonds, page 47
1-1/2 lbs. (675 g) mixed fruit or 2 (1-lb., 456-g) cans fruit salad

Glaze:
1/4 cup (50 g) sugar
2-1/4 teaspoons cornstarch
Dash of salt
1/2 cup (125 ml) orange juice
1 teaspoon grated orange peel
1-1/2 teaspoons orange-flavored liqueur

Grease a 10-inch (25-cm) springform cake pan. Preheat oven to 375°F (190°C).

To make cake, put egg yolks, water, half the sugar and lemon peel into a large bowl. Beat until pale and creamy, 5 to 10 minutes with an electric mixer. Beat egg whites until stiff; fold in remaining sugar. Fold egg white mixture into egg yolk mixture. Sift flour with baking powder. Fold into egg mixture. Turn batter into greased pan. Bake 40 minutes or until a wooden pick inserted in center comes out clean. Turn out cake onto a rack to cool. Cut cooled cake horizontally into 3 layers.

To make filling, melt nougat in a double boiler over low heat. Spread over 1 cake layer. Cover with second layer. Combine almonds, kirsch, water and powdered sugar in a small bowl. Spread over second layer. Cover with third cake layer.

To make topping, warm jam and press through a strainer to obtain jelly. Brush warm jelly over top and sides of cake. Cover sides with sliced almonds, pressing in well. Prepare fresh fruit or drain canned fruit; arrange on top of cake.

To make glaze, mix sugar, cornstarch and salt in a small saucepan. Gradually stir in orange juice until smooth. Heat to boiling, stirring constantly. Boil and stir 2 minutes. Add orange peel and orange-flavored liqueur. Cover and cool. Spoon cooled glaze over fruit.

Fresh Cream Pear Gâteau

Cake:
6 eggs, separated
2/3 cup (150 g) sugar
3/4 cup plus 2 tablespoons (100 g) all-purpose flour
1 teaspoon baking powder
Scant 1/2 cup (50 g) unsweetened cocoa powder
1/2 cup (50 g) ground almonds
4 tablespoons (50 g) butter or margarine

Filling & Topping:
2 lbs. (1 kg.) ripe pears
4-1/2 cups (1 liter) water
1/4 cup (50 g) granulated sugar
Juice of 1 lemon
2/3 cup (225 g) blueberry preserves
2-1/2 cups (600 ml) whipping cream
Scant 1/2 cup (60 g) powdered sugar, sifted
1/2 cup (50 g) toasted sliced almonds, page 47
7 candied cherries

Grease a 10-inch (25-cm) round cake pan. Preheat oven to 375°F (190°C).
To make cake, put egg yolks and a third of the sugar into a large bowl. Beat until pale and creamy, 5 to 10 minutes with an electric mixer. Beat egg whites until stiff. Add remaining sugar and beat again until stiff. Fold into egg yolk mixture. Sift flour, baking powder and cocoa powder together. Mix with almonds. Fold thoroughly into egg mixture. Melt butter or margarine; cool slightly. Carefully fold into chocolate mixture. Turn batter into greased pan; smooth the surface. Bake 40 to 50 minutes or until a wooden pick inserted in center comes out clean. Turn out cake onto a rack to cool.

To make filling and topping, peel pears and divide each one into 8 segments. Remove cores. In a large saucepan, bring water, granulated sugar and lemon juice to a boil. Add pear segments; reduce heat. Cover and simmer about 10 minutes. Drain and let cool.

Cut cooled cake horizontally into 3 layers. Spread 2 cake layers with blueberry preserves. Arrange cooled pear segments on top, reserving 14 segments for decoration. Beat cream and powdered sugar until stiff. Using half the whipped cream mixture, spread thickly over pears on 2 cake layers. Stack 3 cake layers. Spread top and sides of gâteau with whipped cream mixture, reserving some for decoration. Sprinkle sides with sliced almonds. Mark top of gâteau into 14 portions. Place remaining whipped cream mixture in a pastry bag fitted with a fluted nozzle; pipe a rosette on each portion. Decorate with reserved pear segments and halved candied cherries.

Cook's Tip

If you don't have fresh pears, use a large can of pear halves, drained and sliced.

Strawberry Cream Roll

Cake:
3 large eggs, separated
1/4 cup (50 g) granulated sugar
Scant 1/2 cup (50 g) powdered sugar, sifted
1/2 cup plus 2 tablespoons (60 g) all-purpose flour
1/2 teaspoon baking powder

Filling:
1-2/3 cups (225 g) strawberries
2 tablespoons (25 g) granulated sugar
2/3 cup (150 ml) whipping cream
Scant 1/2 cup (50 g) powdered sugar, sifted
Additional powdered sugar

Line a 13x9-inch (33x23-cm) cake pan with waxed paper; grease paper. Preheat oven to 425°F (220°C).
To make cake, put egg yolks and granulated sugar into a large bowl. Beat until pale and creamy, 5 to 10 minutes with an electric mixer. Beat egg whites until frothy. Add powdered sugar; beat until stiff. Fold egg white mixture into egg yolk mixture. Sift flour with baking powder. Fold into egg mixture quickly but thoroughly. Spread batter evenly in prepared cake pan. Bake 10 to 12 minutes or until a wooden pick inserted in center comes out clean.

Place a sheet of waxed paper over a damp cloth towel; sprinkle with a little granulated sugar. Carefully turn out cake onto waxed paper. Peel off lining paper. Trim cake edges. Roll up cake and waxed paper together. Cool.
To make filling, hull and quarter strawberries. Place in a medium bowl and sprinkle with granulated sugar. Let stand 30 minutes. Drain strawberries in a strainer, reserving juice. Beat cream with strawberry juice until stiff. Fold powdered sugar into whipped cream mixture with strawberries.

Unroll cake. Spread with filling. Roll up, using waxed paper to lift cake. Sprinkle with additional powdered sugar.

Jelly Rolls

Cake:
4 eggs, separated, plus 2 egg yolks
Grated peel of 1 lemon
1/2 cup (100 g) sugar
3/4 cup (75 g) all-purpose flour
1/2 teaspoon baking powder

Filling & Topping:
3/4 cup (250 g) apricot jam
Powdered sugar
6 candied cherries

Line a 13x9-inch (33x23-cm) cake pan with waxed paper; grease paper. Preheat oven to 425°F (220°C).
To make cake, put 6 yolks, lemon peel and half the sugar into a large bowl. Beat until pale and creamy, 5 to 10 minutes with an electric mixer. Beat whites until stiff; beat in remaining sugar. Fold egg white mixture into egg yolk mixture. Sift flour with baking powder. Fold into egg mixture. Spread batter evenly in prepared cake pan. Bake 10 to 12 minutes or until a wooden pick inserted in center comes out clean. Leave in pan covered with a damp cloth towel until cooled. Turn out cooled cake onto a clean work surface. Peel off lining paper. Trim cake edges.
To complete rolls, spread apricot jam over cake. Cut into 12 squares and roll up each square with apricot jam inside. Sift powdered sugar over rolls. Decorate each roll with half a candied cherry.

Raspberry Cream Roll

Cake:
4 eggs, separated, plus 2 egg yolks
1/2 cup (100 g) sugar
3/4 cup (80 g) all-purpose flour
1/2 teaspoon baking powder

Filling:
8 oz. (225 g) fresh or frozen raspberries, thawed
1-1/4 cups (300 ml) whipping cream
Scant 1/2 cup (50 g) powdered sugar, sifted

Line a 13x9-inch (33x23-cm) cake pan with waxed paper; grease paper. Preheat oven to 425°F (220°C).

To make cake, put 6 egg yolks and half the sugar into a large bowl. Beat until pale and creamy, 5 to 10 minutes with an electric mixer. Beat egg whites until stiff; beat in remaining sugar. Fold egg white mixture into egg yolk mixture. Sift flour and baking powder over egg mixture; fold in. Spread batter evenly in prepared cake pan. Bake 10 to 12 minutes or until a wooden pick inserted in center comes out clean.

Place a sheet of waxed paper over a damp cloth towel; sprinkle with a little granulated sugar. Carefully turn out cake onto waxed paper. Peel off lining paper. Trim cake edges. Roll up cake and waxed paper together. Cool.

To make filling, reserve a few raspberries for decoration and place the remainder in a medium bowl. Crush raspberries with a wooden spoon. Beat cream and powdered sugar until stiff. Place about a fourth of the whipped cream mixture in a pastry bag fitted with a fluted nozzle. Mix remaining whipped cream mixture with crushed raspberries.

Unroll cooled cake. Spread with raspberry cream. Roll up, using waxed paper to lift cake. Pipe cream rosettes on top of cake and decorate with reserved raspberries.

Chocolate Cream Roll

Cake:
4 eggs, separated, plus 2 egg yolks
1/2 cup (100 g) sugar
3/4 cup (80 g) all-purpose flour
1 teaspoon baking powder
1/4 cup plus 1 tablespoon (40 g) unsweetened cocoa powder

Filling:
4 oz. (100 g) fresh or frozen strawberries, thawed
1-1/4 cups (300 ml) whipping cream
Scant 1/4 cup (50 g) powdered sugar, sifted
1 tablespoon instant chocolate drink powder

Line a 13x9-inch (33x23-cm) cake pan with waxed paper; grease paper. Preheat oven to 425°F (220°C).

To make cake, put 6 egg yolks and half the sugar into a large bowl. Beat until pale and creamy, 5 to 10 minutes with an electric mixer. Beat egg whites until stiff; beat in remaining sugar. Fold egg white mixture into egg yolk mixture. Sift flour, baking powder and cocoa powder over egg mixture; fold in. Spread batter evenly in prepared cake pan. Bake 10 to 12 minutes or until a wooden pick inserted in center comes out clean.

Place a sheet of waxed paper over a damp cloth towel; sprinkle with a little granulated sugar. Carefully turn out cake onto waxed paper. Peel off lining paper. Trim cake edges. Roll up cake and waxed paper together. Cool.

To make filling, puree strawberries in a blender or press through a strainer. Place puree in a medium bowl. Beat cream and powdered sugar until stiff. Mix with pureed strawberries.

Carefully unroll cooled cake. Spread with strawberry cream. Roll up, using waxed paper to lift cake. Sift chocolate powder over cake.

Gooseberry Meringue Tartlets

Pastry:
1-1/4 cups (160 g) all-purpose flour, sifted
Pinch of salt
6 tablespoons (100 g) butter, cut in small pieces
1/4 cup (60 g) sugar
1 tablespoon dairy sour cream
2 egg yolks

Filling:
1 lb. (500 g) gooseberries
1/4 cup (60 g) granulated sugar
1/3 cup (100 ml) brandy
1-1/4 cups (300 ml) milk
3 tablespoons (20 g) cornstarch
Scant 1/4 cup (50 ml) whipping cream
1/4 cup (25 g) powdered sugar

Meringue:
4 egg whites
Generous 1 cup (150 g) powdered sugar, sifted

To make pastry, knead flour, salt, butter, sugar, sour cream and egg yolks to a dough. Wrap in foil and refrigerate 2 hours.
To make filling, wash and stem gooseberries. Cook gently in a covered saucepan with granulated sugar and brandy until soft. Drain. Blend a little milk and cornstarch. Boil remaining milk, cream and powdered sugar. Stir hot milk mixture into cornstarch mixture. Return to heat and bring to a boil, stirring until thick. Cool, stirring often. Preheat oven to 400°F (205°C).

On a floured surface, roll out dough 1/8 inch (3 mm) thick. Cut out rounds to fit eight to ten 3-inch (7.5-cm) tartlet pans. Place dough in pans. Bake blind, page 9, 10 minutes or until golden. Cool in pans. Increase oven temperature to 425°F (220°C). Fill shells with cream mixture; top with gooseberries.
To make meringue, beat egg whites until stiff; beat in powdered sugar. Pipe lattices over tartlets. Brown meringue in oven a few minutes with oven door slightly open.

Raspberry Tartlets

Pastry:
1-1/4 cups (150 g) all-purpose flour
Pinch of salt
7 tablespoons (95 g) butter, cut in small pieces
3-1/2 tablespoons (45 g) sugar
1/2 beaten egg

Filling:
1/2 cup plus 2 tablespoons (150 g) butter
2/3 cup (150 g) sugar
3 egg yolks
1 tablespoon cornstarch
Grated peel and juice of 3 lemons

Decoration:
1/4 cup (75 g) apricot jam
3/4 cup (75 g) toasted sliced almonds, page 47
8 oz. (225 g) fresh or frozen raspberries, thawed
2/3 cup (150 ml) whipping cream
1 tablespoon powdered sugar

To make pastry, sift flour and salt into a medium bowl. Add butter, sugar and egg to flour mixture. Knead to a dough. Press into a ball and wrap in foil or plastic wrap. Refrigerate 2 hours. Preheat oven to 400°F (205°C). On a floured surface, roll out dough 1/8 inch (3 mm) thick. Cut out rounds to fit six to eight 3-inch (7.5-cm) tartlet pans. Place dough in pans without stretching. Bake blind, page 9, 10 to 15 minutes or until golden. Slip tartlets shells out of pans; cool on a rack.
To make filling, put butter, sugar, egg yolks, cornstarch, lemon peel and juice into a medium saucepan. Bring slowly to a boil, stirring constantly until smooth and thickened. Cool.
To decorate, warm jam; brush over sides of tartlet shells. Sprinkle with sliced almonds, pressing them on well. Spoon in filling. Top with raspberries. Whip cream with powdered sugar. Use to pipe a rosette on each tartlet. Decorate with almonds.

Cream Horns

Horns:
3/4 (17-1/4-oz., 489-g) pkg. frozen puff pastry, thawed
1 egg yolk
1 tablespoon milk
1/2 cup (50 g) sliced almonds
Powdered sugar

Filling:
1 cup (150 g) strawberries
1/4 cup (25 g) powdered sugar
2/3 cup (150 ml) whipping cream
Few drops of vanilla extract

Special cream horn molds are required for this recipe.
To make horns, roll out puff pastry dough to a 12x8-inch (30x20-cm) rectangle on a floured surface. Using a pastry wheel or sharp knife, cut dough into 8 long strips, each 1 inch (2.5 cm) wide. Refrigerate 15 minutes. Preheat oven to 425°F (220°C).

Rinse 8 cream horn molds in cold water. Beat egg yolk and milk in a small bowl. Brush 1 edge of each dough strip with yolk mixture. Starting at narrow end of mold, roll dough around molds so the edge brushed with egg overlaps unbrushed edge by about 1/4 inch (5 mm). Press both edges together. Brush pastry horns with remaining beaten egg mixture. Scatter almonds over half the horns. Sprinkle a baking sheet with cold water. Place horns on dampened baking sheet. Bake 15 minutes or until puffed and golden. While still hot, carefully loosen horns from molds; cool on a rack.

When horns are completely cool, sift powdered sugar over those without almonds.
To make filling, wash and hull strawberries. Puree in a blender or press through a strainer. Place puree in a medium bowl. Stir powdered sugar into strawberry puree. Beat cream and vanilla until stiff. Put just over half the whipped cream into a pastry bag fitted with a fluted nozzle; pipe into horns sprinkled with powdered sugar. Mix remaining whipped cream with strawberry puree; pipe into horns sprinkled with almonds.

Cook's Tip

If you want to make Cream Horns but do not have special molds, make them from cardboard and cover the cardboard molds with foil. Allow 2 to 3 minutes longer baking time as foil is not a good heat conductor. During the last few minutes of baking, cover horns with waxed paper so they do not become too brown.

Cherry Cream Cones

Cookie Dough:
1 cup (100 g) all-purpose flour
Pinch of salt
1/2 cup (50 g) ground almonds
Scant 1 cup (100 g) powdered sugar, sifted
2 eggs plus 1 egg white
Few drops of almond extract

Filling:
1 tablespoon kirsch
2/3 cup (225 g) cherry jam
1-1/4 cups (300 ml) whipping cream
Slivers of grated chocolate

Grease a large baking sheet. Preheat oven to 350°F (175°C).
To make cookie dough, sift flour and salt into a medium bowl. Add almonds, powdered sugar, 2 eggs, egg white and almond extract. Beat until smooth. Using the back of a teaspoon, spread 2 teaspoons of mixture into a 5-inch (12.5-cm) circle on greased baking sheet. Repeat with 2 more teaspoons of mixture. You can bake only two at a time on the baking sheet. Bake 5 to 7 minutes or until edges of cookies start turning brown. Repeat until mixture is used up. As soon as cookies come out of oven, remove them from baking sheet and shape into cones using a cream horn mold. Cool on a rack.
To make filling, blend kirsch and cherry jam in a small bowl. Beat cream until stiff. Place a third of the whipped cream in a pastry bag fitted with a fluted nozzle. Mix half the jam mixture with remaining whipped cream and use to half-fill cones. Put a little of remaining cherry jam mixture in each cone and pipe a rosette of cream on top. Decorate with chocolate slivers.

Chocolate Fruit Boats

1/4 cup (25 g) ground almonds

Cake:
1/3 cup (40 g) finely chopped dates
1/2 cup (50 g) finely chopped candied pineapple
1/3 cup (40 g) raisins
1/3 cup (40 g) dried currants
1/3 cup (40 g) toasted chopped almonds, page 47
3 tablespoons rum
1-3/4 cups plus 3 tablespoons (190 g) all-purpose flour, sifted
3/4 cup plus 2 tablespoons (190 g) butter, softened
3/4 cup plus 2 tablespoons (190 g) sugar
Grated peel of 1/2 lemon
3 eggs plus 3 egg yolks

Frosting:
4 oz. (100 g) semisweet chocolate
1/4 cup (25 g) coarsely crushed cookie crumbs

Grease 16 boat-shaped patty molds; sprinkle with almonds.
To make cake, combine dates, candied pineapple, raisins, currants and almonds in a medium bowl. Sprinkle with rum; cover and let stand 2 hours.
After 2 hours, stir 3 tablespoons (20 g) flour into fruit mixture. Preheat oven to 350°F (175°C). In a large bowl, beat butter, sugar and lemon peel until light and fluffy. Beat in eggs and egg yolks one at a time. Add remaining flour. Fold in fruit mixture. Fill prepared patty molds with batter. Bake 15 minutes or until a wooden pick inserted in center comes out clean. Turn out boats onto a rack to cool.
To make frosting, melt chocolate in a double boiler over low heat. Spoon over top of cooled boats. Sprinkle with cookie crumbs before chocolate sets.

Marzipan Wheels

Pastry:
3-1/2 cups (400 g) all-purpose flour
Generous 1 cup (150 g) powdered sugar, sifted
Pinch of salt
1 cup plus 2 tablespoons (250 g) butter, softened
2 egg yolks

Filling & Decoration:
1-3/4 cups (200 g) ground almonds
Few drops of almond extract
Scant 1/4 cup (50 ml) kirsch or sherry
2/3 cup (120 g) finely chopped mixed candied peel
1 egg yolk, beaten
Small pieces of candied lemon peel
Blanched almonds, page 124

To make pastry, sift flour, powdered sugar and salt into a large bowl. Add butter and egg yolks. Knead to a dough. Press into a ball and wrap in foil or plastic wrap. Refrigerate 2 hours. Preheat oven to 400°F (205°C). On a floured surface, roll out dough to a 16x10-inch (40x25-cm) rectangle, 1/4 inch (5 mm) thick.
To make filling, combine almonds, almond extract and kirsch or sherry in a small bowl to make a stiff paste. Spread over dough; sprinkle with mixed candied peel. Roll up dough from long side; cut into 1-inch (2.5-cm) slices. Stand slices upright on a baking sheet, 2 to 3 inches (5 to 8 cm) apart. Brush tops with egg yolk. Place a piece of candied lemon peel and an almond on each slice. Bake 20 minutes or until golden. Cool on a rack.

Chocolate Chimneys

Cookie Dough:
1/4 cup (30 g) all-purpose flour
3/4 cup (100 g) powdered sugar
1 cup (120 g) ground almonds
4 egg whites
1/2 teaspoon ground cinnamon
Grated peel of 1/2 lemon
1/2 cup (125 ml) whipping cream

Frosting & Filling:
5 oz. (140 g) semisweet chocolate
1 cup (250 ml) whipping cream

To make cookie dough, sift flour and powdered sugar into a medium bowl. Add almonds, egg whites, cinnamon and lemon peel; beat until smooth. Cover and refrigerate overnight.
Grease and flour baking sheets. Preheat oven to 375°F (190°C). Stir cream into almond mixture. Spread mixture thinly and evenly over prepared baking sheets. Bake 1 sheet at a time in center of oven 5 to 7 minutes or until mixture is just golden. Remove baking sheets from oven and cut partially cooked dough into 4-1/2-inch (11.5-cm) squares with a pastry wheel or sharp knife. Bake squares 5 minutes longer, or until set but not browned. Remove squares one at a time from baking sheets while still warm. Quickly curl squares around the handle of a wooden spoon, pressing edges together to make chimneys. Remove from wooden handle; cool on a rack.
To make frosting and filling, melt chocolate in a double boiler over low heat. Spoon melted chocolate over cooled chimneys. Beat cream until stiff. Put whipped cream into a pastry bag fitted with a plain or fluted nozzle; pipe cream into chimneys.

Swedish Apple Tartlets

Pastry:
1 cup (100 g) all-purpose flour
4 tablespoons (50 g) butter, cut in small pieces
Scant 1/2 cup (60 g) powdered sugar, sifted
1 egg yolk
About 3 tablespoons ice water

Filling:
3 tablespoons toasted chopped almonds, page 47
2 cooking apples, cooked, pureed and sweetened to taste or
  1 cup applesauce, sweetened to taste
Water
Powdered sugar

To make pastry, sift flour into a bowl. Using a pastry blender or 2 knives, cut in butter until evenly distributed and mixture resembles breadcrumbs. With a fork, lightly mix in powdered sugar, egg yolk and enough ice water to make a dough. Press into a ball and wrap in foil or plastic wrap. Refrigerate 2 hours.

Preheat oven to 350°F (175°C). Grease 6 to 8 fluted tartlet pans or muffin pan cups.

To make filling, mix almonds and apple puree or applesauce in a small bowl.

On a floured surface, roll out two-thirds of dough 1/4 inch (5 mm) thick. With a cookie cutter, cut dough into 6 to 8 rounds to fit tartlet pans or muffin pan cups. Place dough in pans. Distribute apple mixture between tartlet shells. Roll out remaining dough 1/8 inch (3 mm) thick; cut out tartlet tops. Brush edges with water; fit tops over tartlets and press edges together to seal. Using a sharp knife, pierce the side of each tartlet to make an air vent. Bake 35 minutes or until golden. Cool slightly in pans then transfer to a rack to cool completely. Sift powdered sugar over cooled tartlets.

Orange Slices

Cake:
8 tablespoons (100 g) butter, softened
2 tablespoons (25 g) vanilla sugar, page 18
1/2 cup plus 1 tablespoon (120 g) sugar
Pinch of salt
3 eggs, separated, plus 1 egg yolk
Grated peel of 2 oranges
Juice of 1 orange
3/4 cup plus 2 tablespoons (90 g) all-purpose flour
1 teaspoon baking powder
1 cup (100 g) ground almonds
2/3 cup (200 g) orange jelly or marmalade

Frosting:
1-2/3 cups (200 g) powdered sugar, sifted
Scant 1/4 cup (50 ml) orange juice
1 tablespoon Cointreau

Grease and flour a 13x9-inch (33x23-cm) cake pan. Preheat oven to 400°F (205°C).

To make cake, cream butter, vanilla sugar, half the unflavored sugar and salt in a large bowl until pale and fluffy. Beat in 4 egg yolks one at a time. Add orange peel and juice. Beat egg whites until stiff; beat in remaining unflavored sugar. Fold egg white mixture into creamed mixture. Sift flour with baking powder. Stir in almonds; fold into egg mixture. Spread batter evenly in prepared cake pan. Bake 10 minutes or until a wooden pick inserted in center comes out clean. Cool slightly in pan then turn out onto a rack to cool completely.

Cut cooled cake horizontally into 2 layers. Join layers together with orange jelly or marmalade.

To make frosting, combine powdered sugar, orange juice and Cointreau in a small bowl. Pour frosting over cake. Cut into slices when frosting has set.

Cherry Cream Tartlets

Pastry:
1/2 cup plus 1 tablespoon (125 g) butter, softened
3/4 cup (90 g) powdered sugar, sifted
1 teaspoon vanilla sugar, page 18
Pinch of salt
1 egg
2-1/4 cups (250 g) all-purpose flour

Filling:
1 (1-lb., 456-g) can pitted black cherries
2/3 cup (150 ml) whipping cream
1/2 cup (125 ml) milk
4 tablespoons (50 g) butter
1 egg plus 1 egg yolk
3 tablespoons (20 g) cornstarch
Pinch of salt
2 teaspoons sugar

To make pastry, beat butter, powdered sugar, vanilla sugar, salt and egg in a medium bowl. Sift flour over mixture. Knead together to make a dough. Press into a ball and wrap in foil or plastic wrap. Refrigerate 2 hours.

Preheat oven to 400°F (205°C). On a floured surface, roll out dough 1/8 inch (3 mm) thick. With a cookie cutter, cut out rounds to fit ten to twelve 3-inch (7.5-cm) tartlet pans. Place dough in pans without stretching. Bake blind, page 9, 10 minutes or until just golden. Remove tartlets from oven but leave in pans. Reduce oven temperature to 350°F (175°C).
To make filling, drain cherries and pat dry on paper towels. Place a few in each tartlet shell. Put cream, milk, butter, egg and egg yolk, cornstarch, salt and sugar into a small saucepan. Cook gently, stirring constantly until thickened. Pour over cherries.

Bake tartlets 20 to 25 minutes or until topping is lightly browned. Cool slightly in pans, then transfer tartlets to a rack to cool completely.

Lemon Puff Slices

1-1/2 (17-1/4-oz., 489-g) pkgs. frozen puff pastry, thawed

Filling:
1/4 cup plus 3 tablespoons (100 g) sugar
1-3/4 cups (200 g) ground almonds
2 egg yolks
Grated peel and juice of 2 lemons

Glaze:
1/4 cup (75 g) lemon jelly or marmalade

Preheat oven to 425°F (220°C). Divide puff pastry dough in half. On a floured surface, roll out each half to a 23x10-inch (58x25-cm) rectangle. Cut each piece in half across the shorter side. Sprinkle 2 baking sheets with cold water. Place 1 piece of dough on each dampened baking sheet.
To make filling, mix sugar, almonds, 1 egg yolk, lemon peel and juice in a medium bowl. Spread filling over dough, leaving a small margin around the edge. Beat remaining egg yolk. Brush dough edges with egg yolk and place one of the remaining pieces of dough on top of each. Press edges together lightly. Brush tops with egg yolk; pierce several times with a fork. Bake 10 to 15 minutes or until puffed and golden.
To make glaze, warm lemon jelly or marmalade and brush over hot pastry. Cool on a rack.

Cut into slices when cold.

From the Cake Tray

Greek Doughnuts

Yeast Dough:
2 teaspoons sugar
1 cup (250 ml) warm milk (110°F, 43°C)
2 pkgs. active dry yeast
4 cups (450 g) all-purpose flour
1/2 teaspoon salt
1 egg
1-2/3 cups (375 ml) warm water (110°F, 43°C)
Grated peel of 1 lemon
Oil to deep-fry

Syrup:
1 cup (225 g) sugar
1/3 cup (100 g) honey
1/2 cup plus 1 tablespoon (150 ml) water
1 tablespoon lemon juice
1/4 cup (25 g) chopped pistachio nuts

To make yeast dough, stir 1 teaspoon sugar into warm milk and sprinkle with yeast. Let stand 5 minutes or until the surface is frothy. Stir gently to moisten any dry particles remaining on top. Sift flour, remaining sugar and salt into a large bowl. Beat egg, warm water and lemon peel in a medium bowl. Stir in yeast mixture. Pour into flour mixture; beat to an elastic batter. Cover and let rise in a warm place 20 minutes. Beat thoroughly.

In a deep frying pan, heat oil to 350°F (175°C). Using a wet tablespoon, take small spoonfuls of yeast batter and carefully drop into hot oil, 3 or 4 at a time. Dip spoon in cold water before taking each spoonful. Fry doughnuts about 4 minutes, turning once. Drain on paper towels and keep warm while cooking remaining doughnuts.

To make syrup, put sugar, honey, water and lemon juice into a medium saucepan. Stir constantly over low heat until sugar has dissolved. Increase heat and boil 5 minutes, until syrup is quite thick. Pour over warm doughnuts; sprinkle with pistachios.

Hazelnut Combs

1/2 (17-1/4-oz., 489-g) pkg. frozen puff pastry, thawed

Filling:
1-1/4 cups (150 g) ground hazelnuts
1 egg, beaten
1/4 cup plus 2 tablespoons (80 g) sugar
1 tablespoon rum
1 egg yolk, beaten

On a lightly floured surface, roll out pastry dough to a 12-inch (30-cm) square. Cut out nine 4-inch (10-cm) squares.
To make filling, combine hazelnuts, whole egg, sugar and rum in a medium bowl.

Place a strip of filling down the center of each square. Brush 1 side of each square with egg yolk; fold over opposite side. Make even cuts along sealed edge and spread to form a comb. Sprinkle a large baking sheet with cold water; place hazelnut combs on dampened baking sheet. Brush tops with egg yolk. Refrigerate 15 minutes. Preheat oven to 425°F (220°C).

Bake 15 minutes or until golden. Cool on a rack.

Danish Scrolls

Yeast Dough:
Pinch of sugar
1 cup (250 ml) warm milk (110°F, 43°C)
2 pkgs. active dry yeast
4 cups (450 g) all-purpose flour
1/2 teaspoon salt
1 cup (225 g) butter
1 egg
Water

Filling:
3 tablespoons (40 g) firmly packed brown sugar
1/2 teaspoon ground cinnamon
1/3 cup (50 g) raisins

To make yeast dough, stir sugar into milk; sprinkle with yeast. Let stand 5 minutes. Stir gently. Sift flour and salt into a bowl. Melt 4 tablespoons (50 g) butter; cool slightly. Lightly beat butter and egg into yeast mixture. Pour into flour mixture; beat to a smooth dough. Knead dough on a floured surface. Cover and let rise in a warm place 15 minutes. Roll out to an 14x8-inch (35x20-cm) rectangle. Mark into 3 sections. Dot half the remaining butter over top 2 sections. Fold bottom section over middle section and fold top section down over this. Press edges to seal. Turn dough once in a counter-clockwise direction and roll out to an 14x8-inch (35x20-cm) rectangle. Repeat process using remaining butter. Repeat once more without butter. Refrigerate 15 minutes between each rolling. Grease baking sheets. Preheat oven to 400°F (205°C). Roll out dough to a 20x14-inch (50x35-cm) rectangle; brush with water.
To make filling, mix sugar, cinnamon and raisins. Spread over dough. Starting from the long sides, roll dough in to meet at the center. Cut into 1-inch (2.5-cm) slices; place flat on greased baking sheets. Bake 10 minutes then reduce heat to 350°F (175°C) and bake 10 to 15 minutes more or until golden.

Hazelnut Pastries

Yeast Dough:
Pinch of sugar
1 cup (250 ml) warm milk (110°F, 43°C)
2 pkgs. active dry yeast
4-1/2 cups (500 g) all-purpose flour
1/2 teaspoon salt
1 cup (225 g) butter
1 egg

Filling:
1 cup (100 g) ground toasted hazelnuts, page 47
1/4 cup (50 g) sugar
3 tablespoons rum
1/2 teaspoon almond extract
1 egg white

Glaze:
1/4 cup (25 g) powdered sugar, sifted
1 to 2 teaspoons rum

To make yeast dough, use recipe for Danish Scrolls, opposite, reserving extra 1/2 cup (50 g) flour and 3/4 cup (175 g) butter. Work flour into butter. Using flour and butter mixture to dot over dough, refrigerate, fold and roll as in the recipe. Grease baking sheets. Preheat oven to 425°F (220°C). Divide dough in half. Roll out each piece to a 22x9-inch (55x23-cm) rectangle.
To make filling, mix hazelnuts, sugar, rum, almond extract and egg white in a medium bowl. Spread over one dough rectangle. Cover with second rectangle; press edges together.

Cut long side into 1-inch (2.5-cm) wide pieces. Make a 3-inch (7.5-cm) long slit near 1 end of each piece. Twist the other end before putting it through opening. Seal ends well. Place on baking sheets. Bake 15 minutes or until golden. Transfer to a rack.
To make glaze, combine powdered sugar and rum in a small bowl. Drizzle glaze over hot pastries.

Petits Fours à la Ritz

Pastry:
1-3/4 cups (190 g) all-purpose flour
7 tablespoons (95 g) butter, cut in small pieces
1/4 cup plus 1 tablespoon (65 g) sugar
1 egg
About 3 tablespoons ice water

Filling:
4 egg yolks
1/2 cup plus 1 tablespoon (125 g) granulated sugar
Pinch of salt
2 tablespoons (15 g) cornstarch
1 cup (250 ml) milk
1/2 teaspoon vanilla extract
3/4 cup plus 2 tablespoons (200 g) butter, softened
Scant 3/4 cup (80 g) powdered sugar, sifted
1 tablespoon unsweetened cocoa powder
2 tablespoons boiling water
2 teaspoons orange-flavored liqueur
1 tablespoon instant coffee powder
2 teaspoons coffee-flavored liqueur
3 tablespoons brandy

Decoration:
Candied cherries
Chocolate sprinkles
Crystallized violets
Candied coffee beans

To make pastry, sift flour into a large bowl. Using a pastry blender or 2 knives, cut in butter until evenly distributed and mixture resembles breadcrumbs. With a fork, lightly mix in sugar, egg and enough ice water to make a dough. Press into a ball and wrap in foil or plastic wrap. Refrigerate 2 hours.

Preheat oven to 400°F (205°C). On a floured surface, roll out dough 1/8 inch (3 mm) thick. Cut out rounds to fit 24 petits fours pans. Place dough in pans. Arrange pans on baking sheets. Bake blind, page 9, 8 to 10 minutes or until golden. Slip pastry shells out of pans by loosening them carefully with a knife. Cool on a rack.

To make filling, combine egg yolks, granulated sugar, salt, cornstarch and a little milk in a medium bowl. In a medium saucepan, heat remaining milk and vanilla. Stir hot milk into cornstarch mixture and return to saucepan. Bring to a boil, stirring constantly until smooth and thickened. Cool, stirring frequently. Cream butter and powdered sugar in a medium bowl until pale and fluffy. Add butter mixture a spoonful at a time to cooled vanilla mixture, beating well after each addition.

Divide vanilla cream into 3 portions. Dissolve cocoa powder in 1 tablespoon boiling water; stir with orange-flavored liqueur into 1 portion of vanilla cream. Dissolve coffee powder in 1 tablespoon boiling water; stir with coffee-flavored liqueur into another portion of vanilla cream. Mix brandy into final portion. Using a pastry bag fitted with a fluted nozzle, pipe each flavored cream into a third of prebaked petits fours shells. Refrigerate 2 hours to set cream fillings.

To decorate, add candied cherry halves, chocolate sprinkles, crystallized violets or candied coffee beans as illustrated.

Cook's Tip

Petits fours will look especially professional if some are dipped in melted chocolate, then decorated with silver cake decors, chocolate sprinkles or chopped pistachios as illustrated.

Classical Petits Fours

Cake:
5 eggs, separated, plus 1 egg yolk
3/4 cup (80 g) ground almonds
Grated peel of 1 lemon
1/2 cup plus 1 tablespoon (120 g) sugar
Scant 1 cup (120 g) all-purpose flour, sifted
1/2 cup (175 g) apricot jam
8 oz. (225 g) almond paste

Frosting:
1-3/4 cups (225 g) powdered sugar, sifted
1 tablespoon white rum
2 to 3 tablespoons water
Red and yellow food coloring, if desired

Decoration:
Candied cherries
Crystallized violets
Chopped pistachio nuts
Silver cake decors

Line one 14x11-inch (36x28-cm) cake pan with waxed paper; grease paper. Preheat oven to 425°F (220°C).
To make cake, beat 6 egg yolks, almonds, lemon peel and half the sugar in a large bowl until pale and creamy. Beat egg whites until stiff; fold in remaining sugar. Fold egg white mixture and flour into egg yolk mixture. Spread cake batter evenly in prepared cake pan. Bake 10 to 12 minutes or until a wooden pick inserted in center comes out clean. Turn out cake onto clean waxed paper; strip off lining paper. Cool.

Cut cake in half lengthwise. Spread 1 half with half the apricot jam and place second half of cake on top. Cut cake in half lengthwise. Spread strips with remaining jam. Place layers one on top of the other to make 4 layers. Knead almond paste. On a surface sprinkled with powdered sugar, roll out almond paste to fit top of cake. Place on cake. Cover with foil or waxed paper; weigh down with a heavy wooden board and let stand 24 hours. The next day, cut cake into 1-1/2-inch (3.5-cm) squares or shapes.
To make frosting, put powdered sugar and rum into a small bowl. Beat in enough water to give a thick flowing consistency. Spoon frosting over petits fours. Color some of frosting with food coloring if desired. Using a pastry bag fitted with a fine nozzle, pipe designs on petits fours with frosting.
To decorate, add pieces of candied cherries, crystallized violets, chopped pistachios or silver cake decors. Dry out on a rack 1 to 2 hours. Serve in small paper cases.

Cook's Tip

The key to success with these petits fours is to weigh down the cake layers with a heavy board and leave for several hours. Otherwise the sponge will dry out and the petits fours will lose their moistness.

Chocolate Slice

Cake:
5 oz. (130 g) semisweet chocolate
1/2 cup plus 2 tablespoons (130 g) butter, softened
3/4 cup plus 2 tablespoons (200 g) sugar
Pinch each of salt, ground cinnamon and grated lemon peel
6 eggs, separated
1-1/4 cups (130 g) all-purpose flour, sifted

Frosting:
8 tablespoons (120 g) butter
7 oz. (200 g) semisweet chocolate
2 eggs, beaten
Generous 3 cups (400 g) powdered sugar, sifted
Scant 1/4 cup (50 ml) rum

Line a 14x10-inch (35x25-cm) cake pan with waxed paper; grease paper. Preheat oven to 350°F (175°C).

To make cake, melt chocolate in a double boiler over low heat. In a large bowl, cream butter and half the sugar until light and fluffy. Add salt, cinnamon and lemon peel. Beat in egg yolks, one at a time, with melted chocolate. Beat egg whites until stiff; fold in remaining sugar. Fold egg white mixture into creamed mixture with flour. Spread batter evenly in prepared cake pan. Bake 20 minutes or until a wooden pick inserted in center comes out clean.

Sprinkle a sheet of waxed paper with sugar and turn out cake onto it. Peel off lining paper. Cool 2 hours. Cut cooled cake lengthwise into 2 strips.

To make frosting, melt butter; cool slightly. Finely grate chocolate. Mix chocolate, eggs, powdered sugar, butter and rum in a double boiler. Stir constantly over low heat until chocolate has melted and all ingredients are thoroughly combined. Cool.

Use about half the frosting to fill cake. Spread remaining frosting thickly over top. Cut into slices when frosting is firm.

Nougat Slice

Cake:
4 eggs, separated, plus 2 egg yolks
1/2 cup (100 g) sugar
3/4 cup (80 g) all-purpose flour
1 teaspoon baking powder
1/4 cup plus 1 tablespoon (40 g) unsweetened cocoa powder

Filling & Frosting:
1/4 cup (20 g) cornstarch
2 egg yolks
1/4 cup (50 g) sugar
1-1/4 cups (300 ml) milk
1-1/3 cups (285 g) butter
4 oz. (100 g) nougat
6 oz. (175 g) semisweet chocolate
Candied cherries

Line a 13x9-inch (33x23-cm) cake pan with waxed paper; grease paper. Preheat oven to 425°F (220°C).

To make cake, beat yolks and half the sugar until thick. Beat whites until stiff; fold in remaining sugar. Fold into yolk mixture. Sift flour, baking powder and cocoa powder; fold into mixture. Turn batter into pan. Bake 10 minutes or until a wooden pick inserted in center comes out clean. Turn onto waxed paper. Peel off lining paper. Cool. Cut cake lengthwise into 3 strips.

To make filling and frosting, blend cornstarch, yolks, sugar and a little milk. Heat remaining milk in a medium saucepan. Stir hot milk into cornstarch mixture and return to heat. Bring to a boil, stirring constantly until thickened. Cool, stirring frequently. Beat butter until soft. Gradually beat in cornstarch sauce. Melt nougat and 2 oz. (50 g) chocolate in a double boiler over low heat. As soon as mixture melts, remove from heat and gradually beat in butter cream. Spread over 2 strips of cake. Stack strips. Spread nougat cream thinly over cake, reserving some for decoration. Melt remaining chocolate; spread over cake. Decorate as illustrated.

Hungarian Chocolate Roll

Cake:
6 eggs, separated
1/2 cup (100 g) sugar
1/2 teaspoon vanilla extract
1 cup (100 g) all-purpose flour
Scant 3/4 cup (75 g) unsweetened cocoa powder

Filling & Decoration:
1/3 cup (100 g) raspberry jam
2 tablespoons (15 g) cornstarch
2/3 cup (150 ml) milk
1/4 cup (50 g) sugar
8 tablespoons (100 g) butter
1 tablespoon kirsch
1 tablespoon instant chocolate drink powder

Line a 13x9-inch (33x23-cm) cake pan with waxed paper; grease paper. Preheat oven to 400°F (205°C).

To make cake, beat yolks, sugar and vanilla until creamy. Beat whites until stiff; fold into yolk mixture. Sift flour with cocoa powder; fold into egg mixture. Using a pastry bag fitted with a large plain nozzle, pipe batter in strips across width of pan. Bake 10 to 12 minutes or until a wooden pick inserted in center comes out clean. Place waxed paper over a damp cloth towel; sprinkle with a little sugar. Turn out cake onto waxed paper. Peel off lining paper. Roll up cake and waxed paper. Cool.

To make filling and decoration, unroll cake and spread with jam, reserving 2 tablespoons. Blend cornstarch, a little milk and sugar. Bring remaining milk to a boil. Stir hot milk into cornstarch mixture; return to heat. Bring to a boil, stirring constantly until thickened. Cool, stirring frequently. Beat butter until soft. Gradually beat in cornstarch sauce and kirsch. Reserve 1/4 cup (50 ml) butter cream. Spread cake with remaining butter cream. Roll up. Sift chocolate powder over cake. Decorate with whirls of reserved butter cream filled with remaining jam.

Coffee Cream Slice

Cake:
4 eggs, separated, plus 2 egg yolks
1/2 cup (100 g) sugar
1/2 cup (60 g) all-purpose flour
1/2 teaspoon baking powder
3/4 cup (80 g) ground almonds

Filling & Frosting:
1/4 cup (25 g) cornstarch
1/4 cup (50 g) granulated sugar
3 tablespoons instant coffee powder
1-1/4 cups (300 ml) milk
1 cup plus 2 tablespoons (250 g) butter, softened
3 tablespoons (20 g) powdered sugar, sifted
1/2 cup (50 g) coarse cookie crumbs
10 candied coffee beans

Line a 13x9-inch (33x23-cm) cake pan with waxed paper; grease paper. Preheat oven to 425°F (220°C).

To make cake, beat yolks and half the sugar until thick. Beat whites until stiff; beat in remaining sugar. Fold into yolk mixture. Sift flour and baking powder onto egg mixture; fold in with almonds. Spread batter in pan. Bake 10 minutes or until a wooden pick inserted in center comes out clean. Turn onto waxed paper. Peel off lining paper. Cool. Cut cake lengthwise into 3 strips.

To make filling and frosting, mix cornstarch, granulated sugar, coffee powder and a little milk. Heat remaining milk. Stir milk into cornstarch mixture; return to heat. Bring to a boil, stirring constantly until thickened. Cool, stirring frequently. Cream butter and powdered sugar until fluffy. Gradually beat in coffee sauce. Spread coffee cream over 2 strips of cake. Stack strips. Spread coffee cream thinly over cake, reserving some for decoration. Sprinkle with crumbs. Put reserved coffee cream into a pastry bag fitted with a fluted nozzle. Decorate cake with rosettes of coffee cream and candied coffee beans.

Cream Puffs

Cream Puff Paste:
1 cup (250 ml) water
4 tablespoons (60 g) butter or margarine
Pinch of salt
Grated peel of 1/2 lemon
1 cup (150 g) all-purpose flour, sifted
4 eggs, beaten

Filling:
2 cups (475 ml) whipping cream
Scant 1/2 cup (60 g) powdered sugar
Additional powdered sugar

To make cream puff paste, gently heat water, butter or margarine, salt and lemon peel in a heavy saucepan until butter or margarine has melted. Raise heat and bring to a boil then add flour all at once. Remove from heat and beat until mixture forms a ball and comes away from sides of pan. Return to heat and cook 1 minute, stirring constantly. Turn mixture into a large bowl. Cool slightly, then add eggs a little at a time, beating well with each addition. Preheat oven to 425°F (220°C).

Using a pastry bag fitted with a fluted nozzle, pipe paste in different shapes onto a baking sheet. Leave room for expansion during cooking. Bake 20 minutes or until golden and crisp. Do not open oven door during first 10 minutes of baking, or pastry will collapse. While puffs are still warm, split in half to let steam escape. Cool on a rack.

To make filling, beat cream with scant 1/2 cup (60 g) powdered sugar in medium bowl until stiff. Put whipped cream mixture into a pastry bag fitted with a fluted nozzle. Pipe filling into each cooled puff. Sift powdered sugar over cream puffs.

Cook's Tip

Pipe long éclair shapes from the cream puff paste and fill with coffee cream. To make coffee cream, beat 2 cups (475 ml) whipping cream until stiff and add 1 teaspoon instant coffee powder. To make coffee frosting, dissolve 1 teaspoon instant coffee powder in 3 tablespoons hot water. Sift scant 2 cups (225 g) powdered sugar into a medium bowl and add enough coffee to give a coating consistency. Spoon frosting over éclairs.

Bath Buns

1/4 cup plus 2 tablespoons (80 g) sugar
3/4 cup (185 ml) warm milk (110°F, 43°C)
2 pkgs. active dry yeast
4 cups (500 g) all-purpose flour
1/2 teaspoon salt
1/2 teaspoon ground aniseed
Pinch of ground cinnamon
8 tablespoons (120 g) butter
2 eggs
2/3 cup (100 g) finely chopped mixed candied peel
Grated peel of 1/2 lemon
1/2 cup (80 g) raisins
1 egg yolk, beaten
1/2 cup (60 g) sugar crystals

Stir 1 teaspoon sugar into warm milk and sprinkle with yeast. Let stand 5 minutes or until surface is frothy. Stir gently to moisten any dry particles remaining on top. Sift flour, remaining sugar, salt, aniseed and cinnamon into a large bowl. Melt butter; cool slightly. Lightly beat butter and eggs into yeast mixture. Pour into flour mixture. Beat to make a dough. Work in mixed candied peel, lemon peel and raisins. Cover and let rise in a warm place until doubled in size, up to 1 hour. Grease baking sheets.

On a lightly floured surface, knead dough until smooth. Shape into small buns; place well apart on greased baking sheets. Let rise in a warm place until doubled in size. Preheat oven to 400°F (205°C).

Brush buns with egg yolk and sprinkle with sugar crystals. Bake 15 to 20 minutes or until buns are golden and sound hollow when tapped on undersides.

Shrewsbury Biscuits

5 cups (530 g) all-purpose flour
1-1/2 cups (300 g) sugar
2 eggs
Pinch each of salt and ground cinnamon
1-1/2 cups (300 g) butter, cut in small pieces

Sift flour onto a clean working surface or into a large bowl. Make a well in center of flour; add sugar, eggs, salt and cinnamon. Dot butter over flour. Quickly knead ingredients to a smooth dough. Press into a ball and wrap in foil or plastic wrap. Refrigerate 2 hours.

Preheat oven to 350°F (175°C). Line baking sheets with waxed paper; grease paper. On a lightly floured surface, roll out dough 1/8 inch (3 mm) thick. Cut out rounds 2-1/2 to 3 inches (6 to 7.5 cm) across. Place on prepared baking sheets. Bake 15 to 20 minutes or until golden. Cool on baking sheets.

Remove cooled biscuits from baking sheets with a spatula.

Shortbread Fingers

**1-1/4 cups plus 2 tablespoons (320 g)
  butter, softened**
3/4 cup (180 g) sugar
1/4 teaspoon salt
**3-1/3 cups (500 g) all-purpose flour,
  sifted**
Additional sugar

In a large bowl, cream butter, sugar and salt until pale and fluffy. Knead flour into creamed mixture to make a workable dough. Press into a ball and wrap in foil or plastic wrap. Refrigerate 30 minutes.

Preheat oven to 375°F (190°C). Grease a baking sheet. On a lightly floured surface, roll out dough 3/4 inch (1.5 cm) thick. Trim to fit baking sheet. Place on greased baking sheet. Pierce dough several times with a fork. Bake 25 to 30 minutes or until golden. Cut warm shortbread into fingers with a sharp knife. Sprinkle with additional sugar. Cool on baking sheet until firm then cool completely on a rack.

Teacakes

Prepare these using the recipe for Bath Buns, page 67, but use 1 teaspoon sugar to sweeten the mixture instead of 1/4 cup plus 2 tablespoons (80 g). Omit aniseed, cinnamon and lemon peel. Instead of using candied peel and raisins, add 1 cup (150 g) dried currants. Brush the risen teacakes with egg yolk before baking.

Finger Cookies

4 eggs, separated, plus 2 egg yolks
1/2 cup plus 1 tablespoon (125 g) granulated sugar
1 cup (100 g) all-purpose flour
Scant 1/2 cup (50 g) cornstarch
Powdered sugar

Grease non-stick baking sheets or line regular baking sheets with baking parchment; grease parchment well. Preheat oven to 400°F (205°C).

Put 6 egg yolks and granulated sugar into a large bowl. Beat until pale and creamy, 5 to 10 minutes with an electric mixer. Beat egg whites until stiff; fold into egg yolk mixture. Sift flour with cornstarch; fold into egg mixture.

Put mixture into a pastry bag fitted with a large plain nozzle. Pipe 3-1/2-inch (8.5-cm) long fingers onto prepared baking sheets, leaving space between each for spreading during cooking. Bake 7 to 10 minutes or until golden. Cool a few seconds on baking sheets then transfer to a rack to cool completely.

Sift powdered sugar over cooled cookies.

Cook's Tip

Using the same mixture, you can pipe round cookies. After baking, join pairs of cooled cookies with melted chocolate and decorate the tops with more chocolate.

Almond Macaroons

2 cups (225 g) ground almonds
1 cup (225 g) sugar
4 egg whites, beaten

Line baking sheets with rice paper. Preheat oven to 325°F (165°C).

In a medium bowl, stir almonds, sugar and beaten egg whites until blended. Fill a pastry bag fitted with a plain nozzle with mixture. Pipe small rounds onto rice paper, leaving enough space between each for spreading during cooking. Bake 15 to 20 minutes or until light golden. Cool on rice paper. When macaroons are cool, cut around each one and trim off excess rice paper.

Cook's Tip

Macaroons can be made with ground hazelnuts instead of almonds; for the best possible flavor use lightly toasted nuts, page 47.

Marzipan Toasts

Yeast Dough:
1/4 cup (50 g) sugar
1 cup (250 ml) warm milk (110°F, 43°C)
2 pkgs. active dry yeast
4 cups (500 g) all-purpose flour
1/2 teaspoon salt
4 tablespoons (50 g) butter or margarine
2 eggs
Grated peel of 1/2 lemon

Topping:
1 cup (100 g) ground almonds
Scant 3/4 cup (80 g) powdered sugar, sifted
1 egg white
1 tablespoon rum

To make yeast dough, stir 1 teaspoon sugar into warm milk and sprinkle with yeast. Let stand 5 minutes or until the surface is frothy. Stir gently to moisten any dry particles remaining on top. Sift flour, remaining sugar and salt into a large bowl. Melt butter or margarine; cool slightly. Lightly beat butter or margarine, eggs and lemon peel into yeast mixture. Pour into flour mixture, combining to make a dry dough. On a floured surface, knead dough until smooth. Cover and let rise in a warm place 15 minutes. Grease 2 cylindrical-shaped or Balmoral cake pans, or two 8-1/2x4-1/2-inch (22x11-cm) loaf pans.

Knead risen dough lightly. Form into 2 rolls. Shape rolls to fit greased pans. Let rise in a warm place until doubled in size. Preheat oven to 425°F (220°C).

Bake 25 to 35 minutes or until loaves are golden brown and sound hollow when tapped on undersides. Turn out loaves onto a rack to cool overnight.

Preheat broiler. Cut cooled loaves into thick slices. Arrange on broiler pan and toast on 1 side. Cool.

To make topping, put almonds, powdered sugar, egg white and rum into a medium bowl. Mix to a smooth spreading consistency. Spread mixture on untoasted sides of bread slices. Toast under the broiler until lightly browned.

Cook's Tip

If you are in a hurry, buy almond paste and knead with a little rum for the topping.

Turkish Fruit Cake

Cake:
3/4 cup (175 g) butter, softened
1/2 cup (100 g) sugar
1 tablespoon vanilla sugar, page 18
Grated peel of 1 lemon
4 eggs
1 tablespoon Madeira
1-1/2 cups (175 g) self-rising flour
Scant 1/2 cup (50 g) cornstarch
1 teaspoon baking powder
1/2 cup (75 g) raisins
1/3 cup (75 g) washed and coarsely
  chopped candied cherries
1 cup (100 g) coarsely chopped
  pickled walnuts
1/4 teaspoon salt
1/2 teaspoon ground cinnamon
1/2 teaspoon ground cardamom

Frosting:
4 oz. (100 g) semisweet chocolate
1/2 cup (50 g) chopped pistachio nuts

Preheat oven to 350°F (175°C). Grease a 9-1/4x5-1/4-inch (23x13-cm) loaf pan and sprinkle with fine breadcrumbs.
To make cake, cream butter, unflavored sugar, vanilla sugar and lemon peel in a large bowl until pale and fluffy. Stir in eggs and Madeira. Sift flour, cornstarch and baking powder together into a large bowl. Mix in raisins, cherries, pickled walnuts, salt, cinnamon and cardamom. Fold flour mixture into creamed mixture. Turn batter into prepared pan. Bake 1 hour 5 minutes or until a skewer inserted in center comes out clean. Remove cake from pan; cool on a rack.
To make frosting, melt chocolate in a double boiler over low heat. Spread over cake. Sprinkle with pistachios before chocolate sets.

Rum Butter Cake

3/4 cup (180 g) butter, softened
3/4 cup plus 2 tablespoons (200 g) sugar
5 eggs
2-1/4 cups (250 g) all-purpose flour
3/4 cup (80 g) corn flour
1 teaspoon baking powder
Scant 1/4 cup (50 ml) rum
1 tablespoon lemon juice
1 tablespoon orange juice
Grated peel of 1/2 lemon
Grated peel of 1/2 orange

Grease and flour a 9-1/4x5-1/4-inch (23x13-cm) loaf pan. Preheat oven to 375°F (190°C).

In a large bowl, cream butter and sugar until pale and fluffy. Beat in eggs one at a time. Sift all-purpose flour, corn flour and baking powder together; carefully fold into creamed mixture. Gradually fold in rum, lemon and orange juice and peel. Turn batter into prepared pan; smooth the surface. Bake 1-1/4 hours or until a skewer inserted in center comes out clean. Cover with foil if cake is becoming too brown. Remove cake from pan; cool on a rack.

Royal Fruit Loaf

Generous 1 cup (200 g) raisins
1-1/2 cups (175 g) self-rising flour
Scant 1/2 cup (50 g) cornstarch
1 teaspoon baking powder
3/4 cup (175 g) butter or margarine, softened
1/2 cup (100 g) sugar
4 eggs
1/3 cup (50 g) candied lemon peel
1 cup (100 g) chopped almonds
1 tablespoon rum

Grease a 9-1/4x5-1/4-inch (23x13-cm) loaf pan and sprinkle with fine breadcrumbs. Preheat oven to 350°F (175°C).

Toss raisins in a little flour. Sift remaining flour, cornstarch and baking powder together. In a large bowl, cream butter or margarine and sugar until pale and fluffy. Beat in 1 egg. Gradually beat remaining eggs into creamed mixture, stirring in a little flour mixture between each addition. Fold in remaining flour mixture. Stir lemon peel, almonds, raisins and rum into mixture. Turn batter into prepared pan; smooth the surface. Bake 1 hour 5 minutes or until a skewer inserted in center comes out clean. Remove cake from pan; cool on a rack.

Crumb Puffs

3/4 (17-1/4-oz., 489-g) pkg. frozen puff pastry, thawed
1 egg yolk, beaten

Topping:
1-3/4 cups (200 g) all-purpose flour
1/4 cup plus 3 tablespoons (100 g) granulated sugar
Pinch of ground cinnamon
Pinch of salt
1/2 cup plus 2 tablespoons (150 g) butter
Powdered sugar

On a floured surface, roll out pastry dough 1/8 inch (3 mm) thick. Cut out 2-inch (5-cm) rounds. Roll each round in 1 direction only until about 4-1/2 inches (11.5 cm) long and leaf-shaped. Sprinkle a baking sheet with cold water. Arrange dough leaves on dampened baking sheet; brush with egg yolk. Refrigerate 15 minutes. Preheat oven to 400°F (205°C).
To make topping, sift flour, granulated sugar, cinnamon and salt into a medium bowl. Melt butter. Add to flour mixture drop by drop, stirring constantly with the blade of a knife. Using a fork, toss mixture until it resembles large crumbs. Sprinkle crumb topping over leaves. Bake 12 to 15 minutes or until crisp and brown. Cool on a rack.
Sift powdered sugar over cooled puffs.

Chinese Doughnuts

2 tablespoons (25 g) butter or margarine, softened
3/4 cup (175 g) sugar
1 egg
3 tablespoons water
3 cups (350 g) all-purpose flour
1 teaspoon baking powder
Cold water
3/4 cup (75 g) sesame seeds
Oil to deep-fry

In a large bowl, cream butter or margarine and sugar. Add egg and water. Beat until fluffy. Sift flour with baking powder. Work into mixture using first a wooden spoon then your hands as dough stiffens. Knead dough well. Shape into a 20-inch (50-cm) long roll. Cut 1-inch (2.5-cm) slices from roll. Shape slices into small balls. Dip balls into cold water and toss in sesame seeds.
Heat oil to 360°F (180°C) in a deep-frying pan. Cook 6 to 8 doughnuts in oil at once, turning frequently until golden brown, about 5 minutes. Remove from hot oil with a slotted spoon; drain on paper towels.

Butter Swirls

3-1/4 cups (375 g) all-purpose flour
1 cup plus 2 tablespoons (250 g) butter, cut in small pieces
1/2 cup plus 1 tablespoon (125 g) sugar
6 egg yolks
Pinch of salt
Grated peel of 1/2 lemon
Sugar crystals

Grease baking sheets.

Sift flour into a large bowl; dot with butter. Make a well in center of flour; add granulated sugar, 5 egg yolks, salt and lemon peel. Knead ingredients to make a smooth dough. Place in a pastry bag fitted with a plain nozzle. Pipe S shapes at equal intervals onto greased baking sheets. Refrigerate 1 hour.

Preheat oven to 375°F (190°C). Beat remaining egg yolk and brush over cookies. While egg yolk on cookies is still moist, sprinkle with sugar crystals. If any sugar falls onto baking sheets, remove with a damp pastry brush to avoid burning. Bake 8 to 10 minutes or until golden. Cool on baking sheets about 5 minutes. Remove from baking sheets with a spatula; cool completely on a rack.

Aniseed Chräbeli

1 cup plus 2 tablespoons (250 g) sugar
2 eggs
2-1/4 cups (250 g) all-purpose flour, sifted
1 to 2 teaspoons ground aniseed
Grated peel of 1/2 lemon

Sprinkle baking sheets with flour.

In a large bowl, beat sugar and eggs until creamy; stir in flour. Add aniseed and lemon peel. Shape dough into 1/2-inch thick ropes. Cut ropes into 3-inch (7.5-cm) lengths; curve each piece into a half-moon shape. Slash outer edges of half-moons in 3 places with a sharp knife. Place on prepared baking sheets. Cover and let stand overnight at room temperature.

Preheat oven to 375°F (190°C). Bake cookies 12 to 15 minutes or until just golden. Remove from baking sheets while warm; cool on a rack.

Cook's Tip

Half-moons are the traditional shape for Chräbeli. To save time you can cut the ropes into thick slices, make slashes in these and continue as in the recipe.

Chocolate Almond Bars

Cookie Dough:
1 cup plus 2 tablespoons (250 g) butter, softened
Generous 1 cup (150 g) powdered sugar, sifted
2 eggs
3 tablespoons milk
Grated peel of 1 lemon
4-1/2 cups (520 g) all-purpose flour, sifted
1-3/4 cups (200 g) coarsely chopped almonds

Topping:
4 oz. (100 g) semisweet chocolate
1-3/4 cups (200 g) toasted slivered almonds, page 47

To make cookie dough, beat butter, powdered sugar, eggs, milk and lemon peel in a large bowl. Knead flour and almonds into butter mixture to make a dough.

On a floured surface, roll half the dough into a long thin rope, about 1 inch (2.5 cm) in diameter. Flatten rope to give a strip of dough about 1-1/2 inches (3.5 cm) wide. Repeat with remaining half of dough. Wrap in foil or plastic wrap. Refrigerate 2 hours.

Preheat oven to 400°F (205°C). Grease baking sheets. Cut strips of dough into pieces, 2-1/2 inches (6 cm) long. Place cookies on greased baking sheets. Bake 15 minutes or until golden brown. Cool slightly on baking sheets then transfer to a rack with a spatula to cool completely.

To make topping, melt chocolate in a double boiler over low heat. Spread chocolate thickly over cooled cookies. While chocolate is soft, sprinkle with almonds.

Store in an airtight container when chocolate has set.

Sugar Pretzels

Pinch of granulated sugar
1/2 cup (125 ml) warm milk (110°F, 43°C)
1-1/2 pkgs. active dry yeast
2-3/4 cups (320 g) all-purpose flour
1/2 teaspoon salt
Pinch of ground cardamom
6 tablespoons (80 g) butter or margarine
1 egg
1 egg yolk, beaten
1/2 cup (50 g) sugar crystals

Stir granulated sugar into warm milk and sprinkle with yeast. Let stand 5 minutes or until the surface is frothy. Stir gently to moisten any dry particles remaining on top. Sift flour, salt and cardamom into a large bowl. Melt butter or margarine; cool slightly. Lightly beat butter or margarine and whole egg into yeast mixture. Pour into flour mixture, combining to make a firm dough. On a floured surface, knead dough until smooth. Dough does not need to rise. Preheat oven to 450°F (230°C). Grease a baking sheet.

On a floured surface, roll dough to make a long thick rope. Cut into 24 equal pieces. Roll each piece into a thin strip, about 16 inches (40 cm) long. Make strips into pretzel shapes. Brush with egg yolk; press sugar crystals onto 1 side to decorate. Place pretzels on greased baking sheet. Bake 8 to 10 minutes or until golden. Remove from baking sheet carefully. Cool on a rack.

These pretzels taste best served fresh.

Orange & Nutmeg Cookies

1/2 cup plus 2 tablespoons (150 g) butter, softened
1/2 cup (100 g) granulated sugar
Pinch of salt
Generous pinch of grated nutmeg
Grated peel of 1 orange
2 egg yolks
2-1/4 cups (250 g) all-purpose flour, sifted
3/4 cup (75 g) sugar crystals

In a large bowl, beat butter, granulated sugar, salt, nutmeg, orange peel and 1 egg yolk until pale and creamy. Knead flour into butter mixture to make a dough. On a floured surface, shape dough into a roll 1-3/4 inches (4 cm) in diameter. Cover with foil or plastic wrap. Refrigerate 2 hours.

Preheat oven to 400°F (205°C). Grease baking sheets. Beat remaining egg yolk and brush over roll of dough. Roll dough in sugar crystals to coat all over, pressing in well. Cut into slices about 1/4 inch (5 mm) thick. Lay slices flat on greased baking sheets, leaving a little space between each cookie. Bake 12 to 15 minutes or until light golden. Cool 5 minutes on baking sheets then transfer to a rack with a spatula to cool completely.

Cats' Tongues

Cookie Dough:
1 cup plus 2 tablespoons (250 g) butter, softened
1-3/4 cups (220 g) powdered sugar, sifted
1/2 teaspoon vanilla extract
Pinch of salt
1 egg plus 1 egg yolk
2-1/4 cups (250 g) all-purpose flour, sifted

Filling:
4 oz. (100 g) nougat
3 oz. (75 g) semisweet chocolate

Grease and flour baking sheets. Preheat oven to 400°F (205°C). **To make cookie dough,** cream butter, powdered sugar, vanilla and salt in a large bowl until pale and fluffy. Beat in whole egg and egg yolk separately. Fold flour into egg mixture.

Using a pastry bag fitted with a plain nozzle, pipe cookie mixture onto prepared baking sheets. Shape into cats' tongues as you pipe, see illustration, making each about 3 inches (7.5 cm) long. Leave enough space between each for spreading during baking. Bake 8 to 12 minutes or until golden. Cool on a rack. **To make filling,** melt nougat and chocolate in double boiler over low heat. Spread filling over cooled cookies and press together lightly in pairs.

Let filling set before storing cookies in an airtight container.

Austrian Marble Cake

1 cup plus 2 tablespoons (250 g) soft margarine
3/4 cup plus 2 tablespoons (200 g) granulated sugar
4 eggs
1/2 cup (125 ml) milk
3 cups (450 g) all-purpose flour
2 teaspoons baking powder
1/4 cup plus 1 tablespoon (40 g) unsweetened cocoa powder
1/4 cup plus 1 tablespoon (40 g) powdered sugar
Additional powdered sugar

Grease two 7-inch (18-cm) fluted savarin pans. Sprinkle with fine breadcrumbs. Preheat oven to 400°F (205°C).

Cream margarine and granulated sugar in a large bowl until pale and fluffy. Beat in eggs one at a time. Stir in milk. Sift flour with cornstarch and baking powder. Carefully fold into creamed mixture. Divide batter into 2 equal portions. Divide 1 portion between prepared pans. Sift cocoa powder and powdered sugar together and fold into remaining portion. Divide chocolate portion between both pans. Lightly blend both mixtures in pans by swirling carefully with a skewer or knife. Bake 1 to 1-1/4 hours or until skewers inserted in centers of cakes come out clean. Remove cakes from pans; cool on a rack.

Sift additional powdered sugar over cooled cakes.

Frosted Lemon Cake

Cake:
1/2 cup plus 1 tablespoon (125 g) soft margarine
Grated peel of 1 lemon
1/2 cup (100 g) sugar
2 eggs, beaten
Scant 1/4 cup (50 ml) milk
1-3/4 cups (200 g) self-rising flour
1/2 teaspoon baking powder

Syrup:
3 tablespoons water
Juice of 1 lemon
1/4 cup (50 g) sugar
1 tablespoon liqueur such as arrack or ouzo

Frosting:
Scant 1 cup (100 g) powdered sugar, sifted
3 tablespoons lemon juice
Strip of lemon peel

Grease a round 8-inch (20-cm) cake pan and sprinkle with fine breadcrumbs. Preheat oven to 375°F (190°C).

To make cake, cream margarine, lemon peel and sugar in a large bowl until pale and fluffy. Stir in eggs and milk. Sift together flour and baking powder. Fold into egg mixture. Turn batter into prepared pan; smooth the surface. Bake 40 to 50 minutes or until a wooden pick inserted in center comes out clean. Remove cake from pan; cool on a rack.

To make syrup, bring water to a boil with lemon juice and sugar in a small saucepan. Add arrack or ouzo. Pour hot syrup slowly over cooled cake, letting it soak in well.

To make frosting, blend powdered sugar and lemon juice in a small bowl until smooth. Spread thickly over top of cake so it runs down sides. Cut lemon peel into fine strips; sprinkle over cake while frosting is soft.

Quiche Lorraine

Pastry:
1-3/4 cups (200 g) all-purpose flour
1/2 teaspoon salt
7 tablespoons (100 g) butter or margarine, cut in small pieces
3 to 5 tablespoons (50 to 75 ml) ice water

Filling:
8 oz. (225 g) sliced bacon
4 eggs, separated
1 cup (250 ml) whipping cream
Pinch of white pepper
1/4 teaspoon salt
Generous 1 cup (125 g) shredded Edam cheese

To make pastry, sift flour and salt into a large bowl. Using a pastry blender or 2 knives, cut in butter or margarine until evenly distributed and mixture resembles breadcrumbs. With a fork, lightly mix in enough ice water to make a dough. Press into a ball and wrap in foil or plastic wrap. Refrigerate 2 hours.

Grease and flour one 10-inch (25-cm) or two 7-inch (18-cm) flan tins with removable bottoms. Preheat oven to 400°F (205°C). On a floured surface, roll out dough 1/6 inch (4 mm) thick. Place dough in flan tins without stretching.

To make filling, chop bacon slices and scatter over dough. In a medium bowl, beat egg yolks, cream, pepper and salt. Stir in cheese. Beat egg whites until stiff; fold into cheese mixture. Pour egg mixture into quiche shell; smooth the surface. Bake 30 to 40 minutes or until a knife inserted off-center comes out clean. Cool 10 minutes in tins, then transfer to a platter and serve warm.

Quiche is especially good served with a dry white wine.

Cook's Tip

Bacon, combined with eggs and cream, is the traditional filling for a Quiche Lorraine. Equally delicious quiche fillings include smoked or flaked fresh salmon, mushrooms tossed in a little butter, cooked chopped spinach or canned asparagus spears.

Surprise Sausage Flan

3/4 (17-1/4-oz., 489-g) pkg. frozen puff pastry, thawed

Filling:
3 tablespoons oil
1 onion, sliced
1 clove garlic, crushed
1/2 teaspoon salt
1/4 teaspoon black pepper
4 oz. (100 g) ground beef
4 oz. (100 g) ground pork
3 tablespoons fresh white breadcrumbs
1/2 teaspoon anchovy paste
3 link sausages
2 oz. (50 g) garlic sausage, sliced
2 eggs
Scant 1/4 cup (50 ml) milk
1 teaspoon dried marjoram
1/2 teaspoon dried thyme

On a floured surface, roll out puff pastry dough to fit a 9-inch (23-cm) flan tin with a removable bottom. Place dough in tin without stretching. Preheat oven to 400°F (205°C).
To make filling, heat oil in a small skillet. Add onion and fry until soft. Add garlic, salt and pepper; fry 5 minutes. Remove from heat. In a medium bowl, combine ground beef and pork, breadcrumbs, anchovy paste and onion mixture. Spread meat mixture over pastry shell. Broil or fry sausage links until well-browned; slice. Arrange sausage link slices and garlic sausage slices over meat mixture. In a small bowl, beat eggs, milk, marjoram and thyme; pour over sausage filling. Bake 40 minutes. Serve hot.

Savory Upside-Down Pie

1-1/2 lbs. (675 g) ground beef
1 teaspoon salt
1/2 teaspoon black pepper
1 large onion, chopped
3 egg yolks
4 oz. (100 g) sliced bacon
1/2 cup (50 g) crumbled blue cheese
1-1/2 tablespoons each chopped fresh sorrel and chervil or
 1/4 teaspoon each dried herb
1-1/2 cups (100 g) chopped mushrooms
1/2 (17-1/4-oz., 489-g) pkg. frozen puff pastry, thawed

Mix ground beef, salt, pepper and onion in a large bowl. Stir in egg yolks. Preheat oven to 400°F (205°C). Cover bottom of an 8-inch (20-cm) removable-bottomed cake pan with bacon slices. Arrange blue cheese, sorrel, chervil and mushrooms on top. Cover with ground meat mixture, pressing it down firmly. Smooth the surface.

On a floured surface, roll out puff pastry dough to a circle large enough to cover filling. Place over filling; pierce dough all over with a fork. Bake 40 to 50 minutes. Invert pan over a warm plate or a rack and turn out pie. Serve hot.

Spicy Meat Pie

Pastry:
3 cups (350 g) all-purpose flour
1/2 cup plus 2 tablespoons (150 g) butter or margarine,
  cut in small pieces
1 egg yolk
1/2 cup (125 ml) lukewarm water
1 teaspoon salt

Filling:
1 bread roll
1/2 cup (125 ml) hot milk
1 onion
2 oz. (50 g) sliced bacon
12 oz. (350 g) ground pork and veal
1 tablespoon chopped parsley
1/2 cup (125 ml) half-and-half
Pinch each of salt, white pepper, cayenne pepper,
  ground allspice, ground cardamom and dried basil
1/4 teaspoon grated lemon peel
1 egg, beaten

To make pastry, sift flour into a large bowl and dot with butter or margarine. Make a well in the center; add egg yolk, lukewarm water and salt. Starting at the center, knead quickly to make a dough. Press into a ball and wrap in foil or plastic wrap. Refrigerate 2 hours.

To make filling, crumble bread roll into a small bowl; sprinkle with hot milk and set aside. Finely chop onion. Dice bacon. Fry bacon and onion in a small skillet until golden brown, turning constantly. In a medium bowl, combine ground meats, bacon and onion mixture, parsley, half-and-half, salt, pepper, cayenne pepper, allspice, cardamom, basil and lemon peel. Squeeze milk from breadcrumbs; add breadcrumbs to meat mixture. Preheat oven to 425°F (220°C).

On a lightly floured surface, roll out two-thirds of dough to fit an 8-inch (20-cm) layer cake pan, including a border of 1/8 inch (3 mm). Place dough in pan without stretching. Pierce bottom of pastry shell with a fork in several places; spread filling evenly over dough. Roll out remaining dough to fit top of pan. Place over filling; seal edges well. Make a small hole in the center. Brush surface with beaten egg; pierce in several places with a skewer. Using dough trimmings, cut out flowers, leaves and stems; use to decorate pie. Brush with beaten egg.

Bake about 1 hour. Cover with foil after 45 minutes to prevent burning. Place on a serving dish and serve hot.

Cook's Tip

Try the following variation: use only 6 oz. (175 g) veal. Replace the pork with 6 oz. (175 g) finely diced calf's liver, fried lightly with a chopped onion. Add to the filling and continue as above.

Mushroom & Cheese Flan

Pastry:
2-1/4 cups (250 g) all-purpose flour
1/4 teaspoon salt
1/2 cup plus 1 tablespoon (125 g) butter, cut in small pieces
1 egg yolk
3 to 5 tablespoons (50 to 75 ml) ice water

Filling:
1 leek
3 tablespoons oil
2/3 cup (150 g) diced ham
3 cups (225 g) diced mushrooms
1-1/2 tablespoons (20 g) butter
3 tablespoons (20 g) all-purpose flour
1-1/4 cups (300 ml) milk
3 tablespoons chopped fresh mixed herbs, or 1 teaspoon dried herbs
1/4 teaspoon each salt and pepper
1 egg yolk
4 oz. (100 g) Camembert cheese, cut in small pieces
10 stuffed olives, sliced

To make pastry, sift flour and salt. Using a pastry blender or 2 knives, cut in butter evenly. Lightly mix in egg yolk and enough water to make a dough. Wrap and refrigerate 2 hours.
To make filling, trim, wash and dice leek. Heat oil in a large skillet; add ham and cook until lightly browned. Add leek and mushrooms; simmer 10 minutes. Melt butter in a medium saucepan. Stir in flour and cook a few moments. Add milk and bring to a boil, stirring constantly. Remove from heat and cool to lukewarm. Stir herbs, salt, pepper, egg yolk, Camembert and olives into cooled sauce. Preheat oven to 425°F (220°C). On a floured surface, roll out dough to fit a 10-inch (25-cm) flan tin. Place dough in tin. Spread filling over dough. Pour cheese sauce over filling; sprinkle with olives. Bake 40 to 50 minutes or until filling is firm. Serve hot.

Country Leek Flan

Pastry:
1-3/4 cups (200 g) all-purpose flour
Pinch of salt
7 tablespoons (100 g) butter or margarine, cut in small pieces
1 egg
1 to 3 tablespoons ice water

Filling:
1 lb. (450 g) leeks
6 oz. (175 g) sliced bacon
1 tablespoon oil
Salt and freshly ground black pepper
Pinch of curry powder
8 oz. (225 g) pork sausage, sliced
2 eggs
1 cup (250 ml) dairy sour cream

To make pastry, sift flour and salt into a large bowl. Using a pastry blender or 2 knives, cut in butter or margarine until evenly distributed and mixture resembles breadcrumbs. Lightly mix in egg and enough ice water to make a dough. Press into a ball and wrap in foil or plastic wrap. Refrigerate 2 hours.
To make filling, trim, wash and slice leeks. Dice bacon. Heat oil in a large skillet; add bacon and cook until lightly browned. Add leeks. Sprinkle with salt, pepper and curry powder. Cook over medium heat 10 minutes. Preheat oven to 400°F (205°C).

On a floured surface, roll out dough to fit a 9-inch (23-cm) flan tin. Place dough in tin without stretching. Arrange pork sausage slices over pastry shell. Spread with leek filling. In a medium bowl, beat eggs, sour cream and salt and pepper to taste. Pour over filling. Bake 50 to 60 minutes or until filling is firm. Serve hot.

Piquant Cheese Flan

3/4 (17-1/4-oz., 489-g) pkg. frozen puff pastry, thawed

Filling & Topping:
2/3 cup (150 g) finely chopped ham
1 lb. (450 g) cream cheese
1 tablespoon tomato paste
1 tablespoon paprika
Pinch each of salt, white pepper and sugar
Few drops of Worcestershire sauce
1 small clove garlic, crushed
4 tablespoons chopped fresh mixed herbs
12 small hot red peppers, if desired
12 capers

Divide puff pastry dough in half. On a floured surface, roll out each half to an 8-inch (20-cm) round. Sprinkle baking sheets with cold water; place dough rounds on dampened baking sheets. Pierce dough lightly with a fork. Refrigerate 15 minutes. Preheat oven to 425°F (220°C). Bake dough rounds 10 to 15 minutes or until puffed and golden. Cool on a rack.
To make filling and topping, mix ham, half the cream cheese, tomato paste and paprika in a medium bowl. Season with salt, pepper, sugar and Worcestershire sauce. Combine garlic, just over half the remaining cream cheese, herbs and a little salt and pepper in a small bowl. Cover 1 prebaked pastry round with tomato, ham and cream cheese mixture. Place second pastry round on top; spread with herb and cream cheese mixture. Using the blade of a knife, mark into 12 portions.

In a small bowl, beat remaining cream cheese. Put into a pastry bag fitted with a fluted nozzle. Pipe a rosette of cream cheese onto each portion; top with hot red peppers and capers.

Basque Chicken Pie

Filling:
1 red pepper
1 green pepper
1 large onion
2 medium (225 g) tomatoes
3 tablespoons oil
1/2 clove garlic, crushed
1/4 cup (50 g) diced ham
1-1/2 cups (350 g) diced cooked chicken
1 teaspoon salt
1/4 teaspoon pepper

Pie Dough:
Risen Basic Yeast Dough, page 8
1 egg, beaten

To make filling, wash peppers and remove cores, pith and seeds. Finely chop peppers. Peel and chop onion and tomatoes. Heat oil in a medium skillet; gently fry peppers, onion and garlic about 10 minutes. Add tomatoes, ham and chicken; simmer a few minutes. Stir in salt and pepper; remove from heat. Preheat oven to 400°F (205°C). Grease a baking sheet.
To assemble pie, divide dough in half. On a lightly floured surface, roll out dough to two 12-inch (30-cm) rounds. Place 1 round of dough on greased baking sheet. Spread with chicken mixture to within 1/2 inch (1 cm) of edge. Place second round on top; press edges together to seal. Score with a knife; brush with beaten egg. Bake pie 45 minutes or until a rich golden brown. Serve hot or cold.

Cheese Puffs

3/4 cup (80 g) shredded Gruyère cheese
3/4 (17-1/4-oz., 489-g) pkg. frozen
puff pastry, thawed
3 tablespoons milk
1 egg yolk
3/4 cup (80 g) shredded
Emmenthal cheese
1/2 teaspoon paprika

To make cheese bows, sprinkle a third of the Gruyère cheese over a pastry board or clean working surface. Roll out half the pastry dough over cheese to 1/4 inch (5 mm) thick. Beat milk and egg yolk in a small bowl; use half to brush surface of dough. Sprinkle with half the remaining Gruyère cheese. Fold up dough and roll it out again. Sprinkle remaining Gruyère cheese over surface of dough. Fold up and roll out cheese dough 1/8 inch (3 mm) thick. Cut into 3x2-inch (7.5x5-cm) strips. Lay them 4 strips on top of each other. Cut into 1-inch (2.5-cm) wide slices. Twist slices to form bows. Sprinkle a baking sheet with cold water. Arrange bows on dampened baking sheet. Refrigerate 15 minutes. Preheat oven to 425°F (220°C). Bake 8 to 10 minutes or until puffed and golden. Cool on a rack.

To make cheese straws, combine Emmenthal cheese and paprika in a small bowl; reserve 3 tablespoons. Repeat the same process as above with second half of dough using Emmenthal and paprika mixture. Cut into 4-inch (10-cm) long narrow strips. Brush with remaining egg yolk and milk mixture; sprinkle with reserved 3 tablespoons cheese mixture. Bake as above.

Cook's Tip

Delicious canapés can be made with a variation of these Cheese Puffs. Form the cheese dough into small oval shapes. Make a filling of cream cheese beaten with a little cream. When the cheese pastry is cool, join ovals together in pairs with piped cream cheese mixture. Sprinkle with poppy seeds or caraway seeds and garnish as illustrated.

Savory Cream Puffs

Cream Puff Paste:
1 cup (250 ml) water
4 tablespoons (60 g) butter
Pinch of salt
1 cup (150 g) all-purpose flour
4 eggs

Filling:
4 oz. (100 g) cream cheese
1/2 teaspoon paprika
Pinch of celery salt
1 tablespoon chopped chives
1/4 to 1/3 cup (50 to 100 ml) milk

Garnish:
**Stuffed olives, dill pickles, walnut halves, candied cherries,
    strips of red pepper**

To make cream puff paste, heat water, butter and salt in a
medium saucepan over low heat. When butter has melted, increase heat and bring to a boil. Remove pan from heat; add
flour all at once. Mix with a wooden spoon to make a paste.
Return to heat and beat until mixture forms a smooth ball.
Cool. Preheat oven to 425°F (220°C). Grease baking sheets.

Beat eggs into cooled mixture one at a time. Pipe or spoon
mixture in small balls onto greased baking sheets. Bake about
20 minutes or until crisp and golden brown. Remove from
baking sheets. Cut puffs in half; cool on a rack.

To make filling, put cream cheese, paprika, celery salt and
chives into a small bowl. Beat in enough milk to give a piping
consistency. Put filling into a pastry bag fitted with a fluted
nozzle. Use two-thirds of mixture to fill cooled puffs. Top with
rosettes of remaining filling.

Add a selection of garnishes as illustrated.

Surprise Tartlets

3/4 (17-1/4-oz., 489-g) pkg. frozen puff pastry, thawed

Fillings:
4 oz. (125 g) ground steak
1 egg
About 1/2 teaspoon salt
About 1/2 teaspoon white pepper
3/4 cup (50 g) finely chopped mushrooms
1/2 cup (50 g) shredded Cheddar cheese
2 oz. (50 g) liver sausage
2 oz. (50 g) garlic sausage, diced
4 tablespoons chopped parsley
3/4 cup (75 g) finely chopped walnuts
Parsley sprigs, if desired

Sprinkle 12 small boat-shaped pans and 18 round patty pans
with cold water. Preheat oven to 400°F (205°C).

On a floured surface, roll out pastry dough 1/8 inch (3 mm)
thick. Cut out dough to fit pans. Place dough in pans without
stretching. Pierce tartlet shells all over with a fork.

To make fillings, combine steak, egg and some salt and pepper
in a small bowl. In another small bowl, blend mushrooms,
cheese, liver sausage and some salt and pepper. Using a third
small bowl, mix garlic sausage, parsley, walnuts, salt and
pepper. Use mixtures to fill tartlet shells.

Bake tartlets 20 minutes. Serve hot. Garnish with tiny parsley
springs, if desired.

Ham & Cheese Horns

3/4 (17-1/4-oz., 489-g) pkg. frozen
   puff pastry, thawed

Filling:
3/4 cup (75 g) finely diced Gouda cheese
1/2 cup (100 g) finely diced ham
1 egg yolk
1 tablespoon finely chopped parsley
1 tablespoon finely chopped onion
Pinch each of pepper and dried oregano
1 egg, beaten

On a floured surface, roll out pastry
dough to a 23x10-inch (58x25-cm)
rectangle. Cut into about 15 triangles,
each with 2 very long sides, see
illustration.
To make filling, combine cheese,
ham, egg yolk, parsley, onion, pepper
and oregano in a medium bowl. Place
about 2 teaspoons of filling towards
bottom of each triangle. Make a small
cut in short side of triangle, see
illustration, and roll into horn
shapes; they should be loosely
wrapped. Sprinkle baking sheets with
cold water; place horns on dampened
baking sheets. Brush with beaten egg.
Refrigerate 15 minutes. Preheat oven
to 400°F (205°C).
   Bake 25 minutes or until puffed
and golden. Serve warm.

Cook's Tip

**Instead of horn shapes, the puff pastry
dough can be cut into oblong pieces and
used to make small rolls. The rolls can
be filled with well-seasoned ground beef
instead of cheese and ham.**

Crisp Cheese Bites

1/2 cup plus 2 tablespoons (150 g) butter, softened
1-1/2 cups (180 g) shredded Gruyère or Emmenthal cheese
1/2 cup (125 ml) half-and-half
1/2 teaspoon salt
1 teaspoon paprika
1/2 teaspoon baking powder
2-1/4 cups (250 g) all-purpose flour
1 egg yolk, beaten
Poppy seeds, sesame seeds, caraway seeds, chopped pistachio nuts,
   blanched almonds, page 124

Beat butter and cheese in a large bowl. Stir in half-and-half, salt and paprika. Sift baking powder with flour; stir into mixture. Knead lightly to make a smooth dough. Divide dough into 2 or 3 pieces; wrap in foil or plastic wrap. Refrigerate 2 hours.

Preheat oven to 400°F (205°C). Grease baking sheets. On a floured surface, roll out pieces of dough, about 1/4 inch (5 mm) thick. Cut dough into rings, hearts, half-moons or stars. Place on greased baking sheets. Brush with egg yolk and while still moist, sprinkle with poppy seeds, sesame seeds, caraway seeds or chopped pistachios, or top with an almond. Bake 10 to 15 minutes or until golden. Remove carefully from baking sheet with a spatula. Cool slightly on a rack. Serve warm.

Cook's Tip

There is also an Italian variety of these Cheese Bites made with Gorgonzola cheese. Make the cheese dough as above and sprinkle half with sesame seeds. Bake as above. Mix 3/4 cup (75 g) finely shredded Gorgonzola cheese with 5 oz. (125 g) cream cheese, 1 egg yolk, a pinch of salt and cayenne pepper and 1 teaspoon paprika. Fill a pastry bag fitted with a fluted nozzle with cream cheese mixture and decorate the remaining Cheese Bites.

Cheese & Grape Puffs

1 (17-1/4-oz., 489-g) pkg. frozen puff pastry, thawed
2 eggs
3 tablespoons water
1 teaspoon paprika
1/4 teaspoon black pepper
1 teaspoon apple pie spice
8 oz. (225 g) Cheddar cheese
4 oz. (100 g) green grapes
4 oz. (100 g) salami or garlic sausage, sliced

On a lightly floured surface, roll out puff pastry dough to a rectangle about 1/8 inch (3 mm) thick. Cut into about forty 2-inch (5-cm) squares.

In a small bowl, beat eggs, water, paprika, black pepper and apple pie spice. Brush some of egg mixture over dough squares. Preheat oven to 400°F (205°C).

Cut cheese into same number of cubes as you have dough squares. Halve grapes and remove seeds. Cut salami or garlic sausage slices into small pieces. Place a cube of cheese, a grape and a piece of salami or garlic sausage on each dough square.

Bring corners of dough inwards to the center to make an envelope; press together firmly. Cut small rounds from dough trimmings. Place rounds over centers of envelopes where corners meet; press to seal. Brush envelopes with remaining egg mixture. Sprinkle baking sheets with cold water. Arrange puffs on dampened baking sheets. Bake 15 minutes or until lightly browned. Serve warm.

Bacon Twists

1 (8-oz., 226-g) pkg. crescent roll dough
4 oz. (100 g) sliced bacon
1 egg, beaten

Preheat oven to 375°F (190°C). Unroll dough carefully into 4 rectangles; do not separate into triangles.

On a floured surface, roll out each rectangle to 9x4 inches (23x10 cm). Cut each rectangle lengthwise into 3 strips. Stretch bacon slices by pressing along them with the blade of a knife. Cut bacon into 9-inch (23-cm) strips. Twist each piece of bacon with a strip of dough. Place twists on a baking sheet; brush with beaten egg. Bake 15 minutes or until dough is golden. Cool slightly on a rack. Serve warm.

Cook's Tip

You can make these twists with ham instead of bacon. Cut strips of ham and twist with the strips of dough. Brush with beaten egg and bake as described.

Ham Pasties

3/4 (17-1/4-oz., 489-g) pkg. frozen puff pastry, thawed
4 to 5 slices Parma ham
1 egg yolk, beaten

On a floured surface, roll out pastry dough 1/8 inch (3 mm) thick. Cut into eight to ten 4x2-inch (10x5-cm) rectangles. Cut each slice of ham in half lengthwise; roll up. Place rolled slice of ham on each rectangle of dough. Brush edges with egg yolk. Fold over and press together firmly. Brush surface of pasties with egg yolk. Cut very narrow strips from dough trimmings; place in a cross on pasties. Brush with egg yolk. Sprinkle baking sheet with cold water; place pasties on dampened baking sheet. Refrigerate 15 minutes. Preheat oven to 425°F (220°C).

Bake pasties 15 to 20 minutes or until puffed and golden. Serve hot.

Cook's Tip

Instead of rolling the ham, it can be finely chopped.

Emmenthal Tartlets

Pastry:
2-1/4 cups (250 g) all-purpose flour
Pinch of salt
1/2 cup plus 1 tablespoon (125 g) butter, cut in small pieces
1 small egg
3 to 5 tablespoons (50 to 75 ml) ice water

Filling:
3 cups (350 g) finely shredded Emmenthal cheese
3/4 cup (175 ml) milk or half-and-half
2 eggs
Generous pinch each of white pepper and grated nutmeg

To make pastry, sift flour and salt into a large bowl. Using a pastry blender or 2 knives, cut in butter until evenly distributed and mixture resembles breadcrumbs. With a fork, lightly mix in egg and enough ice water to make a dough. Press into a ball and wrap in foil or plastic wrap. Refrigerate 2 hours.
To make filling, combine cheese, milk or half-and-half, eggs, pepper and nutmeg in a medium bowl.

Preheat oven to 400°F (205°C). On a floured surface, roll out dough about 1/8 inch (3 mm) thick. Cut out 16 circles, 4 inches (10 cm) across. Place in 16 fluted tartlet pans or muffin pan cups. Press down edges well. Fill tartlet shells to the brim with cheese mixture; smooth the surface. Bake 25 to 30 minutes or until filling is rich golden brown. Serve hot.

Cook's Tip

For an alternative filling, use a mixture of 1-1/2 cups (175 g) shredded cheese and 3/4 cup (175 g) very finely chopped ham.

Anchovy Bites

3/4 (17-1/4-oz., 489-g) pkg. frozen puff pastry, thawed
1 (2-oz., 56-g) can anchovy fillets
1 egg yolk, beaten
1-1/2 to 3 teaspoons sea salt

On a floured surface, roll out pastry dough 1/4 inch (5 mm) thick. Cut out 2-1/2-inch (6-cm) rounds with a fluted cutter. Place a halved anchovy fillet on half the dough rounds. Brush edges of each round with egg yolk; join rounds together in pairs, sealing edges well. Brush tops with egg yolk; sprinkle with salt. Sprinkle a baking sheet with cold water; arrange rounds on dampened baking sheet. Refrigerate 15 minutes. Preheat oven to 425°F (220°C).

Bake 10 to 15 minutes or until golden. Serve warm.

Cook's Tip

Sardines can be used instead of anchovies for the filling.

Cheese Twists

3/4 (17-1/4-oz., 489-g) pkg. frozen puff pastry, thawed
1 egg
Salt and pepper
1/2 cup (50 g) finely shredded Emmenthal cheese

Divide puff pastry dough into 3 equal pieces. On a floured surface, roll out each piece to a 14x5-inch (35x13-cm) rectangle. Beat egg with salt and pepper. Brush each rectangle generously with seasoned egg. Sprinkle half the cheese over 1 rectangle of dough; cover with second rectangle. Sprinkle with remaining cheese; cover with third rectangle. Press dough firmly together; cut into thin strips about 1/4 inch (5 mm) wide. Sprinkle a baking sheet with cold water. Twist strips of cheese dough; place on prepared baking sheet. Refrigerate 15 minutes. Preheat oven to 400°F (205°C).

Bake 15 minutes or until golden. Serve immediately.

Cook's Tip

When baking puff pastry, always sprinkle the baking sheet or pan with cold water. The steam from the water helps the pastry to rise.

Bacon & Mushroom Pasties

4 oz. (100 g) sliced bacon
1 small onion
2-1/4 cups (175 g) sliced mushrooms
2 teaspoons tomato paste
1/2 teaspoon celery salt
1/2 teaspoon white pepper
2 tablespoons (25 g) butter
3/4 (17-1/4-oz., 489-g) pkg. frozen puff pastry, thawed
1 egg, beaten
Parsley

Dice bacon. Peel and finely chop onion. Fry bacon and onion in a medium skillet until bacon is crisp. Add mushrooms, tomato paste, celery salt, pepper and butter; fry until liquid evaporates. Remove from heat. Preheat oven to 425°F (220°C).

On a floured surface, roll out pastry dough 1/8 inch (3 mm) thick. Cut into eight to ten 4-inch (10-cm) circles. Including as little fat as possible, place a spoonful of filling on 1 half of each circle. Fold over other half to cover, making a half-moon shape. Using the prongs of a fork, press edges together to seal. Brush pasties with beaten egg. Sprinkle a baking sheet with cold water. Arrange pasties on dampened baking sheet. Bake 15 to 20 minutes or until puffed and golden. Serve hot or cold, garnished with a sprig of parsley.

Savory Tartlets

3 sticks pie crust mix
Water

Fillings:
6 oz. (175 g) lean ground beef
Pinch of salt
Pinch of white pepper
1 egg, beaten
Pinch of dried mixed herbs
3/4 cup (50 g) chopped mushrooms
1/2 cup (50 g) diced cheese
2 oz. (50 g) tongue, diced
2 oz. (50 g) garlic sausage, diced
1/2 cucumber
4 oz. (100 g) liver sausage
3 tablespoons chopped parsley

Place pie crust sticks in a large bowl. Add water and make pie dough according to directions on package. On a lightly floured surface, roll out dough to fit twelve 4-inch (10-cm) tartlet pans. Place in pans without stretching. Preheat oven to 400°F (205°C).

To make fillings, combine ground beef, salt, pepper, egg and mixed herbs in a medium bowl. Fill 4 tartlet shells with mixture. Combine mushrooms, cheese, tongue and garlic sausage in a medium bowl. Use to fill 4 more tartlet shells. Grate cucumber; mix with liver sausage and parsley in a medium bowl. Fill remaining 4 tartlet shells.

Place filled tartlet pans on a baking sheet. Cook 20 minutes. Cool in pans 10 minutes. Transfer to a rack to cool completely.

Gypsy-Style Savories

3/4 (17-1/4-oz., 489-g) pkg. frozen puff pastry, thawed

Filling:
2 small onions
4 tomatoes
24 small slices salami
1/2 cup (75 g) chopped ham
Freshly ground black pepper
1/2 teaspoon paprika
1/2 teaspoon mushroom powder, if desired
1 cup (100 g) diced Cheddar cheese
4 tablespoons chopped parsley
Scant 1/4 cup (50 ml) olive oil

Rinse eight to ten 4-inch (10-cm) tartlet pans in cold water. Preheat oven to 400°F (205°C).

On a floured surface, roll out pastry dough 1/8 inch (3 mm) thick. Cut out circles to fit tartlet pans. Place dough in pans without stretching. Pierce bottoms of tartlet shells all over with a fork.

To make filling, peel onions and slice into rings. Peel and slice tomatoes. Remove any paper casing from salami; place slices in tartlet shells. Add chopped ham and onion rings. Season with pepper, paprika and mushroom powder, if desired. Arrange tomato slices on top. Dot with cheese and sprinkle with parsley. Sprinkle with oil. Bake 20 minutes. Serve hot.

Spiced Meat Pasties

Pastry:
2-3/4 cups (300 g) all-purpose flour
1/4 cup (30 g) cornstarch
Pinch of salt
1/2 cup plus 3 tablespoons (150 g) butter, cut in small pieces
3 to 5 tablespoons (50 to 75 ml) ice water

Filling:
1 onion, peeled
2 tablespoons (30 g) butter
3 tablespoons (20 g) all-purpose flour
1/2 cup (125 ml) beef bouillon
1/3 cup (100 ml) whipping cream
Pinch each of salt, black pepper, sugar, curry powder,
   ground ginger, and cayenne pepper
3/4 cup (150 g) diced cold roast pork
1-1/2 cups (100 g) chopped mushrooms
1 tablespoon chopped parsley
1 egg yolk, beaten

To make pastry, sift flour, cornstarch and salt into a large bowl. Using a pastry blender or 2 knives, cut in butter evenly. Lightly mix in enough ice water to make a dough. Press into a ball and wrap in foil or plastic wrap. Refrigerate 2 hours.

To make filling, finely chop onion; place in a skillet with butter. Cook onions over medium heat until light golden. Stir in flour. Cook a few minutes; mix in beef bouillon and cream. Bring to a boil, stirring constantly. Cook 1 minute; reduce heat. Add salt, pepper, sugar, curry powder, ground ginger and cayenne pepper. Stir pork, mushrooms and parsley into onion mixture. Cook a few minutes. Preheat oven to 400°F (205°C).

On a floured surface, roll out dough 1/8 inch (3 mm) thick and cut out circles 4 inches (10 cm) across. Place a little filling in the center of each circle. Brush edges with water and fold over. Using the prongs of a fork, press edges together. Brush pasties with egg yolk. Bake 25 to 30 minutes or until golden. Serve hot.

Piroshki

Yeast Dough:
Pinch of sugar
1 cup (250 ml) warm milk (110°F, 43°C)
2 pkgs. active dry yeast
4 cups (500 g) all-purpose flour
1/4 teaspoon salt
4 tablespoons (50 g) butter
2 eggs

Filling:
1 leek, washed and trimmed
1 small onion, peeled
1 tablespoon oil
8 oz. (225 g) bulk pork sausage
3 tablespoons fresh white breadcrumbs
1 egg yolk, beaten

To make yeast dough, stir sugar into milk and sprinkle with yeast. Let stand 5 minutes or until frothy. Stir gently. Sift flour and salt into a large bowl. Melt butter; cool slightly. Lightly beat butter and eggs into yeast mixture. Pour into flour mixture, combining to make a dough. On a floured surface, knead dough until smooth. Cover and let rise in a warm place 1 hour.
To make filling, cut leek into thin slices. Finely chop onion. Heat oil in a skillet; fry leek and onion 5 minutes. Put sausage and breadcrumbs into a medium bowl; stir in leek and onion mixture. Preheat oven to 400°F (205°C). Grease baking sheets.

On a floured surface, knead risen dough lightly. Roll out to a 21x16-inch (52.5x40-cm) rectangle. Divide dough lengthwise into 7 long pieces measuring 16x3 inches (40x7.5 cm). Cut each strip along long side into 4 equal pieces. Divide filling between pieces of dough. Dampen edges; fold longer side over filling to give 28 filled rectangles. Press edges together well to seal; brush dough with egg yolk. Place on baking sheets. Bake 30 minutes or until golden. Serve hot.

Rich Game Pasties

8 tablespoons (100 g) butter
12 oz. (350 g) ground lean venison or pheasant
1-1/2 cups (100 g) chopped mushrooms
Juice of 2 oranges
1/4 teaspoon dried marjoram
1/4 teaspoon pepper
1/2 teaspoon salt
Scant 1/4 cup (50 ml) brandy
1/3 cup (100 ml) whipping cream
4 tablespoons chopped parsley
3/4 (17-1/4-oz., 489-g) pkg. frozen puff pastry, thawed
Water
1 egg yolk
1 tablespoon milk

Melt butter in a medium skillet; add venison or pheasant. Cook until browned, stirring constantly. Add mushrooms, orange juice, marjoram, pepper and salt to skillet. Cook gently until most of liquid has evaporated. Pour brandy over mixture. Heat a few seconds then flame and let burn out. Cool. Stir cream and parsley into cooled meat mixture.

On a floured surface, roll out pastry dough 1/8 inch (3 mm) thick. Cut into 12 equal squares. Divide filling between squares. Brush edges with a little water; fold over to enclose filling. Press down firmly to seal. Beat egg yolk with milk; brush over pasties. Sprinkle baking sheet with cold water; place pasties on dampened baking sheet. Refrigerate 15 minutes. Preheat oven to 400°F (205°C).

Bake pasties 20 to 25 minutes or until puffed and golden. Serve hot.

Frankfurter Crescents

1 (8-oz., 226-g) pkg. crescent roll dough
8 frankfurters
1 egg yolk, beaten

Preheat oven to 375°F (190°C). Separate dough into 8 triangles.

Place a frankfurter on each triangle and roll up from the wide end. Place on a baking sheet; brush with egg yolk. Bake 15 minutes or until crisp and golden.

Cook's Tip

Frankfurter Crescents are also good made with puff pastry. Roll out dough thinly and cut it into triangles. Roll up dough with the frankfurters inside. Brush with beaten egg yolk and place on a baking sheet which has been sprinkled with cold water. Bake as above.

Chicken Pasties

Pastry:
2-1/4 cups (250 g) all-purpose flour
Pinch of salt
1/2 cup plus 1 tablespoon (125 g) butter, cut in small pieces
1 small egg
3 to 5 tablespoons (50 to 75 ml) ice water

Filling:
2 slices of bread
1 cup (250 ml) milk
1/2 cup (50 g) ground almonds
1 egg plus 1 egg yolk
1/4 cup (50 g) ground cooked chicken
Pinch each of salt, white pepper, nutmeg and cayenne pepper
1 egg yolk, beaten

To make pastry, sift flour and salt into a large bowl. Using a pastry blender or 2 knives, cut in butter evenly. Lightly mix in egg and enough ice water to make a dough. Press into a ball and wrap in foil or plastic wrap. Refrigerate 2 hours.

To make filling, crumble bread into a small bowl; sprinkle with milk and set aside. In a medium bowl, combine almonds, whole egg, 1 egg yolk, chicken, salt, pepper, nutmeg and cayenne pepper. Squeeze milk from breadcrumbs; add breadcrumbs to chicken mixture with enough milk to give a soft but not runny consistency. Preheat oven to 425°F (220°C).

On a floured surface, roll out dough 1/8 inch (3 mm) thick. Cut out 6 to 8 circles measuring 4 inches (10 cm) across and 6 to 8 circles measuring 2-1/2 inches (6 cm) across. Make a thimble-size hole in the center of smaller circles. Place large circles in fluted tartlet pans or muffin pan cups; divide chicken mixture between pans. Brush edges of smaller circles with egg yolk. Place over filling; seal well at edges. Brush tops with egg yolk. Decorate with dough trimmings.

Bake 20 to 30 minutes or until golden. Serve hot.

Vol au Vent Pastry Shell

3/4 (17-1/4-oz., 489-g) pkg. frozen puff pastry, thawed
1 egg, beaten

Line a 6-cup (1.5-liter) bowl with foil. Fill with crumpled paper towels, pressing down lightly. Fold foil over to enclose towels; secure lightly with tape. Turn out foil mold. Sprinkle a baking sheet with cold water. Preheat oven to 425°F (220°C).

On a floured surface, roll out pastry dough to a 20x12-inch (50x30-cm) rectangle. Cut out a round about 7-1/2 inches (19 cm) across; place on dampened baking sheet. Stand foil mold in middle of dough round, narrow end up. Cut out another round of dough large enough to cover mold, about 13 inches (33 cm) across. Brush edges of both dough rounds with beaten egg. Carefully place large round of dough over foil mold; seal edges to dough base. Flute edges with a knife as illustrated. Brush all over with beaten egg. Cut out shapes from remaining dough trimmings; use to decorate pastry. Brush dough decorations with beaten egg. Bake vol au vent 15 to 20 minutes or until puffed and golden.

Remove from oven and using a sharp pointed knife, cut a round lid from top of vol au vent. Remove lid carefully. Cut a hole in foil underneath. Carefully remove paper towels. Crumple foil; remove from vol au vent shell. Fill and serve immediately or cool and then fill.

Cook's Tip

The Vol au Vent Shell will taste delicious if filled with a creamy chicken or veal mixture. You can also use cold lobster cocktail or crab and shrimp mousse. For a dessert, use a sweet filling such as the ones used in Frosted Vanilla Slices, page 198, or Charlotte Royal, page 203.

The Vol au Vent Shell can be reheated if you wish to make it in advance and serve it hot. Heat the filling separately and fill the shell just before serving, or heat the shell already filled.

Hot or cold, sweet or savory, this vol au vent makes a spectacular buffet party dish.

Bacon Pizza

Pizza Dough:
Pinch of sugar
1 cup (250 ml) warm milk (110°F, 43°C)
2 pkgs. active dry yeast
4 cups (500 g) all-purpose flour
1/2 teaspoon salt
4 tablespoons (60 g) butter
1 egg

Topping:
1 lb. (500 g) sliced bacon
Olive oil
1 tablespoon caraway seeds

To make pizza dough, stir sugar into warm milk and sprinkle with yeast. Let stand 5 minutes or until the surface is frothy. Stir gently to moisten any dry particles remaining on top. Sift flour and salt into a large bowl. Melt butter; cool slightly. Lightly beat butter and egg into yeast mixture. Pour into flour mixture, combining to make a dough. On a floured surface, knead dough until smooth, 5 to 10 minutes. Cover and let rise in a warm place 30 minutes. Grease two 9-1/2-inch (24-cm) flan tins.
To make topping, cut bacon into small pieces. On a floured surface, knead risen dough lightly. Divide dough in half and roll out to fit greased flan tins. Place dough in tins. Scatter bacon pieces over dough. Brush edges of pizzas with a little oil. Sprinkle with caraway seeds. Let stand in a warm place 15 minutes. Preheat oven to 425°F (220°C).

Bake 25 minutes or until edges of pizzas are lightly browned. Serve hot.

Neapolitan Pizza

Pizza Dough:
1/2 teaspoon sugar
2/3 cup (150 ml) warm milk (110°F, 43°C)
1 pkg. active dry yeast
2 cups (225 g) all-purpose flour
1/4 teaspoon salt
3 tablespoons olive oil

Topping:
4 tomatoes
1 teaspoon celery salt
1 teaspoon black pepper
2 teaspoons dried oregano
4 oz. (100 g) mozzarella cheese slices
2 onions, chopped
10 anchovy fillets
1 tablespoon capers
3 tablespoons olive oil

To make pizza dough, stir sugar into warm milk and sprinkle with yeast. Let stand 5 minutes or until the surface is frothy. Stir gently to moisten any dry particles remaining on top. Sift flour and salt into a large bowl. Pour in yeast mixture and oil, combining with flour to make a dough. On a floured surface, knead dough 5 to 10 minutes. Grease baking sheets. Roll out dough into two 7-inch (18-cm) rounds. Place on greased baking sheets; turn up edges slightly to make a rim.
To making topping, peel and slice tomatoes; place on pizza rounds. Sprinkle with celery salt, pepper and oregano. Arrange cheese slices, onions, anchovies and capers over tomatoes. Sprinkle with oil. Let pizzas stand 15 minutes. Preheat oven to 350°F (175°C).

Bake 40 minutes or until edges of pizzas are lightly browned. Serve hot.

Puff Pastry Pizzas

1 small onion, peeled
1 clove garlic
1 tablespoon oil
1 (1-lb., 456-g) can tomatoes, drained
1 teaspoon salt
1/2 teaspoon black pepper
1 tablespoon chopped fresh mixed herbs
   or 1 teaspoon dried herbs
3/4 (17-1/4-oz., 489-g) pkg. frozen
   puff pastry, thawed
Salami slices, stuffed olives, capers and
   chopped herbs
or mussels, paprika, stuffed olives,
   mushrooms, onion rings and freshly
   ground black pepper
or strips of red pepper, black olives,
   cocktail onions and anchovy fillets
1-3/4 cups (200 g) shredded
   Emmenthal cheese

Finely chop onion and garlic. Heat oil in a medium saucepan. Add onion and garlic and cook until soft. Break up tomatoes; stir into onion mixture with salt and pepper. Cover pan and simmer mixture 15 minutes. Stir in fresh or dried herbs.

On a floured surface, roll out pastry dough 1/8 inch (3 mm) thick. Cut into 4-inch (10-cm) squares. Sprinkle a baking sheet with cold water; place dough squares on dampened baking sheet. Top each square with tomato mixture. Add garnishing ingredients according to taste. Sprinkle thickly with cheese. Let stand 15 minutes. Preheat oven to 425°F (220°C).

Bake squares 15 to 18 minutes or until edges are golden. Serve hot.

Alsace Cheese Pizzas

Yeast Dough:
1 (13-3/4-oz., 390-g) pkg. hot roll mix
Water

Topping:
2 medium onions
3 tablespoons (40 g) butter
6 oz. (175 g) sliced bacon
1 egg, beaten
12 oz. (350 g) cream cheese
2 tablespoons chopped parsley

Preheat oven to 425°F (220°C).

To make yeast dough, prepare hot roll mix with water according to pizza recipe on package.

To make topping, peel onion and slice into rings. Melt butter in a skillet. Add onion rings; fry lightly. Chop bacon into small pieces; fry a few minutes with onion.

Divide dough into 8 portions. On a floured surface, roll out each portion to a 5-inch (12.5-cm) round. Brush rounds with beaten egg. Cut cream cheese into small pieces and scatter over rounds. Arrange lightly fried onion rings and bacon pieces over cream cheese. Place on a baking sheet. Bake 20 minutes or until edges are crisp and brown.

Sprinkle rounds with parsley and serve hot.

Mushroom Pizza

Pizza Dough:
1/2 teaspoon sugar
2/3 cup (150 ml) warm milk (110°F, 43°C)
1 pkg. active dry yeast
2 cups (225 g) all-purpose flour
1/4 teaspoon salt
3 tablespoons olive oil

Topping:
8 ripe tomatoes
3 cups (225 g) sliced mushrooms
2 oz. (50 g) Gruyère cheese slices
3 tablespoons chopped parsley
3 tablespoons olive oil

To make pizza dough, stir sugar into warm milk and sprinkle with yeast. Let stand 5 minutes or until the surface is frothy. Stir gently to moisten any dry particles remaining on top. Sift flour and salt into a large bowl. Pour in yeast mixture and oil, combining with flour to make a dough. On a floured surface, knead dough until smooth, 5 to 10 minutes. Grease 2 baking sheets. Roll out dough into two 7-inch (18-cm) rounds. Place on greased baking sheets.

To make topping, peel and slice tomatoes. Cover pizza rounds with tomato slices. Arrange mushrooms over tomatoes; cover with sliced cheese. Sprinkle with parsley and oil. Let stand 15 minutes. Preheat oven to 350°F (175°C).

Bake 40 minutes or until edges of pizzas are lightly browned. Serve hot.

Cook's Tip

To peel tomatoes successfully, place in a bowl and pour boiling water over to cover. Leave for about 1 minute then transfer to a bowl of cold water. The skins should slip off easily.

Seafood Pizza

1 (2-oz., 56-g) can anchovy fillets
3 tablespoons milk
3/4 (17-1/4-oz., 489-g) pkg. frozen puff pastry, thawed
3 tablespoons oil
Scant 1/4 cup (50 ml) tomato paste
4 oz. (100 g) pitted green olives
1 lb. (500 g) tomatoes
1 (3-1/2-oz., 99-g) can tuna
1 small onion, peeled and thinly sliced
3 tablespoons capers
1 (3-oz., 85-g) can crabmeat
1/2 cup (50 g) cooked baby shrimp
Pinch each of garlic salt and dried oregano

Drain anchovies and soak in milk to remove excess saltiness. Sprinkle a 10-inch (25-cm) flan tin with cold water. Preheat oven to 400°F (205°C).

On a floured surface, roll out pastry dough to fit dampened flan tin. Place dough in tin without stretching. Stir 1 tablespoon oil into tomato paste. Brush remaining oil over dough. Slice olives. Peel and slice tomatoes. Spread tomato paste mixture over dough; add sliced tomatoes and olives. Flake tuna; arrange over tomatoes with onion slices, drained anchovies, capers, crabmeat and shrimp. Sprinkle pizza with garlic salt and oregano. Bake 35 minutes or until edges of pizza are lightly browned. Serve hot.

Cook's Tip

In many places along the Italian coast, Seafood Pizza is filled with the following ingredients: 8 oz. (225 g) smoked fish, cut into pieces, 12 oz. (350 g) peeled, diced tomatoes, 4 oz. (100 g) diced bacon slices, 1 cup (100 g) cubed cheese and a finely chopped onion. Then 1 egg is beaten with 3 tablespoons olive oil, 1/2 teaspoon salt, a generous pinch of garlic salt and 1 teaspoon paprika. The egg mixture is poured over the filling and the pizza is baked as above.

Sicilian Sfincione

Topping:
2 lbs. (1 kg) tomatoes
2 cloves garlic, crushed
2 small onions, chopped
1 teaspoon salt
Scant 1/4 cup (50 ml) olive oil

Pizza Dough:
Pinch of sugar
1-1/4 cups (300 ml) warm milk (110°F, 43°C)
2 pkgs. active dry yeast
4 cups (500 g) all-purpose flour
1/2 teaspoon salt
1 egg
3 oz. (75 g) pitted ripe olives, chopped
2 teaspoons dried oregano
4 oz. (100 g) crumbled caciocavallo or grated Parmesan cheese
Olive oil, if desired

To make topping, peel and chop tomatoes. Combine tomatoes, garlic, onions, salt and olive oil in a large bowl. Cover and set aside. Flavor will improve while mixture stands.

To make pizza dough, stir sugar into warm milk and sprinkle with yeast. Let stand 5 minutes or until the surface is frothy. Stir gently to moisten any dry particles remaining on top. Sift flour and salt into a large bowl. Lightly beat egg into yeast mixture.

Pour into flour mixture, combining to make a dough. On a floured surface, knead dough until smooth and springy, 5 to 10 minutes. Cover and let rise in a warm place 25 minutes.

Brush baking sheets with oil. Preheat oven to 425°F (220°C). On a floured surface, lightly knead risen dough; divide into 4 to 6 pieces. Roll out pieces into individual rounds; place on oiled baking sheets. Top each round with tomato mixture. Scatter olives and oregano over pizza. Sprinkle caciocavallo or Parmesan cheese over topping.

Bake 20 minutes or until edges are brown. Sprinkle with olive oil on removal from oven, if desired.

Baking Sheet Sfincione

The yeast dough should be rolled out to the size of a large baking sheet, about 13 inches (33 cm) square. Pierce dough several times with a fork to avoid bubbling during baking. Prepare tomato topping as in the previous recipe and spread over dough. Sprinkle the surface with fresh, coarsely chopped peppermint leaves and a teaspoon of chopped basil, if available. Use twice the quantity of ripe olives and sprinkle with 1-1/2 cups (175 g) shredded mozzarella cheese. Bake sfincione 20 to 25 minutes in a preheated 425°F (220°C) oven.

Cook's Tip

Although sfincione are similar to the Neapolitan pizza, it would be unforgivable to call this Sicilian specialty a pizza. Sfincione were originally made from local products and Sicilians maintain that they were baking them before anyone in Italy had thought of making a pizza. Sfincione are typical of the baking of peasants and farm workers. They may be baked in small round cakes or as one cake on a baking sheet.

Pizzas

Salami Pizza

Pizza Dough:
1/2 teaspoon sugar
2/3 cup (150 ml) warm milk (110°F, 43°C)
1 pkg. active dry yeast
2 cups (225 g) all-purpose flour
1/4 teaspoon salt
3 tablespoons olive oil

Topping:
6 ripe tomatoes
6 small hot red peppers, if desired
2 oz. (50 g) Gruyère cheese slices
8 oz. (225 g) salami, sliced
3 tablespoons olive oil
1 teaspoon dried basil
Freshly ground black pepper

To make pizza dough, stir sugar into warm milk and sprinkle with yeast. Let stand 5 minutes or until the surface is frothy. Stir gently to moisten any dry particles remaining on top. Sift flour and salt into a large bowl. Pour in yeast mixture and oil, combining with flour to make a dough. On a floured surface, knead dough 5 to 10 minutes. Grease two 6-inch (15-cm) layer cake pans. Roll out dough into 2 rounds to fit pans. Place dough in greased pans.
To make topping, peel and halve tomatoes; arrange on pizza rounds with cut-sides up. Cut stems off red peppers; halve lengthwise and remove seeds. Cut cheese into 1/2-inch (1-cm) wide strips. Arrange red peppers, strips of cheese and salami slices over tomatoes. Sprinkle with olive oil, basil and freshly ground black pepper. Let pizzas stand 15 minutes. Preheat oven to 350°F (175°C).
  Bake 40 minutes or until edges of pizzas are lightly browned. Serve hot.

Anchovy Pizza

Pizza Dough:
1/2 teaspoon sugar
2/3 cup (150 ml) warm milk (110°F, 43°C)
1 pkg. active dry yeast
2 cups (225 g) all-purpose flour
1/4 teaspoon salt
3 tablespoons olive oil

Topping:
8 ripe tomatoes
4 oz. (100 g) Gruyère cheese slices
2 (2-oz., 56-g) cans anchovy fillets
1-1/2 teaspoons dried oregano
3 tablespoons olive oil

To make pizza dough, stir sugar into warm milk and sprinkle with yeast. Let stand 5 minutes or until the surface is frothy. Stir gently to moisten any dry particles remaining on top. Sift flour and salt into a large bowl. Pour in yeast mixture and oil, combining with flour to make a dough. On a floured surface, knead dough 5 to 10 minutes. Grease 2 baking sheets. Roll out 2 rounds of dough 7 inches (18 cm) in diameter. Place rounds on greased baking sheets.
To make topping, peel and halve tomatoes; place on pizza rounds cut-sides down. Cut cheese slices into squares; arrange between tomato halves with anchovy fillets. Sprinkle topping with oregano and oil. Let stand 15 minutes. Preheat oven to 350°F (175°C).
  Bake 40 minutes or until edges of pizzas are lightly browned. Serve hot.

Mother's Day Cake

Cake:
1 (18-1/2-oz., 526-g) pkg. orange cake mix
Eggs
Water
Oil, if required

Frosting & Decoration:
About 3 tablespoons orange juice
1-3/4 cups (225 g) powdered sugar
Few drops orange food coloring
2 oz. (50 g) semisweet chocolate
2 teaspoons chopped pistachio nuts
12 sugar daisies, bought or made from almond paste

Grease and flour a 9-inch (23-cm) springform cake pan. Preheat oven to 350°F (175°C).
To make cake, prepare orange cake mix with eggs, water and oil, if required, according to package instructions. Spread batter evenly in cake pan. Bake 55 to 60 minutes, following package instructions to test doneness. Cool as indicated on package.
To make frosting and decoration, heat orange juice in a small saucepan. Sift powdered sugar into a small bowl; stir in enough hot orange juice to give a coating consistency. Beat in orange coloring thoroughly. Pour frosting over cooled cake; let set.

Melt chocolate in a double boiler over low heat. Make a small pastry bag from baking parchment, page 16. Place melted chocolate in pastry bag; pipe rings round edge of cake. Sprinkle with pistachios. Stick sugar daisies onto chocolate rings at equal intervals, using a little melted chocolate to seal.

Cook's Tip

Any of these recipes using package cake mixes can also be made from the basic sponge and layer cake mixtures, page 11.

Sweetheart Cakes

Cakes:
1 (18-1/2-oz., 526-g) pkg. yellow cake mix
Eggs
Water
Oil, if required
1/2 cup (175 g) raspberry jam

Frosting & Decoration:
1 (1-1/2-oz., 42-g) pkg. whipped topping mix
1/2 cup (125 ml) cold milk
1/2 teaspoon vanilla extract
3 tablespoons chopped nuts
Sugar flowers and ladybugs
1-1/4 cups (175 g) powdered sugar, sifted
About 1-1/2 tablespoons water
Crystallized violets and silver cake decors

Grease and flour 2 heart-shaped cake pans, 7 or 8 inches (18 or 20 cm) long. Preheat oven to 350°F (175°C).
To make cake, prepare yellow cake mix with eggs, water and oil, if required, according to package instructions. Spread batter evenly in pans. Bake 35 to 40 minutes, following package instructions to test doneness. Cool as indicated on package.

Cut one of the cooled cakes horizontally into 2 layers. Spread 1 layer with raspberry jam; cover with second layer.
To make frosting and decoration, prepare whipped topping mix with milk and vanilla according to package instructions. Completely cover jam-filled cake with two-thirds of whipped topping, spreading smoothly with a spatula. Put remaining topping into a pastry bag fitted with a fluted nozzle. Pipe rosettes around top of cake; decorate with chopped nuts, sugar flowers and ladybugs as illustrated.

In a small bowl, blend powdered sugar with enough water to give a coating consistency. Spread over second cake. Decorate with crystallized violets and silver cake decors.

Children's Birthday Cake

Cake:
1 (18-1/2-oz., 526-g) pkg. chocolate cake mix
Eggs
Water
Oil, if required

Frosting:
3/4 cup (175 g) butter, softened
2 cups (250 g) powdered sugar, sifted
3 tablespoons unsweetened cocoa powder
2 tablespoons boiling water

Decoration:
Marshmallows
Colored cake decors and M&M's

Grease and flour two 8-inch (20-cm) layer cake pans. Preheat oven to 350°F (175°C).
To make cake, prepare chocolate cake mix with eggs, water and oil, if required, according to package instructions. Spread batter evenly in cake pans. Bake 35 to 40 minutes, following package instructions to test doneness. Cool as indicated on package.
To make frosting, cream butter and powdered sugar in a medium bowl until light and fluffy. Dissolve cocoa powder in water; stir into butter mixture. Fill cake, using about a third of the frosting. Cover cake with remaining frosting, swirling it with a spatula.
To decorate cake, make figures from marshmallows as illustrated; join with wooden picks. Cut a few marshmallows in half and press 1 side into colored cake decors. Place marshmallows and M&M's on cake.

Birthday Car

Cake:
1 (18-1/2-oz., 526-g) pkg. lemon cake mix
Eggs
Water
Oil, if required
1/2 cup (175 g) raspberry jam

Frosting & Decoration:
1-3/4 cups (225 g) powdered sugar, sifted
2 to 3 tablespoons boiling water
1 to 2 teaspoons unsweetened cocoa powder, sifted
Silver cake decors and M&M's

Grease and flour a 13x9-inch (33x23-cm) cake pan. Preheat oven to 350°F (175°C).
To make cake, prepare lemon cake mix with eggs, water and oil if required, according to package instructions. Spread batter evenly in cake pan. Bake 35 to 40 minutes, following package instructions to test doneness. Cool as indicated on package.
  Cut cooled cake horizontally into 2 layers; place 1 layer on top of the other. Using a cardboard pattern, cut out the shape of a car from the cake, cutting through both cake layers. Spread 1 layer with jam. Cut out windows in the other layer; place on top of first layer. Cut out 2 extra wheels from cake trimmings. Place on top of car wheels using jam to join.
To make frosting, put powdered sugar into a small bowl. Beat in enough water to give a coating consistency. Cover car with about two-thirds of the white frosting. Stir 1 to 2 teaspoons cocoa powder into remaining frosting. Make a small pastry bag from baking parchment, page 16. Fill pastry bag with chocolate frosting; outline car as illustrated.
  Decorate car with silver cake decors and M&M's while frosting is soft.

Alphabet Cookies

Cookie Dough:
1-1/2 cups (180 g) all-purpose flour
1 egg, beaten
1/4 cup plus 2 tablespoons (90 g) sugar
2 tablespoons (25 g) vanilla sugar, page 18
4 tablespoons (60 g) butter, cut in small pieces

Frosting:
1-2/3 cups (200 g) powdered sugar, sifted
3 to 5 tablespoons (50 to 75 ml) lemon juice
2 oz. (50 g) jelly bears

To make cookie dough, sift flour onto a pastry board or into a large bowl. Add egg, unflavored sugar, vanilla sugar and butter; knead to a dough. Press into a ball and wrap in foil or plastic wrap. Refrigerate 2 hours.

Preheat oven to 400°F (205°C). Grease a baking sheet. Cut small pieces from cookie dough; form into sausage shapes about 1/2 inch (1 cm) thick. Make a letter from each sausage and flatten slightly. Place on greased baking sheet. Bake 8 to 10 minutes or until golden.

To make frosting, put powdered sugar into a small bowl. Beat in enough lemon juice to give a spreading consistency. Frost warm cookie letters. Stick jelly bears onto frosting before it sets.

Cook's Tip

When you are making the letters for older children or adults, use candied coffee beans for the decoration.

Chocolate Faces

Cake:
4 eggs, separated, plus 2 egg whites
1/2 cup plus 1 tablespoon (120 g) sugar
Grated peel of 1/2 lemon
1 tablespoon water
3/4 cup (80 g) all-purpose flour
1/2 teaspoon baking powder
1/3 cup (100 g) apricot jam

Frosting & Decoration:
4 oz. (100 g) semisweet chocolate
1 egg white
Scant 1/2 cup (50 g) powdered sugar, sifted
M&M's

Line a baking sheet with baking parchment. Preheat oven to 350°F (175°C).

To make cake, beat egg yolks, 2 tablespoons sugar, lemon peel and water in a large bowl until frothy. Beat 6 egg whites until stiff; beat in remaining sugar. Fold into egg yolk mixture. Sift flour and baking powder over egg mixture; fold in.

Put batter into a pastry bag fitted with a large plain nozzle. Pipe quite large half-spheres onto baking parchment. Bake 12 to 15 minutes or until a wooden pick inserted in a cake comes out clean. Cool on a rack. Join pairs of cooled cakes with jam.

To make frosting and decoration, melt chocolate in a double boiler over low heat; spoon over cakes. Beat egg white in a small bowl until frothy; add enough powdered sugar to give a piping consistency. Make a pastry bag from baking parchment, page 16. Fill with frosting; pipe faces onto cakes as illustrated. Use M&M's for eyes securing them to cakes with a little frosting.

Traditional Wedding Cake

Cake:
1 cup plus 2 tablespoons (250 g) butter, softened
1 cup plus 2 tablespoons (250 g) sugar
5 eggs
Grated peel and juice of 1 lemon
1-1/2 tablespoons rum
2-1/4 cups (250 g) all-purpose flour, sifted
1/2 teaspoon ground cinnamon
Generous pinch of grated nutmeg
2/3 cup (150 g) candied cherries, washed, dried and coarsely chopped
2-1/3 cups (400 g) dried currants
2-1/3 cups (400 g) raisins
Generous 1 cup (200 g) chopped mixed candied peel
1/2 cup (50 g) chopped almonds

Royal Frosting:
3 large egg whites
5-1/4 cups (675 g) powdered sugar
1 teaspoon lemon juice
Sugar flowers

Grease a 10-inch (25-cm) cake pan. Line pan with waxed paper; grease paper thoroughly. Preheat oven to 275°F (135°C).
To make cake, beat butter and sugar in a very large bowl until pale and fluffy. Beat in eggs one at a time with lemon peel and juice and rum. Add a little flour if necessary to prevent mixture curdling. Mix remaining flour, cinnamon, nutmeg, cherries, currants, raisins, candied peel and almonds. Add to creamed mixture; fold in thoroughly. Turn batter into prepared cake pan; smooth the surface. Wrap a double thickness of brown paper around pan; secure it with string. This will prevent the outside of the cake from becoming overcooked before the middle has cooked through.

Bake cake 4-1/2 to 5-1/2 hours. Test for doneness with a skewer before removing cake from oven. If necessary, bake a little longer. Let cool a short while in pan, then turn out onto a rack to cool completely. Remove lining paper from cooled cake.
To make frosting, beat egg whites in a large bowl until frothy; brush a little beaten egg white over surface of cake. Gradually beat powdered sugar and lemon juice into remaining egg whites to make a firm frosting. Reserve about a third of frosting for decoration. Frost top and sides of cake, spreading smoothly with a spatula. Place reserved frosting in a pastry bag fitted with a small fluted nozzle; decorate with sugar flowers as illustrated.

Cook's Tip

The wedding cake will taste best if baked at least 3 to 4 weeks before the wedding and wrapped tightly in foil. The cake will keep in foil for up to 1 year. Frost and decorate just before using. In England, it is customary in many families to make a 2- or 3-tier wedding cake and to keep the second tier for the christening of the first child.

The wedding cake is often covered with a layer of almond paste before it is frosted; this gives a smoother surface for the frosting.

Three-Tier Wedding Cake

Cake & Frosting:
Double quantity Traditional Wedding Cake, opposite

Decoration:
Colored cake decors, candied cherries, crystallized violets, angelica and round wafer cookies

Generously grease a 10-inch (25-cm), a 7-inch (18-cm) and a 5-inch (13-cm) cake pan. Line each pan with waxed paper; grease paper. Preheat oven to 275°F (135°C).

To make cake, prepare according to recipe for Traditional Wedding Cake. Bake cakes, checking smallest cake after 2-1/2 to 3 hours, middle cake after 3 to 4 hours and largest after 4-1/2 to 5-1/2 hours. Test each cake with a skewer. If necessary, bake a little longer. Let cool a short while in pans, then turn out cakes onto racks to cool completely. Remove lining paper from cooled cakes and wrap in foil; keep 3 to 4 weeks.

To frost cake, beat egg whites in a large bowl until frothy; brush a little beaten egg white over surface of cakes. Gradually beat powdered sugar and lemon juice into remaining egg whites to make a firm frosting. Cover tops and sides of all 3 cakes with frosting, reserving about a third for decoration. When frosting is completely set, place cakes one on top of the other to make tiers.

To decorate cake, place reserved frosting in a pastry bag fitted with a small fluted nozzle and in a small baking parchment pastry bag, page 16. Using the illustration as a guide, decorate cake with piped frosting, colored cake decors, candied cherries, crystallized violets and angelica. Cut some of the wafer cookies into fourths and cover thinly with frosting. Use to decorate second tier of cake as illustrated. Place 3 frosted wafers on top of cake to form a crown and decorate.

Frozen Raspberry Cream Cake

Cake:
3 eggs
1/4 cup plus 1 tablespoon (65 g) sugar
Pinch of salt
1/2 cup (50 g) all-purpose flour
1/2 teaspoon baking powder
1/4 cup (25 g) ground almonds
2 tablespoons (25 g) butter, melted

Filling & Topping:
1-2/3 cups (225 g) raspberries
1-1/2 tablespoons kirsch
2-1/2 cups (600 ml) whipping cream
1 cup plus 2 tablespoons (250 g) sugar
Chocolate Curls, page 15

Grease and flour an 8-inch (20-cm) cake pan. Preheat oven to 375°F (190°C).
To make cake, put eggs, sugar and salt into a medium bowl. Beat until pale and creamy, 5 to 10 minutes with an electric mixer. Sift flour with baking powder; fold into egg mixture with almonds and butter. Pour batter into prepared pan. Bake 25 to 30 minutes or until a wooden pick inserted in center comes out clean. Turn out onto a rack; cool 24 hours.

Cut cooled cake into 2 layers. Line sides of an 8-inch (20-cm) cake pan with foil. Place 1 cake layer in pan.
To make filling and topping, place raspberries in a small bowl, reserving a few for decoration. Spoon kirsch over fruit; cover and let stand 1 hour. Crush raspberries. Whip cream with sugar until stiff. Refrigerate a fourth of cream mixture; stir crushed raspberries into remainder. Pour over cake; place second cake layer on top. Freeze cake 5 to 10 hours. Remove frozen cake from freezer; let stand 15 minutes then turn out of pan. Spread a little of reserved cream mixture thinly over top and sides of cake. Decorate with rosettes of remaining cream, reserved raspberries and chocolate curls. Serve immediately.

Frozen Hazelnut Cream Cake

Cake:
3 eggs
1/4 cup plus 1 tablespoon (65 g) sugar
1/4 cup (25 g) all-purpose flour
1/2 teaspoon baking powder
1 tablespoon unsweetened cocoa powder
2/3 cup (75 g) finely ground toasted hazelnuts, page 47

Filling & Topping:
2-1/2 cups (600 ml) whipping cream
1 cup (225 g) sugar
3/4 cup (75 g) ground toasted hazelnuts, page 47
Whole hazelnuts

Grease and flour an 8-inch (20-cm) cake pan. Preheat oven to 375°F (190°C).
To make cake, put eggs and sugar into a medium bowl. Beat until pale and creamy, 5 to 10 minutes with an electric mixer. Sift flour with baking powder and cocoa powder; fold into egg mixture with hazelnuts. Pour batter into prepared cake pan. Bake 25 to 30 minutes or until a wooden pick inserted in center comes out clean. Turn out onto a rack; cool 24 hours.

Cut cooled cake into 2 layers. Line sides of an 8-inch (20-cm) cake pan with foil. Place 1 cake layer in pan.
To make filling and topping, whip cream with sugar until stiff. Refrigerate a third of the whipped cream mixture; stir a third of the ground hazelnuts into the remainder. Pour over cake; place second cake layer on top. Place cake in freezer 5 to 10 hours.

Remove frozen cake from freezer; let stand 15 minutes then turn out of pan. Spread a little of the reserved whipped cream mixture thinly over top and sides of cake. Sprinkle with remaining ground hazelnuts. Decorate with rosettes of remaining cream and whole hazelnuts. Serve immediately.

Baked Alaska

Cake:
1 egg
2 tablespoons (25 g) sugar
1/4 cup (25 g) all-purpose flour, sifted

Filling:
1/2 cup (50 g) ground almonds
3 tablespoons (50 g) apricot jam
1 tablespoon rum
1/3 cup (50 g) chopped candied
    lemon peel
1 pint (475 ml) raspberry ripple
    ice cream
1 pint (475 ml) raspberry ice cream

Meringue & Decoration:
4 egg whites
2/3 cup (150 g) sugar
8 candied cherries
2 teaspoons sliced almonds

Grease and flour a 6-inch (15-cm) layer cake pan. Preheat oven to 375°F (190°C).

To make cake, beat egg and sugar in a small bowl until pale and creamy. Fold in flour. Spread batter evenly in pan. Bake 20 to 25 minutes or until a wooden pick inserted in center comes out clean. Turn out cake onto a rack to cool. Line a baking sheet without edges with brown paper. Place cooled cake on brown paper.

To make filling, combine almonds, jam, rum and candied peel in a small bowl. Spread over cake. Place raspberry ripple ice cream on center of cake. Cut raspberry ice cream into slices; place around raspberry ripple ice cream. Smooth into a mound. Freeze 30 minutes or until firm. Preheat oven to 475°F (245°C).

To make meringue, beat egg whites until stiff; fold in sugar. Place meringue mixture in a pastry bag fitted with a fluted nozzle. Pipe over cake, completely enclosing ice cream and base. Decorate with candied cherries and sliced almonds. Brown in oven 3 to 4 minutes. Using brown paper lining, pull Alaska to edge of baking sheet and carefully ease onto serving dish. Serve immediately.

Baked Chocolate Alaska

Make a cake batter as above, using twice the ingredients. Bake cake in a 6x9-inch (15x23-cm) shallow cake pan. Trim cake to fit a block of Neapolitan ice cream; spread cake with 3 tablespoons red currant jelly. Place ice cream on top. Beat 4 egg whites until stiff; fold in 2/3 cup (150 g) sugar and 1 teaspoon sifted unsweetened cocoa powder. Pipe meringue mixture over ice cream and cake. Brown in a preheated 475°F (245°C) oven 3 to 4 minutes. Sift cocoa powder over meringue. Serve immediately.

Desserts with a Difference

Cherry Meringue Nests

Meringue:
6 egg whites
1 cup (225 g) granulated sugar
Scant 3/4 cup (75 g) powdered sugar
1/4 cup (30 g) cornstarch

Topping:
1 tablespoon instant coffee powder
1 tablespoon boiling water
1 cup (250 ml) whipping cream
3 tablespoons sugar
1 (1-lb., 456-g) can pitted red cherries
1 pint (475 ml) vanilla ice cream

Line baking sheets with baking parchment or waxed paper.
Grease waxed paper. Preheat oven to 225°F (105°C).
To make meringue, beat egg whites in a large bowl until stiff.
Slowly beat in granulated sugar until mixture is stiff and glossy.
Sift powdered sugar with cornstarch; fold into egg white mix-
ture. Fill a pastry bag fitted with a fluted nozzle with meringue
mixture; pipe rosettes onto baking sheets. Bake with oven door
slightly open 3 to 4 hours or overnight. Cool on a rack.
To make topping, dissolve coffee powder in boiling water; cool.
Whip cream with sugar until stiff; stir in cooled coffee mixture.
Using a pastry bag fitted with a fluted nozzle, pipe rings of
coffee cream onto cooled meringue nests. Drain cherries; pat
dry with paper towels. Place a few cherries in coffee cream; top
with a scoop of ice cream. Decorate with remaining cherries.
Serve immediately.

Orange Cream Tartlets

Pastry:
2 cups (200 g) all-purpose flour
Pinch of salt
8 tablespoons (100 g) butter, cut in small pieces
Scant 1 cup (100 g) powdered sugar
2 egg yolks
Few drops of vanilla extract
About 1 tablespoon ice water

Filling & Topping:
1 (6-fl.oz., 177-ml) can frozen orange juice concentrate
Scant 1/4 cup (50 ml) white wine
1/2 cup (100 g) sugar
1 envelope unflavored gelatin
1-1/4 cups (300 ml) whipping cream
Scant 1/2 cup (50 g) instant chocolate drink powder, sifted
1 pint (475 ml) raspberry and vanilla ice cream
1/2 cup (50 g) toasted sliced almonds, page 47

To make pastry, sift flour and salt into a large bowl. Using a
pastry blender or 2 knives, cut in butter evenly. Lightly mix in
powdered sugar, egg yolks, vanilla and enough water to make a
dough. Wrap in foil or plastic wrap. Refrigerate 2 hours. Preheat
oven to 400°F (205°C). On a floured surface, roll out dough
thinly to fit twelve 3-inch (7.5-cm) tartlet pans. Bake blind,
page 9, 10 minutes or until golden. Cool shells on a rack.
To make filling and topping, heat orange juice, wine and sugar
in a small saucepan over low heat. Add gelatin; warm gently to
dissolve. Remove from heat. Pour into a medium bowl; cool
slightly and refrigerate. Whip cream until stiff. When orange
mixture is beginning to set, fold in half the whipped cream. Fill
tartlet shells with orange cream. Refrigerate until firm.
   Stir chocolate powder into remaining whipped cream. Just
before serving, place a slice of ice cream on each tartlet. Using a
pastry bag fitted with a fluted nozzle, pipe a rosette of chocolate
cream onto ice cream. Sprinkle with almonds.

Exotic Fruit Meringues

Meringues:
6 egg whites
1/2 cup (100 g) granulated sugar
Scant 1 cup (100 g) powdered sugar
1/4 cup (30 g) cornstarch
1/4 cup plus 1 tablespoon (40 g) unsweetened cocoa powder

Topping:
1 cup (250 ml) whipping cream
3 tablespoons (20 g) powdered sugar, sifted
6 kiwi fruit
1 pint (475 ml) vanilla and coffee ice cream

Line a baking sheet with baking parchment or waxed paper.
Grease waxed paper. Preheat oven to 225°F (105°C).
To make meringues, beat egg whites in a large bowl until stiff.
Beat in granulated sugar. Sift powdered sugar with cornstarch
and cocoa powder; fold into egg white mixture. Place in a pastry
bag fitted with a plain nozzle; pipe 14 oval meringues onto prepared baking sheet. Bake with oven door slightly open 3 to 4
hours or overnight. Cool on a rack.
To make topping, whip cream with powdered sugar until stiff.
Place in a pastry bag fitted with a fluted nozzle; pipe rings of
whipped cream mixture onto cooled meringues. Peel and slice
kiwi fruit; arrange on top of whipped cream. Place slices of ice
cream over kiwi fruit. Serve immediately.

Chocolate Ice Waffles

Waffle Batter:
4 tablespoons (60 g) butter, softened
2 tablespoons (25 g) sugar
1 teaspoon vanilla sugar, page 18
Pinch of salt
2 eggs
1 cup (125 g) all-purpose flour, sifted
1/2 teaspoon baking powder
3/4 cup (175 ml) buttermilk
Melted butter

Filling & Topping:
2/3 cup (150 ml) whipping cream
1 tablespoon sugar
4 oz. (100 g) semisweet chocolate
1 pint (475 ml) chocolate ripple ice cream
Chopped pistachio nuts

To make waffle batter, beat butter, unflavored sugar, vanilla
sugar and salt in a medium bowl until pale and fluffy. Beat in
eggs one at a time. Fold in flour and baking powder then mix in
buttermilk. Batter will be thick.
   Heat waffle iron; brush lightly with butter. Pour in batter and
cook waffles individually until golden brown.
To make filling and topping, whip cream with sugar until stiff.
Put into a pastry bag fitted with a fluted nozzle and refrigerate.
Melt chocolate in a double boiler over low heat. Let cool but not
set. Just before serving, place a wedge of ice cream on half the
waffles; cover each with a second waffle. Decorate with rosettes
of piped whipped cream, chocolate and chopped pistachios.

Desserts with a Difference

Strawberry Cream Puffs

Cream Puff Paste:
1/2 cup (125 ml) water
2 tablespoons (30 g) butter
Pinch of salt
2/3 cup (95 g) all-purpose flour, sifted
2 eggs, beaten

Filling:
1 (8- to 10-oz., 225- to 275-g) pkg. frozen strawberries
3 tablespoons (40 g) granulated sugar
1 tablespoon rum
2/3 cup (150 ml) whipping cream
1/4 cup (25 g) powdered sugar, sifted
1 pint (475 ml) strawberry ice cream

Grease a baking sheet. Preheat oven to 425°F (220°C).
To make cream puff paste, heat water, butter and salt in a medium saucepan until butter has melted. Increase heat and bring quickly to a boil; remove from heat. Add flour all at once; beat until dough forms a ball and comes away from sides of pan cleanly. Return to heat; cook 1 minute, stirring constantly. Cool slightly; beat in eggs a little at a time. Fill a pastry bag fitted with a large fluted nozzle with paste; pipe 16 small rosettes onto greased baking sheet. Bake 20 minutes or until puffed and golden. Cut a lid from each cream puff. Cool on a rack.
To make filling, combine strawberries, granulated sugar and rum in a small bowl. Set aside to thaw.

Whip cream with half the powdered sugar until stiff. Fill bottom halves of puffs with thawed strawberry mixture. Place scoops of ice cream over strawberries. Using a pastry bag fitted with a fluted nozzle, pipe whipped cream onto ice cream; top with cream puff lids. Sprinkle with remaining powdered sugar. Serve immediately.

Coffee Meringue Kisses

Meringue:
2 tablespoons instant coffee powder
Hot water
8 egg whites
3/4 cup plus 2 tablespoons (200 g) granulated sugar
Generous 1 cup (150 g) powdered sugar
1/4 cup (30 g) cornstarch

Filling:
1 (8-oz., 225-g) can pitted cherries
2 teaspoons cornstarch
1/4 cup (50 g) granulated sugar
1/2 teaspoon ground cinnamon
1-1/4 cups (300 ml) whipping cream
1 tablespoon powdered sugar, sifted

Line baking sheets with baking parchment or waxed paper. Grease waxed paper. Preheat oven to 250°F (120°C).
To make meringue, dissolve coffee powder in just enough hot water to blend it. Cool. In a large bowl, beat egg whites until stiff. Slowly add granulated sugar, beating constantly. Sift powdered sugar and cornstarch onto egg whites; fold in with blended coffee. Fill a pastry bag fitted with a fluted nozzle with meringue mixture; pipe rosettes onto prepared baking sheets. Bake 3 to 4 hours with oven door slightly open. Remove meringues from baking sheets; cool on a rack.
To make filling, drain cherries and reserve juice. Mix cornstarch with a little cherry juice. Bring remaining cherry juice to a boil with granulated sugar and cinnamon in a small saucepan. Reduce heat slightly and add cornstarch mixture; stir until thickened. Add cherries, bring back to a boil. Remove sauce from heat; cool. Whip cream with powdered sugar until stiff. Put into a pastry bag fitted with a fluted nozzle. Pipe a ring of cream mixture onto the flat side of half the meringues. Fill centers with cooled cherry sauce; top with second meringue.

Fruit & Rum Babas

Savarin Dough:
3 tablespoons (40 g) sugar
1 cup (250 ml) warm milk (110°F, 43°C)
1-1/2 pkgs. active dry yeast
3 cups (350 g) all-purpose flour
4 eggs
2 tablespoons (25 g) vanilla sugar, page 18
1/2 teaspoon salt
1/2 cup plus 2 tablespoons (150 g) butter, melted

Syrup:
2/3 cup (150 g) sugar
1 cup (250 ml) water
Grated peel of 1 lemon
1/3 cup (100 ml) rum
1/2 cup (125 ml) white wine

Filling:
1 cup (250 ml) whipping cream
1 tablespoon powdered sugar, sifted
1 teaspoon unsweetened cocoa powder, sifted
12 oz. (350 g) drained canned fruit, pineapple, gooseberries, cherries, kumquats, kiwi fruit
1/2 cup (50 g) sliced almonds

To make savarin dough, stir 1 teaspoon unflavored sugar into warm milk and sprinkle with yeast. Let stand 5 minutes or until frothy. Stir gently to moisten any dry particles remaining on top. Sift flour into a large bowl. Beat eggs with remaining unflavored sugar in a medium bowl until frothy. Mix in vanilla sugar, salt and slightly cooled melted butter. Stir yeast mixture into egg mixture. Pour into flour, mixing well to make a loose dough. Cover and let rise in a warm place 10 minutes. Grease and flour about twenty-four 3-inch (7.5-cm) savarin pans.

Beat risen dough. Half-fill prepared pans with dough. Cover and let rise in a warm place 15 minutes or until dough reaches tops of pans. Preheat oven to 400°F (205°C). Bake 30 minutes or until babas are a rich brown. Turn out onto a rack.

To make syrup, heat sugar, water, lemon peel, rum and white wine in a small saucepan over low heat. Stir constantly until sugar has completely dissolved. Increase heat and bring to a boil; cook 5 to 10 minutes. Place warm babas upside down on a plate; spoon warm syrup over babas. They must be completely soaked with syrup.

To make filling, whip cream with powdered sugar until stiff. Place half the whipped cream mixture in another bowl. Stir in cocoa powder. Fill a pastry bag fitted with a fluted nozzle with the plain whipped cream. Pipe rosettes of cream in the centers of half the babas. Pipe rosettes of chocolate cream into remaining babas. Cut fruit into small pieces; decorate babas with fruit. Sprinkle with almonds.

Cook's Tip

If you have only 12 savarin pans, bake the babas in 2 batches. Instead of savarin pans you can use ring molds or make more savarin pans out of aluminum foil.

Banana Meringues

Meringue:
4 egg whites
1/4 cup plus 3 tablespoons (100 g) granulated sugar
Scant 1/2 cup (70 g) powdered sugar
2 tablespoons (15 g) cornstarch

Filling:
1-1/4 cups (300 ml) whipping cream
1/4 cup (25 g) powdered sugar, sifted
1 tablespoon unsweetened cocoa powder, sifted
6 bananas

Topping:
4 oz. (100 g) semisweet chocolate
1/4 cup (50 g) firmly packed soft brown sugar

Line a baking sheet with baking parchment or waxed paper. Grease waxed paper. Preheat oven to 250°F (120°C).
To make meringue, beat egg whites in a medium bowl until stiff. Slowly add granulated sugar, beating constantly. Sift powdered sugar and cornstarch onto egg white mixture; fold in. Fill a pastry bag fitted with a plain nozzle with meringue mixture; pipe 12 banana shapes onto prepared baking sheet. Bake 3 to 4 hours with oven door slightly open. Remove meringues from baking sheet; cool on a rack.
To make filling, whip cream with powdered sugar until stiff; stir in cocoa powder. Put chocolate cream into a pastry bag fitted with a fluted nozzle; pipe onto cooled meringues. Peel bananas and cut in half lengthwise. Place a halved banana on each cream-topped meringue.
To make topping, melt chocolate in a double boiler over low heat. Pour chocolate over bananas; sprinkle with brown sugar before chocolate sets.

Ice Cream Roll

Cake:
4 eggs, separated, plus 2 egg yolks
1/2 cup (100 g) sugar
3/4 cup (80 g) all-purpose flour
1/2 teaspoon baking powder
1 cup (350 g) orange marmalade

Filling:
2/3 cup (150 ml) whipping cream
1 tablespoon sugar
1 pint (475 ml) Neapolitan or vanilla ice cream

Line a 13x9-inch (33x23-cm) cake pan with waxed paper; grease paper. Preheat oven to 425°F (220°C).
To make cake, put 6 egg yolks and half the sugar into a large bowl. Beat until pale and creamy, 5 to 10 minutes with an electric mixer. Beat whites until stiff. Gradually add remaining sugar, beating until smooth and glossy. Fold into yolk mixture. Sift flour with baking powder; fold carefully into egg mixture. Spread batter evenly in prepared pan. Bake 10 to 12 minutes or until a wooden pick inserted in center comes out clean.

Sprinkle a cloth towel with sugar; turn out hot cake onto sugared towel. Peel off lining paper; trim cake edges. Heat marmalade and press gently through a strainer to obtain jelly. Spread jelly evenly over warm cake. With the help of the cloth towel, roll up cake tightly. Cool on a rack.
To make filling, whip cream with sugar until stiff. Put into a pastry bag fitted with a fluted nozzle and refrigerate. Cut cooled jelly roll into 1/2-inch (1-cm) slices. Place a 1/2-inch (1-cm) slice of ice cream between each pair of cake slices until both jelly roll and ice cream are used up. Decorate with rosettes of whipped cream mixture.

Italian Cassata

Batter for Basic Layer Cake, page 11

Filling:
1-1/2 cups (350 g) small-curd
   cottage cheese
3 tablespoons whipping cream
1/4 cup (60 g) sugar
1 tablespoon orange-flavored liqueur
3 tablespoons (25 g) finely chopped
   candied fruit

Frosting:
About 1/3 cup (100 ml) strong
   black coffee
8 oz. (225 g) semisweet chocolate
8 tablespoons (100 g) butter,
   cut in small pieces
Candied fruit

Prepare cake batter. Turn batter into a greased 9-1/4x5-1/4-inch (23x13-cm) loaf pan. Bake in a preheated 325°F (165°C) oven 45 minutes or until a wooden pick inserted in center comes out clean. Cool on a rack. Trim cake if necessary; cut cooled cake horizontally into 4 layers.

To make filling, press cottage cheese through a strainer into a medium bowl. Add cream, sugar and liqueur; stir until smooth. Mix in candied fruit. Spread filling over 3 layers of cake; stack layers on top of each other. Top with fourth cake layer; press slightly so cake is compact. Refrigerate 2 hours.

To make frosting, put coffee into a double boiler. Add chocolate; stir over low heat until chocolate has melted. Add butter. Stir until mixture becomes completely smooth and creamy. Refrigerate frosting until it begins to set. Cover sides and top of cake with about two-thirds of frosting. Fill a pastry bag fitted with a fluted nozzle with remaining frosting. Decorate cake with rosettes and garlands as illustrated. Cut candied fruit into small pieces; arrange on frosting.

Wrap cake loosely in foil; refrigerate 1 day before serving.

Christmas Stollen

Yeast Dough:
Scant 2 cups (450 ml) warm milk (110°F, 43°C)
1 cup (225 g) sugar
3 pkgs. active dry yeast
8 cups (1.2 kg) all-purpose flour
1/2 teaspoon salt
2 eggs
1/2 teaspoon vanilla extract
Grated peel of 1 lemon
2 cups (350 g) raisins
1 cup (100 g) chopped almonds
2/3 cup (100 g) chopped candied lemon peel
1/3 cup (50 g) chopped candied orange peel
2 tablespoons rum
1 cup (225 g) butter

Topping:
1/2 cup plus 2 tablespoons (150 g) butter
Generous 1 cup (150 g) powdered sugar

To make yeast dough, put warm milk into a medium bowl; stir in 1 tablespoon sugar. Sprinkle with yeast; let stand 5 minutes or until the surface is frothy. Stir gently to moisten any dry particles remaining on top. Sift 6-2/3 cups (1 kg) flour, salt and remaining sugar into a large bowl. Lightly beat eggs into yeast mixture with vanilla and lemon peel. Pour into flour mixture, combining to make a firm dough. On a floured surface, knead dough until smooth. Cover and let rise in a warm place 1 hour. Mix raisins, almonds and candied peel in a medium bowl; sprinkle with rum. Cover and let steep.

Work butter and remaining flour together; knead into risen dough. Cover and let stand in a warm place 15 minutes.

Work fruit and rum mixture quickly into dough. Cover and let stand in a warm place 15 minutes. Line baking sheets with waxed paper; grease paper.

Divide dough into 3 portions. On a floured surface, gently roll each piece into a 12-inch (30-cm) long oval which is thinner in the middle than at the edges. Fold dough over lengthwise, making a 6-inch (15-cm) length. This gives the typical stollen shape. Place dough on baking sheet. Repeat with remaining 2 pieces of dough. Cover and let stand in a warm place 20 minutes, until increased in size. Preheat oven to 350°F (175°C). Bake stollen 30 to 35 minutes or until a rich golden brown.

To make topping, melt butter. Brush melted butter over hot stollen. Sift powdered sugar generously over stollen.

Almond Stollen

Omit the raisins, lemon peel, candied orange peel and rum. Prepare the dough as for Christmas Stollen. After the second rising, knead in 2 cups (225 g) chopped almonds and 1-1/3 cups (225 g) chopped candied lemon peel. Let stand 15 minutes longer then continue as for Christmas Stollen.

Traditional Fruit Loaf

Starter Dough:
3 tablespoons milk
1/3 cup (100 ml) water
1 teaspoon oil
1 teaspoon sugar
3 tablespoons warm water (110°F, 43°C)
1 teaspoon active dry yeast
2 teaspoons salt
1/2 cup (50 g) white bread flour
1/2 cup (50 g) rye flour

Filling:
1/2 cup (75 g) dried prunes, pitted
1 cup (175 g) dried pears
1/2 cup (75 g) dried figs
1/3 cup (50 g) raisins
1/3 cup (50 g) dried currants
1/3 cup (50 g) chopped mixed candied peel
1-1/4 cups (300 ml) hot black tea
1/4 cup (50 g) sugar
1/2 teaspoon ground cinnamon
Pinch each of ground cloves, ground aniseed and salt
3 tablespoons rum
3 tablespoons lemon juice
1-3/4 cups (200 g) all-purpose flour, sifted
1/2 cup (50 g) finely chopped hazelnuts
1/2 cup (50 g) finely chopped walnuts

Decoration:
1/4 cup (25 g) blanched halved almonds, page 124
Candied cherries
Angelica

To make starter dough, combine milk, 1/3 cup (100 ml) water and oil in a small saucepan; bring to a boil. Cool until lukewarm. Stir sugar into 3 tablespoons warm water and sprinkle with yeast. Let stand 5 minutes or until the surface is frothy. Stir gently to moisten any dry particles remaining on top. Add to milk mixture with salt. Combine milk mixture, white bread flour and rye flour in a large bowl until blended. Cover and let stand 12 to 18 hours.

To make filling, chop prunes, pears and figs. Place in a medium bowl with raisins, currants and candied peel. Pour freshly made tea over mixed fruit; cover and let soak overnight.

Add sugar, cinnamon, cloves, aniseed, salt, rum and lemon juice to fruit mixture. Stir mixture thoroughly; cover and let stand 30 minutes. Grease a deep 8-inch (20-cm) cake pan. Preheat oven to 350°F (175°C).

Add fruit mixture to starter dough with flour, hazelnuts and walnuts. Mix thoroughly until blended. Turn batter into greased cake pan. Decorate as illustrated with halved almonds, candied cherries and strips of angelica. Bake 1 hour 10 minutes or until a skewer inserted in center comes out clean. Cool in pan 1 hour; turn out onto a rack to cool completely.

Italian Panettone

2/3 cup (150 ml) warm milk (110°F, 43°C)
1/4 cup (50 g) sugar
2 pkgs. active dry yeast
3-1/2 cups (400 g) all-purpose flour
1 teaspoon salt
8 tablespoons (100 g) butter
3 egg yolks
Pinch of grated nutmeg
Grated peel of 1/2 lemon
2/3 cup (100 g) chopped mixed candied peel
1/3 cup (50 g) raisins
1 egg yolk, beaten

Put warm milk into a medium bowl; stir in a pinch of sugar. Sprinkle with yeast. Let stand 5 minutes or until the surface is frothy. Stir gently to moisten any dry particles remaining on top. Sift flour, salt and remaining sugar into a large bowl. Melt butter; cool slightly. Stir butter into yeast mixture; lightly beat in 3 egg yolks, nutmeg and lemon peel. Pour into flour mixture, combining to make a soft dough. On a floured surface, knead dough about 10 minutes. Cover and let rise in a warm place until doubled in size, about 1 hour. Line a deep 7-inch (18-cm) cake pan with waxed paper; grease paper.

Turn out dough onto a lightly floured surface; knead in candied peel and raisins. Form dough into a ball; place in prepared pan. Cover and let stand in a warm place until dough reaches top of pan. Preheat oven to 400°F (205°C).

Brush risen dough with egg yolk. Using a sharp knife, cut a cross on the top. Bake 20 minutes. Reduce heat to 350°F (175°C) and bake 45 minutes longer or until cake is a rich brown. Cool slightly in pan before turning out onto a rack to cool completely.

Remove lining paper just before cutting cake.

Honey Cakes

Cake:
1 lb. (500 g) honey
1/2 cup (125 ml) water
1 lb. (500 g) molasses
6 cups (700 g) whole-wheat flour
2-1/2 cups (300 g) rye flour
1 tablespoon baking powder
1 teaspoon baking soda
1 tablespoon milk

Filling:
4 oz. (100 g) almond paste, cut in small pieces
1/2 cup plus 1 tablespoon (130 g) sugar
1 egg white
1 tablespoon rum
2/3 cup (100 g) chopped candied fruit
1 cup (100 g) chopped almonds
Milk

Frosting & Decoration:
11 oz. (300 g) semisweet chocolate
Candied cherries, angelica

To make cake, put honey, water and molasses in a saucepan; gradually bring to a boil. Cool in a large bowl. Work in flours and baking powder. Dissolve baking soda in milk; stir into flour mixture. Wrap dough and let stand 2 days at room temperature.
To make filling, mix almond paste, sugar, egg white, rum, candied fruit and almonds in a bowl over a saucepan of hot water.

Preheat oven to 375°F (190°C). Grease 3 baking sheets. Divide dough into 3 portions. On a floured surface, roll out each piece 3/4 inch (1.5 cm) thick. Cut 2 heart shapes from each piece. Spread filling over centers of half the hearts. Brush edges with milk. Top with a second heart; press edges together. Bake 30 to 35 minutes or until firm to the touch. Cool on racks.
To make frosting, melt chocolate in a double-boiler over low heat. Spread over cakes; add candied cherries and angelica.

Marzipan Figures

2 lbs. (1 kg) almond paste

Coloring:
Red and yellow food coloring
1 tablespoon unsweetened cocoa powder
2 teaspoons boiling water

Decoration:
1 egg white
Scant 1/2 cup (50 g) powdered sugar, sifted
4 oz. (100 g) semisweet chocolate
Blanched halved almonds, page 124

On a surface sprinkled with a little powdered sugar, knead almond paste. Divide into 4 equal pieces.

To color almond paste, leave 1 piece of almond paste as it is. Color the second piece with red food coloring. Color the third piece with yellow food coloring. Blend cocoa powder with boiling water; knead into fourth piece. To avoid drying out, wrap marzipan in foil or plastic wrap until you are ready to use it.

Cut pieces from colored marzipan. Using the illustration as a guide, shape animals or figures from marzipan. If the parts of the figures do not stick together, use wooden picks, making sure they are removed before figures are eaten.

To decorate, beat egg white in a small bowl until frothy; mix in powdered sugar. Melt chocolate in a double boiler over low heat. Make 2 small pastry bags from baking parchment, page 16. Fill each pastry bag with one of the frostings; use to draw faces as illustrated. For piglet, use almond halves to make feet and ears.

Use figures to decorate cakes or serve as candy.

Cook's Tip

The color of almond paste varies depending on the brand or whether it is homemade. White almond paste is made with egg whites instead of egg yolks.

Gingerbread House

Gingerbread:
2 lbs. (1 kg) creamed honey or honey spread
1 cup (250 ml) water
6 cups (650 g) rye flour
4 cups (500 g) whole-wheat flour
Generous 1 cup (200 g) chopped mixed candied peel
1 teaspoon ground ginger
1 teaspoon ground cinnamon
1/2 teaspoon grated nutmeg
1 teaspoon baking soda
20 to 30 blanched almonds, page 124

Frosting:
2 egg whites
3-1/2 cups (500 g) powdered sugar, sifted
1 tablespoon lemon juice
Colored cake decors

To make gingerbread, put creamed honey or honey spread and water into a medium saucepan. Bring to a boil, stirring constantly. Cool. Place rye flour and whole-wheat flour in a large bowl; sprinkle with candied peel, ginger, cinnamon and nutmeg. Make a well in the center; pour in almost cold honey mixture. Knead to make a soft dough. Mix in baking soda. Put dough in a plastic bag; seal. Let stand 1 to 2 days at room temperature to give gingerbread a better flavor.

For the walls and roof, cut out a cardboard pattern using the diagram on page 16. Lightly grease 2 baking sheets. Preheat oven to 400°F (205°C).

On a lightly floured surface, roll part of honey dough into 18 sausage shapes 16 inches (40 cm) long and 3/4 inch (1.5 cm) thick. Place sausage shapes side by side on 1 greased baking sheet, leaving about 1/8 inch (3 mm) between each. They should form a 16x10-inch (40x25-cm) rectangle. During baking, gaps will close to form walls. Bake 20 to 30 minutes.

Roll out remaining dough 1/2 inch (1 cm) thick. Cut out 1 piece of dough about 10x6 inches (25x15 cm) and a second piece 14x11 inches (35x28 cm). Reserve trimmmings. These will make base and roof of house. Place pieces on baking sheet; pierce all over with a fork. Bake 12 to 18 minutes.

From the 16x10-inch (40x25-cm) piece which was baked first, cut out with a sharp knife, front, back and side walls of house, using cardboard pattern. Cut out a door and window in the front wall. From flat pieces of gingerbread, cut out a base and 2 roof pieces using cardboard pattern. Roll out remaining uncooked dough 1/4 inch (5 mm) thick. Cut out 20 small oblong cookies; place an almond on each. Also cut out pieces for the chimney and strips for the fence as illustrated. Bake 12 to 15 minutes.

To make frosting, beat egg whites lightly in a medium bowl until frothy. Gradually beat in powdered sugar to make a thick frosting. Beat in lemon juice.

Assemble sections of house, using frosting to hold pieces together; let frosting dry completely at each stage before constructing the next section. Coat roof and chimney with frosting to resemble freshly fallen snow. Decorate house with ginger cookies, cake decors and almonds.

Gingerbread Family

Gingerbread:
7 tablespoons (90 g) margarine
Generous 3/4 cup (275 g) honey
1/2 cup plus 1 tablespoon (115 g) sugar
1-1/2 teaspoons ground ginger
1/4 teaspoon ground allspice
1/4 teaspoon ground cinnamon
1 tablespoon unsweetened cocoa powder
6 cups (675 g) all-purpose flour
1 teaspoon baking soda
Pinch of salt
2 eggs

Frosting:
1 egg white
1-1/4 to 1-3/4 cups (175 to 225 g) powdered sugar, sifted
3 oz. (75 g) semisweet chocolate
Blanched almonds, page 124, pistachio nuts,
  candied cherries, raisins

To make gingerbread, put margarine, honey, sugar, ginger, allspice, cinnamon and cocoa powder into a small saucepan. Stir over low heat until sugar has completely dissolved. Cool. Sift flour and baking soda into a large bowl. Add salt, eggs and cooled honey mixture. Knead to make a smooth dough. Cover and let stand overnight at room temperature.

Grease baking sheets. Preheat oven to 400°F (205°C). On a lightly floured surface, roll out dough 1/4 inch (5 mm) thick. Cut out figures using a gingerbread cutter. Place figures on greased baking sheets. Bake 12 to 15 minutes. Remove from baking sheets while still warm; cool on a rack.
To make frosting, beat egg white with powdered sugar in a medium bowl until stiff. Melt chocolate in a double boiler over low heat. Using a baking parchment pastry bag, page 16, decorate figures with piped frosting and melted chocolate. Add nuts and fruit as illustrated.

Shortbread Christmas Tree

Shortbread:
2-3/4 cups (300 g) all-purpose flour, sifted
Scant 1 cup (200 g) powdered sugar, sifted
1/2 cup plus 3 tablespoons (150 g) butter, softened
1 egg, beaten

Filling:
1 cup (250 ml) milk
1 tablespoon granulated sugar
3 tablespoons (20 g) imported custard powder
2 egg whites
3 tablespoons (20 g) powdered sugar, sifted

Decoration:
1/3 cup (50 g) apricot jam
1-1/3 cups (100 g) shredded coconut
Chocolate and colored frosting
Colored sprinkles, cake decors, silver cake decors and chopped nuts
Additional jam

Using cardboard, cut out a Christmas tree 13 inches (33 cm) high and 11 inches (28 cm) wide at the widest point.
To make shortbread, knead flour, powdered sugar, butter and egg to a dough. Wrap in foil and refrigerate 2 hours.
To make filling, prepare custard with milk, granulated sugar and custard powder, following package instructions; cool. Beat egg whites until stiff; fold in powdered sugar. Fold mixture into custard. Preheat oven to 375°F (190°C). Grease a baking sheet.

On a floured surface, roll out shortbread dough; cut out 2 trees. Cut out several small shapes such as stars and moons from trimmings. Place shortbread shapes on greased baking sheet. Bake 15 to 20 minutes or until golden. While still warm, cover 1 tree with custard filling; place second tree on top. Cool.
To decorate, warm jam; spread on tree. Sprinkle with shredded coconut. Frost as desired and decorate small shortbread shapes. Stick onto tree with jam.

Doughnut Mice

Yeast Dough:
2 tablespoons (25 g) sugar
1-1/4 cups (300 ml) warm milk (110°F, 43°C)
2 pkgs. active dry yeast
1/3 cup (50 g) raisins
4 cups (500 g) all-purpose flour
1/2 teaspoon salt
2/3 cup (100 g) finely chopped candied peel
2 egg yolks

Decoration:
32 blanched halved almonds, page 124
64 raisins
Oil to deep-fry
Powdered sugar

To make yeast dough, stir 1 teaspoon sugar into warm milk and sprinkle with yeast. Let stand 5 minutes or until the surface is frothy. Stir gently to moisten any dry particles remaining on top. Wash and dry raisins; chop finely. Sift flour and salt into a large bowl; mix in raisins and candied peel. Beat egg yolks and remaining sugar in a medium bowl. Stir in yeast liquid. Pour into flour mixture, combining to make a dough. On a floured surface, knead dough until smooth and elastic, 5 to 10 minutes. Place dough in a large oiled bowl. Cover and let rise in a warm place 20 minutes.

Sprinkle a baking sheet with flour; set aside. Knead risen dough lightly. Shape into a long roll; cut into 32 equal pieces. With floured hands, make a small mouse shape from each piece as illustrated.

To decorate, stick 2 almond halves in the heads for ears and 2 raisins for eyes. Place mice on prepared baking sheet; let stand 15 minutes.

Heat oil in a deep-frying pan to 350°F (175°C). Cook mice a few at a time. After 2 minutes turn them with a slotted spoon and cook 2 minutes more or until golden brown all over. Lift out with slotted spoon; drain on paper towels.

Make a small tail for each mouse from string. Knot string, stick a wooden pick through the knot and use this to secure tail to mouse. Sprinkle mice with powdered sugar; serve warm. Be careful to remove tails and wooden picks before eating mice.

Cook's Tip

If it is too much trouble to make the mouse tails from string, you can spear a wooden pick into the mouse. This way you can use the pick to hold the doughnut mouse while you eat it.

Almond Ring Cookies

4 hard-cooked egg yolks
3/4 cup plus 2 tablespoons (200 g) butter, softened
2/3 cup (80 g) powdered sugar, sifted
Few drops of vanilla extract
Pinch of salt
2-1/2 cups plus 2 tablespoons (300 g) all-purpose flour, sifted
Scant 1 cup (120 g) almonds
1/4 cup plus 3 tablespoons (100 g) granulated sugar
2 egg yolks
1/2 cup (175 g) red currant jelly
Additional powdered sugar

Press hard-cooked egg yolks through a strainer into a large bowl. Beat in butter and powdered sugar until thoroughly mixed. Add vanilla, salt and flour; mix to a firm dough. Press into a ball and wrap in foil or plastic wrap. Refrigerate 2 hours.

Pour boiling water over almonds to blanch. Peel almonds and chop coarsely; place in a medium bowl. Add sugar. Stir to coat chopped almonds. Preheat oven to 400°F (205°C).

On a floured surface, roll out dough 1/8 inch (3 mm) thick. Using a cookie ring cutter, cut out rings about 2 inches (5 cm) across. Beat 2 egg yolks. Brush 1 side of rings with egg yolk; sprinkle with sugared almond mixture. Place almond-side up on a baking sheet. Bake 10 to 15 minutes or until golden. Remove with a spatula; cool on a rack.

Join cooled rings together with red currant jelly. Sift powdered sugar over rings.

Austrian Jam Rings

Cookie Dough:
3-1/2 cups (400 g) all-purpose flour
3/4 cup plus 2 tablespoons (200 g) butter, cut in small pieces
3 egg yolks
1/2 cup (100 g) sugar
2 tablespoons (25 g) vanilla sugar, page 18
Grated peel of 1 lemon
1/2 cup (50 g) ground hazelnuts

Filling:
1/3 cup (100 g) strawberry jam
Juice of 1 lemon
Powdered sugar

To make cookie dough, sift flour into a large bowl; add butter. Put egg yolks, unflavored sugar, vanilla sugar, lemon peel and hazelnuts in the center; knead to make a dough. Press into a ball and wrap in foil or plastic wrap. Refrigerate 2 hours.

Preheat oven to 400°F (205°C). Grease a baking sheet. On a floured surface, roll out dough about 1/4 inch (5 mm) thick. Cut into an equal number of 2-1/2-inch (6-cm) rounds and rings. Place on greased baking sheet. Bake 10 minutes or until golden brown. Carefully lift rounds and rings from baking sheet with a spatula; cool on a rack.

To make filling, combine jam and lemon juice. Spread jam mixture over cookie rounds. Sift powdered sugar generously over cookie rings. Place a sugared ring cookie on each round.

Chocolate Orange Cookies

Cookie Dough:
4 oz. (100 g) semisweet chocolate
1/2 cup plus 1 tablespoon (125 g) butter or margarine, softened
1/2 cup plus 1 tablespoon (125 g) sugar
Pinch of salt
1 egg
Grated peel of 1 orange
1-3/4 cups (200 g) all-purpose flour
1 teaspoon baking powder

Frosting:
Scant 1 cup (100 g) powdered sugar
2 to 3 tablespoons orange juice

To make cookie dough, coarsely grate chocolate. Beat butter or margarine, sugar, salt, egg and orange peel in a medium bowl. Sift in flour and baking powder; add grated chocolate. Knead ingredients quickly to a workable dough. Press into a ball and wrap in foil or plastic wrap. Refrigerate 2 hours.

Preheat oven to 400°F (205°C). Grease baking sheets. On a floured surface, roll out dough 1/4 inch (5 mm) thick. Cut out 2-inch (5-cm) rounds. Place on greased baking sheets leaving room for spreading during cooking. Bake 10 to 15 minutes. Remove from baking sheets with a spatula; cool on a rack.

To make frosting, put powdered sugar into a small bowl. Beat in enough orange juice to give a coating consistency. Spread frosting over cookies; let set.

Swiss Honey Bars

1 cup (350 g) creamed honey or honey spread
1-1/2 cups (350 g) sugar
3/4 cup (90 g) finely chopped almonds
3/4 cup (90 g) finely chopped hazelnuts
3/4 cup (90 g) finely chopped walnuts
3/4 cup (250 g) chopped mixed candied peel
Grated peel of 1 lemon
5 cups (575 g) all-purpose flour, sifted
1 teaspoon ground cinnamon
2 teaspoons ground cloves
Generous pinch of grated nutmeg
1/2 teaspoon baking soda
3 tablespoons liqueur such as arrack or ouzo
3 tablespoons cherry brandy
2 tablespoons water

In a medium saucepan, bring creamed honey or honey spread and 1 cup plus 2 tablespoons (250 g) sugar to a boil, stirring constantly. Combine almonds, hazelnuts, walnuts, candied peel, lemon peel and flour in a large bowl. Stir in cinnamon, cloves, nutmeg and baking soda. Pour in hot honey mixture and mix well to make a dough. Knead in arrack or ouzo and cherry brandy. Press into a ball and wrap in foil or plastic wrap. Let stand at room temperature 1 day.

Preheat oven to 350°F (175°C). Grease 2 baking sheets. Divide dough in half. On a floured surface, roll out each half of dough to a square or rectangle 1/2 inch (1 cm) thick. Place on baking sheets. Bake 30 to 35 minutes or until a rich brown.

In a small saucepan, bring remaining sugar and water to a boil. Spread quickly over warm cake; cut into bars on baking sheets. Let cool.

Ginger Slices

6 whole preserved gingers
1/2 cup plus 3 tablespoons (150 g) butter or margarine, softened
1/2 cup (100 g) sugar
1 egg
Pinch of salt
1/2 teaspoon ground ginger
2-3/4 cups (300 g) all-purpose flour
1 egg yolk
Water

Chop three of the whole gingers very finely; dice the others. In a medium bowl, cream butter or margarine, sugar, whole egg, salt, ground ginger and finely chopped ginger. Sift in flour; work quickly together to make a smooth dough. Form into a ball and wrap in foil or plastic wrap. Refrigerate 2 hours.

Preheat oven to 400°F (205°C). Divide dough into 3 pieces. On a lightly floured surface, roll out 1 piece of dough at a time 1/4 inch (5 mm) thick. Cut out oblongs 2-1/2x1-1/2 inches (6x3.5 cm). Place on baking sheets. Beat egg yolk with a little water; brush over cookies. Sprinkle with diced ginger. Bake 15 minutes or until golden. Remove from baking sheets with a spatula; cool on a rack.

Frosted Pretzels

Cookie Dough:
3/4 cup plus 2 tablespoons (200 g) butter, softened
Scant 1 cup (100 g) powdered sugar, sifted
1 egg yolk
Pinch of salt
Few drops of vanilla extract
2-3/4 cups (300 g) all-purpose flour

Frosting:
1 egg white
Scant 1/4 cup (50 ml) rum
2 teaspoons lemon juice
1-2/3 cups (200 g) powdered sugar, sifted

To make cookie dough, cream butter and powdered sugar to a smooth paste in a medium bowl. Add egg yolk, salt and vanilla. Sift flour; knead into mixture to make a dough. Press into a ball and wrap in foil or plastic wrap. Refrigerate 2 hours.

Preheat oven to 350°F (175°C). Cut off 1 piece of dough at a time and shape, leaving remaining dough in refrigerator. On a floured surface, roll each piece of dough pencil thin and 10 inches (25 cm) long. Twist into a pretzel as illustrated. Place pretzels on a baking sheet. Bake 12 to 15 minutes or until golden. Cool slightly on baking sheet then transfer to a rack with a spatula.

To make frosting, combine egg white, rum, lemon juice and powdered sugar in a medium bowl. Brush warm pretzels as thickly as possible with rum frosting.

Cook's Tip

To vary the flavor, make the frosting with a liqueur instead of rum.

Danish Cookies

1 cup (250 g) butter or margarine
3/4 cup plus 2 tablespoons (200 g) sugar
1/3 cup (125 g) light corn syrup
Generous 1/2 cup (75 g) chopped almonds
1/2 cup (75 g) chopped candied lemon peel
1/2 teaspoon ground cloves
2 teaspoons ground cinnamon
1/2 teaspoon ground ginger
1/2 teaspoon baking soda
1 teaspoon boiling water
4 cups (500 g) all-purpose flour, sifted

In a small saucepan, melt butter or margarine, sugar and corn syrup over low heat. Remove from heat; pour into a large bowl. Stir in almonds, candied peel, cloves, cinnamon and ginger. Dissolve baking soda in boiling water; stir into corn syrup mixture. Cool.

Knead flour into mixture to make a dough. Form dough into 2 rolls and wrap in foil or plastic wrap. Refrigerate 24 hours.

Grease baking sheets. Preheat oven to 400°F (205°C). Cut rolls of dough into slices 1/4 inch (5 mm) thick. Place on greased baking sheets leaving space between them for spreading during cooking. Bake 8 to 10 minutes. Remove from baking sheets with a spatula; cool on a rack.

Almond Spice Bars

4 eggs
1 cup plus 2 tablespoons (250 g) sugar
3-1/2 cups (400 g) all-purpose flour
1/2 teaspoon baking powder
3-1/2 cups (400 g) ground almonds
2/3 cup (100 g) chopped mixed candied peel
1 teaspoon ground cinnamon
Generous pinch each of ground cloves, nutmeg and allspice
1 egg yolk
Water
Blanched halved almonds, see below

Beat eggs and sugar in a large bowl until pale and creamy. Sift flour with baking powder; add ground almonds, candied peel, cinnamon, cloves, nutmeg and allspice. Stir flour mixture into egg mixture to make a dough. Press into a ball and wrap in foil or plastic wrap. Refrigerate 2 hours.

Preheat oven to 350°F (175°C). Grease baking sheets. On a floured surface, roll out dough about 1/4 inch (5 mm) thick. Cut into equal-sized bars; place on baking sheets. Beat egg yolk with a little water and use to brush bars. Place an almond half in each corner of bars. Bake 20 minutes or until golden. Remove from baking sheets with a spatula; cool on a rack.

Cook's Tip

To blanch almonds, cover with boiling water and set aside for a short time. The nuts can then be easily squeezed out of their brown skins.

Norwegian Christmas Rings

3 eggs
1 egg yolk
1-1/4 cups (160 g) powdered sugar, sifted
1 cup plus 2 tablespoons (250 g) butter, softened
Few drops of vanilla extract
3 cups (350 g) all-purpose flour
1 egg yolk, beaten
Sugar crystals

Boil 3 eggs 10 to 12 minutes, plunge into cold water; peel. Press hard-cooked eggs through a fine strainer into a large bowl. Stir in 1 egg yolk and powdered sugar. Gradually work in butter and vanilla. Add flour; knead to make a soft dough. Press into a ball and wrap in foil or plastic wrap. Refrigerate 3 hours.

Preheat oven to 375°F (190°C). Divide dough into small pieces. Form each piece into a roll about 4 inches (10 cm) long. Brush ends of rolls with beaten egg yolk; join ends to make rings. Brush tops generously with beaten egg yolk; sprinkle with sugar crystals. Place on baking sheets. Bake 10 to 12 minutes or until golden. Remove from baking sheets with a spatula; cool on a rack.

Honey Hearts

1/2 cup plus 1 tablespoon (115 g) sugar
3 tablespoons (40 g) butter
2/3 cup (225 g) honey
1 large egg
Pinch of salt
3 tablespoons (25 g) chopped mixed candied peel
1/2 teaspoon ground cinnamon
1/4 teaspoon ground cloves
4 cups (450 g) all-purpose flour
1 teaspoon baking powder
1/3 cup (100 g) red currant jelly
4 oz. (100 g) semisweet chocolate

Grease baking sheets. Preheat oven to 425°F (220°C).

In a medium saucepan, heat sugar, butter and honey, stirring constantly until all ingredients have melted. Remove from heat and pour into a large bowl. Stir frequently until lukewarm.

Beat egg with salt. Add candied peel to honey mixture with beaten egg, cinnamon and cloves. Sift flour with baking powder. Add to honey and spice mixture; combine to make a dough. Knead well. On a floured surface, roll out dough about 1/4 inch (5 mm) thick. Cut out small heart shapes; place on greased baking sheets. Bake 8 to 10 minutes or until golden.

While still warm, join hearts in pairs with red currant jelly. Let cookies cool completely on a rack. Melt chocolate in a double boiler over low heat. Dip cooled cookies into melted chocolate so they are half-covered with chocolate.

Apricot Rings

3-1/2 cups (400 g) all-purpose flour
1/2 cup (120 g) granulated sugar
Pinch of salt
Grated peel of 1 lemon
2 tablespoons (25 g) vanilla sugar, page 18
1 egg
3 tablespoons rum
1 cup plus 2 tablespoons (250 g) butter, cut in small pieces
Powdered sugar
2/3 cup (225 g) apricot jam

Sift flour into a large bowl. Make a well in the center of flour; add unflavored sugar, salt, lemon peel, vanilla sugar, egg and rum. Dot butter over flour; knead to a soft dough. Press into a ball and wrap in foil or plastic wrap. Refrigerate 2 hours.

Preheat oven to 350°F (175°C). Grease baking sheets. On a floured surface, roll out cookie dough, a little at a time 1/8 inch (3 mm) thick. Using a plain cutter and a ring cutter of the same size, cut out equal quantities of rounds and rings. Place on baking sheets. Bake 10 to 15 minutes or until golden. Remove from baking sheet with a spatula; cool slightly on a rack.

Sift powdered sugar generously onto rings. Warm jam over low heat; spread jam smoothly onto warm rounds. Place sugared rings on top of rounds. Add a little more jam to centers of rings. Cool completely before storing in an airtight container.

Italian Biscotti

1/2 cup plus 2 tablespoons (150 g) butter, softened
3/4 cup plus 2 tablespoons (200 g) sugar
Few drops of vanilla extract
1/2 egg
2 tablespoons milk
Generous pinch each of ground cardamom and ground cinnamon
Grated peel of 1/2 lemon
2 tablespoons (15 g) ground almonds
1-1/4 cups (150 g) all-purpose flour
4 oz. (100 g) semisweet chocolate

Beat butter, sugar and vanilla in a medium bowl until pale and creamy. Mix in egg, milk, cardamom, cinnamon, lemon peel and almonds. Sift flour over mixture; knead to make a dough. Form into rectangular blocks, measuring 1-1/2x1-1/2 inches (3.5x3.5 cm) at each end. Wrap in foil or plastic wrap. Refrigerate 2 hours.

Preheat oven to 375°F (190°C). Cut blocks of cookie dough into 1/4-inch (5-mm) slices; place on a baking sheet. Bake 15 minutes or until golden. Remove cookies with a spatula; cool on a rack.

Melt chocolate in a double boiler over low heat. Dip cooled cookies into melted chocolate so they are half-coated diagonally. Let dry on waxed paper.

Crumbly Almond Hearts

1 cup plus 2 tablespoons (250 g) butter, softened
1 cup (120 g) powdered sugar, sifted
2 egg yolks
1 cup (100 g) ground almonds
3 cups (350 g) all-purpose flour, sifted
40 blanched halved almonds, page 124

Beat butter, powdered sugar and 1 egg yolk in a large bowl until pale and creamy. Add ground almonds and flour. Knead quickly to a firm dough. Press into a ball and wrap in foil or plastic wrap. Refrigerate 2 hours.

Preheat oven to 400°F (205°C). On a floured surface, roll out dough 1/4 inch (5 mm) thick. Cut out 40 small heart shapes; place on a large baking sheet.

Beat second egg yolk; brush over cookies. Place 2 almond halves on each cookie. Bake 10 to 12 minutes or until golden. Cool slightly on baking sheet then cool completely on a rack.

Swedish Yule Cookies

1 cup plus 2 tablespoons (250 g) butter, softened
3/4 cup (175 g) sugar
1 egg
3-1/2 cups (400 g) all-purpose flour
1 teaspoon baking powder
1/2 teaspoon salt
1/4 teaspoon ground cinnamon
1 egg white, beaten

Beat butter, 1/2 cup (125 g) sugar and egg in a large bowl until fluffy. Sift flour with baking powder and salt. Gradually add flour mixture to butter mixture. Knead to make a dough. Press into a ball and wrap in foil or plastic wrap. Refrigerate 3 hours.

Preheat oven to 400°F (205°C). Divide dough into 3 pieces; knead each in turn. Refrigerate 2 pieces of kneaded dough. On a floured surface, roll out third piece of kneaded dough 1/8 inch (3 mm) thick. Cut out 2-1/2-inch (6-cm) rounds. Place on a baking sheet. Repeat with refrigerated dough.

Combine remaining sugar and cinnamon. Brush cookies with egg white; sprinkle generously with sugar and cinnamon mixture. Bake 8 to 10 minutes or until golden. Cool on a rack.

Cook's Tip

When sprinkling the cookies with cinnamon and sugar, some will fall onto the baking sheet. Before baking, remove this with a pastry brush so it does not burn.

Dutch Zebras

1 cup plus 2 tablespoons (250 g) butter, softened
3/4 cup plus 2 tablespoons (200 g) granulated sugar
1/2 teaspoon salt
4 egg yolks
2-1/4 cups (250 g) all-purpose flour
3/4 cup (100 g) cornstarch
1/2 teaspoon baking powder
3 tablespoons rum
1/4 cup (30 g) unsweetened cocoa powder, sifted
3 tablespoons sugar crystals

In a large bowl, cream butter, granulated sugar and salt until light and fluffy. Add egg yolks one at a time, beating until smooth after each addition. Sift flour with cornstarch and baking powder. Fold into butter mixture. Knead to a firm dough. Halve dough; knead rum into 1 half and cocoa powder into the other half. Place each portion of dough in a bowl and cover with foil or plastic wrap. Refrigerate 1 hour.

Preheat oven to 375°F (190°C). Grease baking sheets. On a floured surface, carefully roll out light and dark dough separately 1/16 inch (1.5 mm) thick. Halve each piece. Place pieces of light and dark dough alternately one on top of the other to make 4 layers. Press together firmly; cut into small oblong shapes. Sprinkle each cookie with sugar cystals; press sugar in slightly. Place cookies on greased baking sheets. Bake 15 to 20 minutes or until light dough is golden. Remove from baking sheets with a spatula; cool on a rack.

Coconut Macaroons

5 egg whites
2 cups (250 g) powdered sugar, sifted
2 cups (225 g) ground almonds
2-2/3 cups (225 g) shredded coconut
Grated peel of 1/2 lemon
1-1/2 tablespoons rum
Additional powdered sugar, sifted
4 oz. (100 g) semisweet chocolate

Line baking sheets with rice paper. Preheat oven to 300°F (150°C).

Beat egg whites in a large bowl until stiff. Fold in half the powdered sugar and ground almonds. Add coconut, remaining powdered sugar, lemon peel and rum; work into a sticky dough. Put mixture into a pastry bag fitted with a large plain nozzle; pipe walnut-size drops onto rice paper. Sprinkle macaroons with additional powdered sugar. Bake 20 minutes. Macaroons should have a golden crust on the outside but remain soft inside. Cool on a rack.

Melt chocolate in a double boiler over low heat. Dip cooled macaroons in melted chocolate to coat about a third of each one. Let chocolate set before serving.

Viennese Vanilla Crescents

Scant 1/2 cup (50 g) blanched almonds, page 124
Scant 1/2 cup (50 g) hazelnuts
2-1/2 cups (280 g) all-purpose flour
1/4 cup plus 1 tablespoon (70 g) granulated sugar
Pinch of salt
3/4 cup plus 2 tablespoons (200 g) butter, cut in small pieces
2 egg yolks
1/4 cup plus 2 tablespoons (75 g) vanilla sugar, page 18
1/4 cup (25 g) powdered sugar, sifted

Finely grate almonds and hazelnuts. Sift flour into a large bowl; add almonds, hazelnuts, unflavored sugar, salt, butter and egg yolks. Knead to a soft dough. Press into a ball and wrap in foil or plastic wrap. Refrigerate 2 hours.

Preheat oven to 375°F (190°C). Form dough a little at a time into pencil-thin ropes. Cut ropes into 2-inch (5-cm) pieces; curve into crescents. Place on a baking sheet. Bake 10 minutes or until golden.

Mix vanilla sugar with powdered sugar in a plastic bag or shallow dish. Toss warm crescent cookies in sugar mixture until coated. Cool on a rack.

Cook's Tip

To store the cookies, place in layers between waxed paper in an airtight container; this will avoid breakage.

Nutmeg Cookies

8 tablespoons (125 g) butter, softened
1/2 cup (125 g) sugar
1 egg
Grated peel of 1/2 lemon
Generous pinch of grated nutmeg
Pinch each of ground cinnamon and ground cloves
1 cup (125 g) all-purpose flour, sifted
1 cup (125 g) finely chopped hazelnuts
2 cups (125 g) fresh white breadcrumbs
1 egg yolk, beaten
Scant 1/2 cup (50 g) blanched almonds, page 124

Beat butter, sugar, egg, lemon peel, nutmeg, cinnamon and cloves in a medium bowl. Mix flour, hazelnuts and breadcrumbs; add to butter mixture. Knead quickly to make a dough. Press into a ball and wrap in foil or plastic wrap. Refrigerate dough 2 hours.

Preheat oven to 400°F (205°C). Grease baking sheets. On a floured surface, roll out dough 1/4 inch (5 mm) thick. With a cookie cutter or cardboard pattern, cut out small scalloped arcs 2-1/2 inches (6 cm) long and 1 inch (2.5 cm) wide. Place on baking sheets; brush with egg yolk. Place an almond on each cookie. Bake 10 to 15 minutes or until golden. Cool on a rack.

Cinnamon Stars

4 small egg whites
1-3/4 cups (225 g) powdered sugar, sifted
2-3/4 cups (300 g) ground almonds
2 tablespoons ground cinnamon
Grated peel of 1/2 lemon
Granulated sugar

Put egg whites into a medium heatproof bowl; beat until frothy. Add powdered sugar. Set bowl over a saucepan of simmering water and continue beating until mixture becomes thick and holds its shape. Remove bowl from saucepan. Reserve 6 tablespoons of mixture. Fold almonds, cinnamon and lemon peel into remaining mixture. Let cool 1 hour.

Preheat oven to 325°F (165°C). Grease and flour baking sheets. Sprinkle a work surface with granulated sugar; roll out mixture about 1/4 inch (5 mm) thick. Mixture will be soft and must be rolled out very carefully. Cut into stars with a cookie cutter; place on prepared baking sheets. Spread reserved egg white mixture carefully over stars. Bake 15 to 20 minutes or until just firm. Remove cookies from baking sheets with a spatula; cool on a rack.

Checkered Cookies

1-1/4 cups (300 g) butter, softened
Generous 1 cup (150 g) powdered sugar, sifted
Pinch of salt
3-1/2 cups (400 g) all-purpose flour, sifted
1/4 cup (30 g) unsweetened cocoa powder, sifted
1 egg white, lightly beaten

Beat butter, powdered sugar and salt in a large bowl until pale and creamy. Knead in flour to make a dough. Divide dough in half. Knead cocoa powder into 1 half. Press each half into a ball and wrap separately in foil or plastic wrap. Refrigerate 2 hours.

Divide each piece of dough into 5 pieces. On a floured surface, roll 1 color into 5 long thin rolls. With the other color, roll 4 pieces into long thin rolls. Arrange 9 rolls into a checkerboard design, brushing and sealing with a little egg white. Roll out remaining dough large enough to wrap around assembled dough. Seal with egg white. Wrap in foil or plastic wrap. Refrigerate until firm, about 1 hour.

Preheat oven to 375°F (190°C). Cut dough into 1/4-inch (5-mm) thick slices; place on a baking sheet. Bake 10 to 15 minutes or until light dough is golden. Remove cookies from baking sheet with a spatula; cool on a rack.

Too dry! (altitude?)

Pan Honey Cake

1 lb. (500 g) honey
1/2 cup (125 ml) oil
1 cup (250 g) sugar
6 cups (700 g) all-purpose flour
1 tablespoon baking powder
2 cups (250 g) ground almonds
2 teaspoons ground cinnamon
1/2 teaspoon ground allspice
Pinch of ground cloves
Pinch of salt
3 eggs, beaten
Generous 1 cup (200 g) chopped mixed
  candied peel
3 tablespoons evaporated milk
Blanched halved almonds, page 124,
  candied cherries and candied
  lemon peel

Bring honey, oil and sugar to a boil in a medium saucepan, stirring constantly. Cool. Sift flour and baking powder into a large bowl. Mix in ground almonds, cinnamon, allspice, cloves, salt, eggs and candied peel. Add cooled honey mixture; knead to a dough. If dough is too soft, add a little more flour. Press dough into a ball and wrap in foil or plastic wrap. Refrigerate 1 hour.

Preheat oven to 375°F (190°C). Grease two 13x9-inch (33x23-cm) cake pans. With floured hands, press dough into greased pans. Smooth the surface; brush with evaporated milk. Lightly cut 3-inch (7.5-cm) squares in dough with a sharp knife. Decorate each square with almonds, cherries and pieces of candied lemon peel as illustrated. Bake 25 to 30 minutes or until golden brown. Cool slightly in pans. Cut into squares and cool completely on a rack.

Aniseed Cookies

4 eggs, separated
1-3/4 cups (225 g) powdered sugar, sifted
Pinch of salt
2-3/4 cups (300 g) all-purpose flour
2 teaspoons ground aniseed

Grease and flour baking sheets.

Beat egg yolks, powdered sugar and salt in a large bowl until pale and creamy. Beat egg whites until very stiff; fold into egg yolk mixture. Sift flour and aniseed onto egg mixture; fold in quickly but thoroughly. Fill a pastry bag fitted with a plain nozzle with cookie mixture. Pipe in small rounds onto prepared baking sheets. Let stand overnight to dry out.

Preheat oven to 325°F (165°C). Bake cookies 20 minutes. Cool on a rack.

Cook's Tip

To make Cinnamon Cookies use 2 teaspoons ground cinnamon instead of ground aniseed.

French Madeleines

1 cup (125 g) self-rising flour
1/2 cup (125 g) sugar
8 tablespoons (125 g) butter
3 eggs
Pinch of salt
1/2 cup (60 g) ground almonds
2 teaspoons orange-flower water
1/4 teaspoon vanilla extract

Traditionally, madeleines are baked in small shell-shaped pans. If you do not have madeleine pans, use individual muffin pan cups or brioche pans.

Sift flour and sugar into a large bowl. Melt but do not brown butter; cool. Mix eggs into flour and sugar with a wooden spoon; gradually add cooled butter, salt, ground almonds, orange-flower water and vanilla. Cover and refrigerate 1 hour. Grease pans with butter. Preheat oven to 400°F (205°C).

Half-fill greased pans with cake batter. Bake 10 to 15 minutes or until golden. Cool on a rack.

Cinnamon Spice Cookies

Cookie Dough:
1 lb. (500 g) honey
1-1/4 cups (300 g) sugar
3 eggs, beaten
2 teaspoons baking soda
1 teaspoon ground cinnamon
1/2 teaspoon ground cloves
Generous pinch each of ground nutmeg, coriander, ginger,
   allspice and cardamom
1 teaspoon white pepper
8 cups (1 kg) all-purpose flour

Frosting:
Scant 1 cup (100 g) powdered sugar, sifted
3 to 4 tablespoons water

To make cookie dough, warm honey over low heat until liquid; pour into a large bowl. Stir in sugar, eggs, baking soda, cinnamon, cloves, nutmeg, coriander, ginger, allspice, cardamom and pepper. Mix in flour gradually. Knead thoroughly to make a dough. Preheat oven to 375°F (190°C). Grease baking sheets.

Form dough into small balls about 1 inch (2.5 cm) across; place on greased baking sheets. Bake 10 to 15 minutes or until golden brown. Cool on a rack.

To make frosting, blend powdered sugar and water in a small saucepan. Bring to a boil, stirring constantly. Coat cookies with hot frosting.

Chocolate Macaroons

4 oz. (100 g) semisweet chocolate
4 egg whites
3/4 cup plus 2 tablespoons (200 g) sugar
2 cups (225 g) ground almonds

Line a baking sheet with baking parchment or rice paper. Preheat oven to 350°F (175°C).

Grate chocolate. Beat egg whites in a medium bowl until stiff. Beat in sugar gradually; continue beating until mixture is thick and glossy. Fold in ground almonds and grated chocolate. Drop spoonfuls of mixture onto prepared baking sheet, leaving space between each macaroon for spreading during cooking. Bake 15 to 20 minutes. Do not let macaroons become too dark or they will taste bitter. Cool on baking sheet. Carefully peel cooled macaroons off baking parchment or cut around each macaroon on the edible rice paper.

Christmas Night Gâteau

Cake:
4 eggs, separated
Scant 1/4 cup (50 ml) water
3/4 cup (180 g) sugar
1 tablespoon vanilla sugar, page 18
1-2/3 cups (250 g) all-purpose flour
2 teaspoons baking powder

Filling & Topping:
Generous 1/4 cup (40 g) unsweetened cocoa powder
1 tablespoon boiling water
2 tablespoons rum
1/4 cup (75 g) cranberry jelly
1 envelope unflavored gelatin
3 tablespoons water
2-1/2 cups (600 ml) whipping cream
2/3 cup (150 g) sugar

Decoration:
4 oz. (100 g) semisweet chocolate
8 candied cherries
1 teaspoon powdered sugar
1/4 cup (25 g) toasted sliced almonds, page 47

Grease the inside bottom of a 9-inch (23-cm) cake pan. Preheat oven to 375°F (190°C).
To make cake, put egg yolks, water, half the unflavored sugar and vanilla sugar into a medium bowl. Beat until pale and creamy, 5 to 10 minutes with an electric mixer. Beat egg whites until stiff; fold in remaining unflavored sugar. Carefully fold into egg yolk mixture. Sift flour with baking powder; carefully fold into egg mixture. Turn batter into prepared pan; smooth the surface. Bake cake 30 to 40 minutes or until a wooden pick inserted in center comes out clean. Turn out cake onto a rack; let stand overnight if possible. Cut cooled cake horizontally into 3 layers.

To make filling and topping, combine cocoa powder, boiling water and rum in a medium bowl; cool. Warm cranberry jelly; cool slightly. Dissolve gelatin in 3 tablespoons water over low heat. Whip cream with sugar until stiff. Mix a fourth of whipped cream mixture with cooled cocoa mixture. Spread chocolate cream thickly on 1 cake layer; place second layer on top. Mix cranberry jelly with dissolved gelatin. Stir into a third of remaining whipped cream mixture. Cover second cake layer with jam and cream mixture; top with last cake layer. Use about two-thirds of remaining whipped cream mixture to cover cake. Place the rest in a pastry bag fitted with a fluted nozzle; pipe 16 rosettes around top of cake.

To make decoration, melt half the chocolate in a double boiler over low heat. Spread thinly over waxed paper or foil. When chocolate has set, dip a small star-shaped cutter into hot water and cut out 16 stars from chocolate. Place a chocolate star and halved candied cherry on each rosette. Coarsely grate remaining chocolate and sprinkle over center of cake. Sift powdered sugar lightly over chocolate. Decorate sides of cake with almonds.

Cook's Tip

You can also make Chocolate Curls to decorate the cake. Spread the melted chocolate onto a clean flat surface. When the chocolate has just set, scrape off shavings with the blade of a knife. Let the shavings set hard then sprinkle onto the cake.

Chocolate Log

Cake:
4 eggs, separated, plus 2 egg yolks
1/4 cup plus 2 tablespoons (80 g) sugar
Grated peel of 1/2 lemon
3/4 cup (80 g) all-purpose flour, sifted

Filling & Topping:
12 oz. (350 g) semisweet chocolate
1 cup (225 g) butter, softened
1 cup (125 g) powdered sugar, sifted
1 tablespoon rum
3 candied cherries
1 teaspoon chopped pistachio nuts

Preheat oven to 425°F (220°C). Line a 15-1/2x10-1/2-inch (39x27-cm) cake pan with waxed paper; grease paper.

To make cake, beat 6 egg yolks with 1 tablespoon sugar and lemon peel in a medium bowl until pale and creamy. Beat egg whites until stiff; fold in remaining sugar. Fold egg white mixture into egg yolk mixture. Carefully fold flour into egg mixture. Spread batter evenly in prepared cake pan. Bake 8 to 10 minutes or until a wooden pick inserted in center comes out clean. Sprinkle a clean cloth towel with sugar. Turn out cake onto cloth towel; peel off lining paper. Trim cake edges. Cover cake with a clean piece of waxed paper; carefully roll up cake with the help of the cloth towel, keeping clean waxed paper inside. Cool on a rack.

To make filling and topping, melt chocolate in a double boiler over low heat. Spread about a fourth of the chocolate thinly over waxed paper; let set. Let remaining melted chocolate cool. Cream butter and powdered sugar in a medium bowl until pale and fluffy. Reserve 3 tablespoons of butter cream. Beat cooled chocolate and rum into remaining butter cream. Carefully unroll cooled cake; spread two-thirds of chocolate butter cream over cake. Roll up again. Using a pastry bag fitted with a fluted nozzle, pipe remaining chocolate butter cream along the length of the cake in long lines.

Using a warmed knife, cut out small leaves from the thin sheet of chocolate. Decorate log with reserved butter cream, halved candied cherries, chocolate leaves and pistachios as illustrated. Cut a slice from the cake and place it against one side of the cake to make a short branch.

Brussels Fruit Cake

1-1/4 cups (200 g) finely chopped crystallized pineapple
1-1/4 cups (200 g) finely chopped crystallized pears
1/2 cup (90 g) finely chopped candied lemon peel
1 cup (250 g) halved red and green candied cherries
2 cups (225 g) finely chopped walnuts
1 cup (110 g) finely chopped pecans
1 cup (110 g) finely chopped almonds
1 cup (110 g) finely chopped hazelnuts
2-1/3 cups (400 g) raisins
Scant 1/2 cup (100 ml) sherry
1 cup (225 g) butter, softened
2 cups (450 g) sugar
Pinch each of salt and grated nutmeg
6 eggs
4 cups (450 g) self-rising flour, sifted
Additional sherry
Additional crystallized and candied fruit

In a large bowl, mix pineapple, pears, candied peel, cherries, walnuts, pecans, almonds, hazelnuts, raisins and sherry. Cover and let stand overnight.

Line two 9-1/4x5-1/4-inch (23x13-cm) loaf pans with waxed paper; grease paper. Preheat oven to 325°F (165°C). In a large bowl, cream butter, sugar, salt and nutmeg until pale and fluffy. Beat in eggs one at a time. Fold in flour. Stir in fruit and nut mixture. Turn batter into prepared pans. Bake 2 to 2-1/4 hours or until a skewer inserted in center comes out clean. Cool cakes in pans. Turn out cooled cakes; remove waxed paper.

Moisten 2 pieces of cheesecloth with sherry; use to wrap cakes. Wrap in foil; refrigerate 4 weeks. Every week, moisten cheesecloth with more sherry. Decorate cakes with additional crystallized and candied fruit before serving.

Soft Fruit Loaf

Loaf:
2 cups (500 g) cottage cheese
4 cups (500 g) all-purpose flour
2 teaspoons baking powder
3 eggs
2/3 cup (150 g) sugar
1 tablespoon vanilla sugar, page 18
Pinch of salt
1 tablespoon grated lemon peel
1 tablespoon chopped almonds
1 tablespoon raisins
3 tablespoons (25 g) chopped mixed candied fruit
3 tablespoons (25 g) chopped mixed candied peel

Topping:
1 tablespoon (15 g) butter
1 tablespoon powdered sugar
1 tablespoon vanilla sugar, page 18

Grease and flour a baking sheet. Preheat oven to 375°F (190°C).

To make loaf, press cottage cheese through a strainer or puree in a blender. Sift flour with baking powder onto a working surface or into a large bowl; form a well in the center. Add cottage cheese, eggs, unflavored sugar, vanilla sugar, salt, lemon peel, almonds, raisins and candied fruit and peel. Mix to a firm dough; knead lightly. Shape into a loaf; place on prepared baking sheet. Bake 50 to 60 minutes or until a wooden pick or skewer inserted in center comes out clean. Transfer to a rack.

To make topping, melt butter and brush over warm loaf. Mix powdered sugar and vanilla sugar; sift generously over loaf.

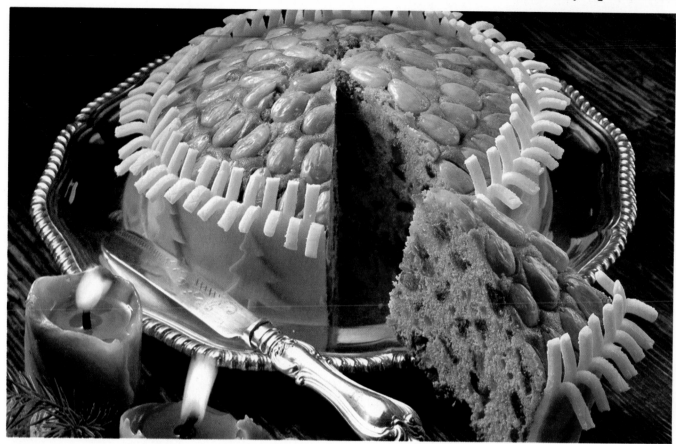

Festive Light Christmas Cake

Cake:
1 cup plus 2 tablespoons (250 g) butter, softened
1 cup plus 2 tablespoons (250 g) sugar
1/4 teaspoon vanilla extract
Generous pinch of salt
1-1/2 tablespoons rum
6 eggs
3 cups (350 g) all-purpose flour
1 teaspoon baking powder
2-1/3 cups (400 g) seedless golden raisins
1/2 cup (50 g) ground almonds
2/3 cup (100 g) chopped candied lemon peel
1 cup (100 g) blanched halved almonds, page 124

Glaze:
3 tablespoons sugar
1/3 cup (100 ml) water

Decoration:
3 tablespoons apricot jam
8 oz. (225 g) almond paste
Food colorings
1 egg white

Line a 9-inch (23-cm) cake pan with waxed paper; grease paper. Preheat oven to 300°F (150°C).
To make cake, beat butter, sugar, vanilla, salt and rum in a large bowl until pale and creamy. Beat in eggs one at a time. If mixture curdles, add 1 tablespoon flour. Sift remaining flour with baking powder; mix with raisins, ground almonds and candied peel. Fold flour mixture gradually into egg mixture. Turn batter into prepared pan; smooth the surface with the back of a wet spoon. Arrange almond halves in a circular pattern on top. Bake 4-1/4 to 4-3/4 hours or until a skewer inserted in center comes out clean. Leave cake in pan about 15 minutes then turn out onto a rack to cool. Remove lining paper when cake is completely cool.
To make glaze, heat sugar and water in a small saucepan, stirring constantly until sugar is completely dissolved. Boil 2 to 3 minutes. Cover top of cake with glaze; let cool.
To make decoration, warm jam and brush over sides of cake. Measure circumference of cake with a piece of string. On a surface sprinkled lightly with powdered sugar, roll three-fourths of almond paste into a long rope the length of the string. Flatten with a rolling pin to 1/2 inch (2 cm) more than height of cake. Trim almond paste; cut 1/2-inch (2-cm) strips along top edge as illustrated. Press strip of almond paste firmly onto sides of cake.
Knead food coloring into remaining almond paste. Cut out small Christmas trees; attach to cake with unbeaten egg white.

Cook's Tip

If you tie a double thickness of brown paper around the outside of the cake pan before baking, this will prevent the edges of the cake from becoming brown and overcooked before the inside is cooked through. The undecorated cake will keep well if wrapped in foil or waxed paper and stored in an airtight container.

Date & Almond Stollen

Yeast Dough:
1/4 cup (60 g) sugar
1 cup (250 g) warm milk (110°F, 43°C)
2 pkgs. active dry yeast
4 cups (500 g) all-purpose flour
Pinch of salt
2 eggs
1/2 cup plus 2 tablespoons (150 g) butter, softened
1/2 cup (50 g) chopped almonds
Grated peel of 1 lemon

Filling:
1/4 cup (25 g) cornstarch
Scant 2 cups (450 ml) milk
1 egg yolk
1/4 cup plus 3 tablespoons (100 g) sugar
1-1/4 cups (250 g) finely chopped dates
1 tablespoon (15 g) butter

Frosting:
1 egg white
1-2/3 cups (200 g) powdered sugar, sifted
Juice of 1 lemon
3 tablespoons toasted sliced almonds, page 47

To make yeast dough, stir 1 teaspoon sugar into warm milk and sprinkle with yeast. Let stand 5 minutes or until the surface is frothy. Stir gently to moisten any dry particles remaining on top.

Sift flour and salt into a large bowl. In a medium bowl, beat eggs, remaining sugar, butter, almonds and lemon peel. Stir in yeast mixture. Add to flour mixture, combining to make a dough. On a floured surface, knead dough until smooth, 5 to 10 minutes. Cover and let rise in a warm place 30 minutes.

To make filling, blend cornstarch with a little milk, egg yolk and sugar in a medium bowl. Put dates and remaining milk into a small saucepan; bring to a boil. Stir milk and dates into cornstarch mixture; add butter. Return to saucepan and bring to a boil, stirring constantly until thickened. Cool, stirring occasionally to prevent a skin forming. Grease a baking sheet.

On a floured surface, knead dough; roll out 1/2 inch (1 cm) thick. Spread date mixture evenly over dough. Roll opposite edges to meet at center; press together to flatten center. Place on greased baking sheet; let stand 20 minutes. Preheat oven to 400°F (205°C). Bake stollen 1 hour or until a rich brown. Transfer to a rack.

To make frosting, put egg white into a medium bowl; beat in powdered sugar and lemon juice. Frost stollen while still warm. Sprinkle with sliced almonds before frosting sets.

Cook's Tip

This stollen tastes best when eaten fresh. However, if wrapped tightly in foil, it will keep for 3 to 4 days.

Rich Chocolate Fudge

4 tablespoons (50 g) butter, softened
2 egg yolks
Scant 1 cup (100 g) powdered sugar, sifted
Grated peel of 1/2 orange
12 oz. (350 g) semisweet chocolate
1/2 cup (125 ml) strong black tea, cooled
Scant 1/2 cup (50 g) instant chocolate drink powder, sifted

Line a 7-inch (18-cm) square pan with foil or waxed paper.

In a medium bowl, beat butter, egg yolks and powdered sugar until pale and creamy. Stir in orange peel. Melt chocolate in a double boiler over low heat. Stir cooled tea and melted chocolate into butter mixture; pour into prepared pan. Refrigerate until firm.

When firm, cut fudge into 1-inch (2.5-cm) squares; dip in chocolate powder.

Cook's Tip

This fudge is delicious when flavored with 2 teaspoons rum in place of the grated orange peel. Add the rum to the melted chocolate then continue as above.

Quince Diamonds

4 lbs. (1.75 kg) quinces
1-1/4 cups (300 ml) water
Grated peel of 1 orange
Grated peel of 1 lemon
1 teaspoon ground cinnamon
1 tablespoon cherry brandy
About 4 cups (1 kg) sugar
2/3 cup (100 g) chopped mixed candied peel

Rub quinces thoroughly with a damp cloth. Cut each quince into 4 pieces and remove stems and cores. Place in a large saucepan with water; cook over low heat 45 minutes. Press cooked quinces through a strainer. Measure pulp into cups and make a note of the amount obtained. Put pulp into a large bowl; add orange and lemon peel, cinnamon and cherry brandy. Cover and let stand overnight.

Add 1-1/4 cups (300 g) sugar to mixture for every 1-3/4 cups (500 g) of pulp; mix well. Heat pulp mixture in a large saucepan over medium heat until sugar has dissolved. Continue to cook over low heat until mixture reaches a thick consistency and comes away from sides of pan. Stir occasionally while cooking. Preheat oven to 225°F (105°C). Line two 7x11-inch (18x28-cm) cake pans with waxed paper; grease paper well.

Stir candied peel into quince pulp. Divide mixture between 2 prepared pans; smooth the surface. Dry out 3 to 4 hours in oven with oven door slightly open. Cool completely then cut into diamond shapes; coat in remaining sugar.

Marzipan Fig Balls

1 tablespoon arrack or rum
9 oz. (250 g) almond paste
8 dried figs
1/4 cup (75 g) orange jelly or marmalade
1/2 cup (100 g) firmly packed brown sugar

On a surface sprinkled lightly with powdered sugar, knead arrack or rum into almond paste. Cut each fig into 4 pieces. Wrap each piece of fig in marzipan; shape into a ball. Warm orange jelly or marmalade over low heat. If using marmalade, press it through a strainer to obtain jelly. Roll marzipan balls in warm jelly then in brown sugar. Let candies dry completely on waxed paper. Put into paper candy cups.

Store in an airtight container between layers of waxed paper.

Cook's Tip

Instead of figs, you can stuff the marzipan balls with diced dried apricots, diced dates or a candied cherry.

Caramel Creams

1-1/4 cups (300 g) sugar
1/2 cup (125 ml) boiling water
2 tablespoons (25 g) butter
1/2 cup (125 ml) whipping cream
1 tablespoon vanilla sugar, page 18

Line a 7-inch (18-cm) square pan with foil; brush with oil.

Carefully cook unflavored sugar in a skillet over very low heat, stirring constantly until caramelized. Gradually add boiling water. Stir in butter, cream and vanilla sugar. Bring mixture to boiling point and continue to cook until temperature reaches 240°F (115°C). Pour mixture into prepared pan.

When caramel begins to set, cut into 3/4-inch (1.5-cm) squares with a sharp pointed knife. Separate candies so they do not stick together. Let cool completely.

Cook's Tip

If the caramels are intended as a gift, they will look attractive wrapped separately in pieces of colored cellophane paper.

Apricot Coins

1-1/4 cups (200 g) dried apricots
Boiling water
3 cups (250 g) shredded coconut
Juice of 1 lemon
1-2/3 to 2-1/2 cups (200 to 300 g) powdered sugar, sifted

Place apricots in a medium bowl; cover with boiling water. Cover and soak about 2 hours.

Drain apricots well; grind finely. Mix with 2-1/3 cups (200 g) shredded coconut; grind again. Alternatively, apricots and coconut may be processed in a blender or food processor. In a medium bowl, combine apricot and coconut mixture and lemon juice. Add enough powdered sugar to give a workable dough.

Shape dough into a roll about 1-1/2 inches (3.5 cm) in diameter. Cut off coins, 1/4 inch (5 mm) thick. Sprinkle remaining coconut onto a plate; turn coins in it until thoroughly coated. Place coins between layers of waxed paper in an airtight container. Let dry out at least 2 days.

Cook's Tip

Instead of apricots, you can make the coins with dried plums. If using plums with pits, allow twice the amount and remove the pits after weighing.

Chocolate Almond Crisps

2/3 cup (100 g) raisins
1-1/2 to 3 tablespoons rum
14 oz. (400 g) semisweet chocolate
1-1/4 cups (150 g) toasted chopped almonds, page 47
3 tablespoons (30 g) finely chopped candied lemon peel

Put raisins in a medium bowl; spoon rum over raisins. Cover and let steep overnight.

Line a baking sheet with foil or waxed paper. Melt chocolate in a double boiler over low heat. Cool slightly then add to raisin and rum mixture with almonds and candied peel. Take small amounts of mixture with a teaspoon; place in mounds on prepared baking sheet. Let dry slightly then refrigerate until firm.

Cook's Tip

You can also make the crisps using meringue crumbs. Crush about 6 meringues with a rolling pin and use them instead of raisins.

Chocolate Ducats

10 oz. (275 g) plain cookies
3 oz. (80 g) semisweet chocolate
8 tablespoons (100 g) butter, softened
3/4 cup plus 2 tablespoons (200 g) sugar
1 egg
Scant 1/2 cup (50 g) unsweetened cocoa powder, sifted
1-1/2 tablespoons cherry brandy

Put cookies a few at a time into a plastic bag; crush them with a rolling pin so they break into pieces the size of chopped nuts. There will be about 4 cups of cookie crumbs. Melt chocolate in a double boiler over low heat. Beat butter, sugar and egg in a medium bowl until pale and creamy. Add melted chocolate, cocoa powder, cherry brandy and cookie crumbs; mix well. Refrigerate mixture until firm enough to work with.

Shape mixture into a roll about 2 inches (5 cm) in diameter. Wrap in plastic wrap or foil. Refrigerate 12 hours or until completely set.

Cut 1/2-inch (1-cm) slices from roll. Wrap ducats carefully in gold wrapping paper or foil.

Cook's Tip

This chocolate mixture also makes a deliciously rich dessert. Turn into an 8-1/2x4-1/2-inch (22x11-cm) foil-lined loaf pan and refrigerate as above. Cut in thin slices and serve with cream.

Marzipan Hearts

1 lb. (500 g) almond paste
2-1/2 cups (300 g) powdered sugar, sifted
2 egg whites, beaten
1 egg yolk, beaten
Candied cherries
Strips of candied orange and lemon peel

Preheat oven to 425°F (220°C). On a clean work surface, knead almond paste with 1-2/3 cups (200 g) powdered sugar. Sprinkle work surface lightly with some additional powdered sugar and roll out marzipan 1/2 inch (1 cm) thick. Cut out small heart shapes with a cookie cutter. Roll out marzipan trimmings and cut thin strips long enough to form the outline of a heart. Brush edges of hearts with egg white; place strips on top to make a raised edge. Flute with the prongs of a fork; brush raised edges with egg yolk. Place on a baking sheet. Bake 3 to 5 minutes.

Combine remaining egg white and powdered sugar in a small bowl to make a frosting. Spoon over centers of hearts. Let set. Decorate with candied cherries and strips of candied peel.

Cook's Tip

Use a selection of cookie cutters to make different marzipan shapes.

Chocolate Fruits

7 oz. (200 g) semisweet chocolate
9 oz. (250 g) crystallized pineapple rings
1-1/2 cups (250 g) dried apricots
1/2 cup (60 g) blanched almonds, page 124

Melt chocolate in a double boiler over low heat. Let chocolate cool until about to set and then warm again gently. Cut pineapple rings into wedges as illustrated.

Dip pineapple pieces and apricots into chocolate to half-coat fruit. Drain on a rack. Stick an almond onto each apricot while chocolate is soft.

Cook's Tip

These fruit candies will taste even better if you make a fruit mixture from raspberries, strawberries or oranges, following the recipe for Quince Diamonds, page 139. Mix raspberry or strawberry puree with a little grated lemon peel and lemon juice; mix the orange pulp with chopped pistachio nuts and some orange-flavored liqueur such as Cointreau. After drying out the fruit mixture in the oven, cut into quite large diamond shapes and coat with melted chocolate.

Stuffed Dates

4 oz. (100 g) almond paste
Generous 1/4 cup (40 g) finely chopped pistachio nuts
1 tablespoon orange-flavored liqueur
2 to 3 tablespoons sugar
1-1/4 cups (225 g) pitted dates
Additional sugar

On a surface sprinkled lightly with powdered sugar, knead almond paste with pistachios and liqueur. Form marzipan into small balls; dip in sugar.

Press marzipan balls into pitted dates. Mark marzipan into ridges with a knife; sprinkle with a little additional sugar.

Cook's Tip

Stuffed Dates have a really festive air if half-coated in melted chocolate. You can also mix about 2/3 cup (100 g) finely chopped crystallized pineapple into the marzipan mixture, form into small balls and coat in melted chocolate.

Chocolate Cherry Nougat

12 oz. (300 g) nougat
4 oz. (100 g) semisweet chocolate
1 cup (100 g) sliced almonds
Generous 1/4 cup (40 g) chopped pistachio nuts
1/3 cup (50 g) finely chopped candied lemon peel
1/2 cup (100 g) coarsely chopped candied cherries
2 teaspoons cherry brandy
8 oz. (200 g) unsweetened chocolate

Line an 8-1/2x4-1/2-inch (22x11-cm) loaf pan with foil.

Melt nougat and semisweet chocolate in a double boiler over low heat. Stir almonds, pistachios, candied peel and cherries and cherry brandy into chocolate mixture. Put mixture into prepared loaf pan; smooth the surface. Refrigerate until set.

Melt unsweetened chocolate in a double boiler over low heat. Remove chocolate nougat from pan when set; strip off foil. Coat nougat with melted chocolate. Let set. Cut nougat into 1/4-inch (5-mm) slices before serving.

Marzipan Pralines

3/4 cup (80 g) finely chopped walnuts
1 tablespoon rum
1 tablespoon maraschino
14 oz. (400 g) almond paste
14 oz. (400 g) semisweet chocolate
40 walnut halves

On a surface sprinkled lightly with powdered sugar, knead walnuts, rum and maraschino into almond paste. Roll out marzipan 1/2 inch (1 cm) thick. Using a sharp knife, cut out shapes as illustrated.

Melt chocolate in a double boiler over low heat. Let cool until almost set then warm again gently. Spear marzipan pieces onto a fork and dip in chocolate until thoroughly coated. Let drain slightly on a rack. Press a walnut half into chocolate while still soft. Let chocolate dry slightly. Refrigerate until completely set.

Cook's Tip

Omit the chocolate frosting and top each Marzipan Praline with a whole almond.

Jam Doughnuts

1/4 cup (50 g) granulated sugar
1 cup (250 ml) warm milk (110°F, 43°C)
2 pkgs. active dry yeast
4 cups (500 g) all-purpose flour
1/2 teaspoon salt
2 to 3 tablespoons oil
2 egg yolks
1-1/2 tablespoons rum
1/4 to 1/2 cup (75 to 100 g) plum jam
Oil to deep-fry
Powdered sugar

Stir 1 teaspoon granulated sugar into warm milk and sprinkle with yeast. Let stand 5 minutes or until the surface is frothy. Stir gently to moisten any dry particles remaining on top. Sift flour, remaining granulated sugar and salt into a large bowl. In a medium bowl, lightly beat oil, egg yolks and rum; stir in yeast mixture. Pour into flour mixture, beating until a light dough. Cover and let rise in a warm place 20 minutes.

On a floured surface, roll out dough 1 inch (2.5 cm) thick. Cut out 2-3/4-inch (6.5-cm) rounds. Place a teaspoonful of jam on each round; draw dough together carefully over jam and pinch firmly. Let doughnuts rise in a warm place 15 minutes.

Heat oil for frying to 360°F (180°C) in a deep-frying pan. When doughnuts have risen, place them smooth side down in hot oil. Cover and cook 3 minutes, turning until golden brown all over. Drain doughnuts on paper towels. Sift powdered sugar over hot doughnuts.

Deep-Fried Pretzels

1/4 cup (50 g) sugar
1 cup (250 ml) warm milk (110°F, 43°C)
2 pkgs. active dry yeast
4 cups (500 g) all-purpose flour
1/2 teaspoon salt
7 tablespoons (100 g) margarine
1 egg
Grated peel of 1/2 lemon
Generous pinch each of ground allspice and ground ginger
Oil to deep-fry
Additional sugar

Stir 1 teaspoon sugar into warm milk and sprinkle with yeast. Let stand 5 minutes or until the surface is frothy. Stir gently to moisten any dry particles remaining on top. Sift flour and salt into a large bowl. Melt margarine; cool slightly. Beat margarine, remaining sugar, egg, lemon peel, allspice and ginger in a medium bowl until fluffy. Stir in yeast mixture; add to flour mixture, combining to make a soft dough. Cover and let rise in a warm place 20 minutes.

Divide dough into golf-ball size pieces. With floured hands, shape pieces of dough into balls. Roll balls into 16-inch (40-cm) lengths; form into pretzel shapes as illustrated. Let stand 15 minutes on a floured board.

Heat oil for frying to 360°F (180°C) in a deep-frying pan. Place 3 pretzels at a time in hot oil; fry until crisp and golden all over. Drain on paper towels. Sprinkle with additional sugar while hot.

Rum-Frosted Rings

Cream Puff Paste:
1 cup (250 ml) water
4 tablespoons (60 g) butter
Pinch of salt
1 cup (150 g) all-purpose flour, sifted
4 eggs, beaten
Oil to deep-fry

Frosting:
Generous 1 cup (150 g) powdered sugar, sifted
3 tablespoons rum
1 tablespoon water

Cut a sheet of baking parchment to fit into a deep-frying pan; brush with oil.
To make cream puff paste, heat water gently with butter and salt in a medium saucepan until butter has melted. Increase heat and bring to a boil. Add flour all at once; remove from heat. Stir until dough comes away from sides of pan and forms a ball. Return to heat and cook 1 minute, stirring constantly. Place in a medium bowl; cool slightly. Stir in eggs one at a time.

Heat oil to 360°F (180°C) in deep-frying pan. Place cream puff paste in a pastry bag fitted with a large fluted nozzle. Pipe rings onto oiled baking parchment; the rings should not be too large. Lift paper with rings attached and carefully invert into hot oil. Remove paper when rings become free of it. Fry rings on both sides until golden. Drain on paper towels. Repeat until all rings are cooked. Cool.
To make frosting, combine powdered sugar, rum and water in a small bowl. Spoon frosting over cooled rings.

Almond Doughnuts

Yeast Dough:
1/4 cup plus 2 tablespoons (80 g) sugar
1 cup (250 ml) warm milk (110°F, 43°C)
2 pkgs. active dry yeast
4 cups (500 g) all-purpose flour
1/2 teaspoon salt
4 tablespoons (60 g) margarine
3 eggs
Generous 1/4 cup (40 g) ground almonds
Oil to deep-fry

Frosting:
1 egg white
2/3 cup (70 g) powdered sugar, sifted
1 tablespoon rum
3 tablespoons toasted sliced almonds, page 47

To make yeast dough, stir 1 teaspoon sugar into warm milk and sprinkle with yeast. Let stand 5 minutes or until the surface is frothy. Stir gently to moisten any dry particles remaining on top. Sift flour and salt into a large bowl. Melt margarine; cool slightly. Beat margarine, remaining sugar, eggs and almonds in a medium bowl until frothy. Stir in yeast mixture; add to flour mixture, combining to make a soft dough. Cover and let rise in a warm place 20 minutes.

Knead dough well on a floured surface. Divide into golf-ball size pieces; shape into balls. Make a hole in the middle of each ball with the handle of a wooden spoon. Twist spoon to form doughnuts into rings. Let rise in a warm place 15 minutes.

Heat oil for frying to 360°F (180°C) in a deep-frying pan. Place risen doughnuts four at a time in hot oil; fry on both sides until crisp and golden. Drain on paper towels; cool.
To make frosting, combine egg white, powdered sugar and rum in a small bowl. Spoon frosting over cooled doughnuts; sprinkle with sliced almonds while frosting is soft.

Brandy Fritters

3-1/2 cups (400 g) all-purpose flour
1/2 teaspoon baking powder
2 tablespoons (30 g) butter or margarine, cut in small pieces
1/4 cup (50 g) granulated sugar
Pinch of salt
2 eggs
1/2 cup (125 ml) milk
1 tablespoon brandy such as grappa
Oil to deep-fry
Powdered sugar

Sift flour with baking powder into a large bowl; dot with butter or margarine. Add granulated sugar, salt, eggs, milk and brandy; knead to a smooth dough.

Heat oil for frying to 360°F (180°C) in a deep-frying pan. On a floured surface, roll out dough 1/8 inch (3 mm) thick. Cut into 1-1/2-inch (3.5-cm) squares. Add 10 fritters at a time to hot oil. Fry 4 to 6 minutes or until golden, turning halfway through cooking with a slotted spoon.

Lift out cooked fritters with slotted spoon; drain on paper towels. Sift powdered sugar over warm fritters.

Rhine Rum Fritters

6 tablespoons (80 g) butter or margarine
1/4 cup (50 g) granulated sugar
1 egg
3 tablespoons rum
2-1/4 cups (250 g) all-purpose flour
Scant 1/4 cup (50 ml) milk
Pinch of salt
Oil to deep-fry
Powdered sugar

Melt butter or margarine. Beat butter or margarine, granulated sugar, egg and rum in a medium bowl until frothy. Sift flour into a medium bowl. Form a well in the center; add milk, salt and egg mixture. Knead to a workable dough.

Heat oil for frying to 360°F (180°C) in a deep-frying pan. On a floured surface, roll out dough 1/8 inch (3 mm) thick. Using a pastry wheel, cut out diamond shapes. Add 6 fritters at a time to hot oil. Fry 4 to 5 minutes or until golden, turning halfway through cooking with a slotted spoon.

Lift out cooked fritters with slotted spoon; drain on paper towels. Sift powdered sugar over warm fritters.

Cinnamon Balls

6 tablespoons (80 g) butter or margarine, softened
1/4 cup plus 2 tablespoons (80 g) sugar
Grated peel of 1/2 lemon
Pinch of salt
4 eggs
3-1/2 cups (400 g) all-purpose flour
1 teaspoon baking powder
Oil to deep-fry
Additional 1/2 cup (100 g) sugar
2 teaspoons ground cinnamon

In a large bowl, cream butter or margarine and 1/4 cup plus 2 tablespoons (80 g) sugar until pale and fluffy. Add lemon peel and salt. Beat in eggs one at a time. Sift flour with baking powder; fold into mixture with a metal spoon to make a dough.

Heat oil for frying to 360°F (180°C) in a deep-frying pan. Using 2 floured teaspoons, form dough into small balls. Add about 8 balls at a time to hot oil. Fry 5 to 6 minutes or until golden, turning halfway through cooking with a slotted spoon.

Lift out cooked balls with slotted spoon; drain on paper towels. Mix 1/2 cup (100 g) sugar and cinnamon; sprinkle over balls while still warm.

Dutch Raisin Doughnuts

1/4 cup plus 3 tablespoons (100 g) sugar
1/2 cup (125 ml) warm milk (110°F, 43°C)
3 pkgs. active dry yeast
4 cups (500 g) all-purpose flour
Pinch of salt
6 tablespoons (75 g) butter, softened
2 eggs
Grated peel of 1 lemon
Grated peel of 1 orange
Generous 1/2 cup (100 g) raisins
1/3 cup (50 g) dried currants
Hot water
1/2 cup (75 g) finely chopped candied orange peel
Oil to deep-fry

Stir 1 teaspoon sugar into warm milk and sprinkle with yeast. Let stand 5 minutes or until the surface is frothy. Stir gently to moisten any dry particles remaining on top. Sift flour and salt into a large bowl. In a medium bowl, beat butter, remaining sugar, eggs, lemon and orange peel. Stir in yeast mixture; add to flour mixture, combining to make a stiff dough. On a floured surface, knead dough a few minutes. Cover and let rise in a warm place 15 minutes.

Simmer raisins and currants 2 minutes in a little hot water; drain. Knead into dough with candied orange peel. Let dough stand in a warm place 30 minutes.

Heat oil for frying to 320°F (160°C) in a deep-frying pan. Using 2 floured tablespoons, form dough into small doughnuts. Add about 6 doughnuts at a time to hot oil. Fry about 10 minutes or until golden brown, turning halfway through cooking with a slotted spoon. Lift out cooked doughnuts with slotted spoon; drain on paper towels.

Easter Bread

Yeast Dough:
1/4 cup plus 3 tablespoons (100 g) sugar
2-1/4 cups (550 ml) warm milk
 (110°C, 43°C)
4 pkgs. active dry yeast
9 cups (1 kg) all-purpose flour
Pinch of salt
3/4 cup plus 2 tablespoons (200 g) butter
2 eggs
Grated peel of 1 lemon

Fruit Loaf:
1 cup (100 g) chopped almonds
1-1/4 cups (200 g) chopped
 candied lemon peel
2 cups (300 g) seedless golden raisins
1-1/2 tablespoons rum
4 tablespoons (50 g) butter, melted
1/4 cup (50 g) sugar

Braided Wreath:
1 egg yolk, beaten
1/2 cup (50 g) slivered almonds
1/4 cup (50 g) sugar
3 tablespoons rum

To make yeast dough, stir 2 teaspoons sugar into warm milk and sprinkle with yeast. Let stand 5 minutes or until the surface is frothy. Stir gently to moisten any dry particles remaining on top. Sift flour and salt into a large bowl. Melt butter; cool slightly. Lightly beat butter, eggs and lemon peel into yeast mixture. Pour into flour mixture, combining to make a dough. On a floured surface, knead dough 5 to 10 minutes until smooth and elastic. Cover and let rise in a warm place 1 hour.

To make fruit loaf, combine almonds, candied peel, raisins and rum in a small bowl. Cover and let stand 30 minutes.

Divide risen dough in half; knead each half lightly. Knead fruit mixture into 1 half; let stand 15 minutes. Grease a baking sheet. Shape fruit dough into a loaf; place on greased baking sheet. Let stand in a warm place 30 minutes. Preheat oven to 375°F (190°C). Cut a cross on top of loaf. Bake 30 to 40 minutes or until a rich brown. While still hot, brush loaf with butter and sprinkle with sugar.

To make braided wreath, divide remaining dough into 3 equal pieces; roll into long ropes. Braid ropes; shape into a wreath. Brush with egg yolk. Combine almonds, sugar and rum in a small bowl; spread over wreath. Bake as for fruit loaf.

Bremer Fruit Loaf

1/2 cup (100 g) sugar
1 cup (250 ml) warm milk (110°F, 43°C)
3 pkgs. active dry yeast
6 cups (750 g) all-purpose flour
1 teaspoon each salt and ground cardamom
1-1/2 cups (400 g) butter
1 tablespoon vanilla sugar, page 18
1-1/4 cups (150 g) chopped almonds
2/3 cup (125 g) chopped candied lemon peel
Grated peel and juice of 1 lemon
2-2/3 cups (500 g) raisins

You can bake the Bremer Fruit Loaf either in a loaf pan or on a baking sheet. The following recipe uses both ways. Grease a 12x4-inch (30x10-cm) loaf pan and a baking sheet.

Stir 1 teaspoon unflavored sugar into warm milk and sprinkle with yeast. Let stand 5 minutes or until the surface is frothy. Stir gently to moisten any dry particles remaining on top. Sift flour, salt and cardamom into a large bowl. Melt butter; cool slightly. In a medium bowl, beat butter, remaining unflavored sugar and vanilla sugar. Stir in yeast mixture. Pour into flour mixture, combining to make a dough. Knead in almonds, candied peel,

lemon peel and juice and raisins. On a floured surface, knead dough until smooth and elastic. Cover and let rise in a warm place 40 minutes.

Lightly knead risen dough; divide in half. Place 1 half in greased loaf pan. Let stand in a warm place 30 minutes. Shape remaining half into a long loaf; place on greased baking sheet. Let stand in a warm place 30 minutes. Preheat oven to 375°F (190°C). When loaves are well risen, bake 45 to 50 minutes or until a skewer inserted in center of loaves comes out clean. Cool on a rack.

Cook's Tip

You can also bake fruit rolls from this dough. After the first rising, break off small pieces of dough and roll into balls. Place on a greased baking sheet and flatten slightly. Cover and let stand in a warm place 15 minutes. Before baking, brush with beaten egg yolk and sprinkle with sugar. Bake 20 to 30 minutes in a preheated 375°F (190°C) oven.

Russian Mazurka

Cake:
5 eggs, separated
3/4 cup (175 g) sugar
2 small lemons
2 cups (250 g) toasted ground hazelnuts, page 47

Topping:
1 cup (250 ml) whipping cream
3 tablespoons (20 g) powdered sugar, sifted
3 tablespoons rum
Colored sugar Easter eggs

Grease a round 8-inch (20-cm) cake pan. Preheat oven to 350°F (175°C).
To make cake, put egg yolks and sugar into a large bowl. Beat until pale and creamy, 5 to 10 minutes with an electric mixer. Grate peel of both lemons. Squeeze juice from one. Add peel and juice to egg yolk mixture. Grind hazelnuts to a powder; gradually fold into egg yolk mixture. Beat egg whites until stiff; fold into mixture carefully with a metal spoon. Turn batter into greased cake pan; smooth the surface. Bake 40 minutes. As soon as sides of cake begin to come away from pan, turn off oven and let cake stand 15 minutes in warm oven. Turn out onto a rack to cool.
To make topping, beat cream with powdered sugar and rum in a medium bowl until stiff. Spread whipped cream mixture thickly over top of cooled cake. Decorate with Easter eggs.

Country Rice Flan

Pastry:
2-1/2 cups (300 g) all-purpose flour
3/4 cup plus 2 tablespoons (200 g) butter, cut in small pieces
1/4 cup plus 3 tablespoons (100 g) sugar
1 egg

Filling:
3-3/4 cups (900 g) milk
3/4 cup (175 g) granulated sugar
2 tablespoons (25 g) butter
4 tablespoons (50 g) short-grain rice, washed and drained
4 eggs
4 oz. (100 g) cream cheese
1/2 cup (75 g) chopped candied lemon peel
1/4 teaspoon ground cinnamon
Grated peel of 1 lemon
Grated peel of 1 large orange
Powdered sugar mixed with a little ground cinnamon

To make pastry, sift flour into a large bowl. Using a pastry blender or 2 knives, cut in butter evenly. Lightly mix in sugar and egg to make a dough. Cover and refrigerate 2 hours.
To make filling, bring milk to a boil with granulated sugar and butter in a medium saucepan. Stir in rice; reduce heat and simmer gently 1 hour. Stir occasionally until mixture is thick and creamy. Remove from heat. In a large bowl, beat eggs, cream cheese, candied peel, cinnamon and lemon and orange peel. Gradually stir in rice mixture; cool. Preheat oven to 400°F (205°C). On a floured surface, roll out two-thirds of dough to fit an 8-inch (20-cm) flan tin with a removable bottom. Place dough in tin without stretching. Pierce bottom of pastry shell all over with a fork; fill with rice mixture. Roll out remaining dough. Cut into strips and place on top of flan in a lattice pattern. Bake 50 minutes, covering with foil if becoming too brown. Leave in tin until filling is set. Sift powdered sugar and cinnamon mixture over warm flan. Serve immediately.

Coffee Cream Tart

Pastry:
1-1/2 cups (150 g) all-purpose flour
8 tablespoons (100 g) butter, softened
1/4 cup (50 g) sugar
1 cup (100 g) ground hazelnuts
1 egg
About 1-1/2 tablespoons ice water

Filling & Topping:
1 tablespoon instant coffee powder
3/4 cup (185 ml) hot water
2 envelopes unflavored gelatin
2 eggs, separated
1/2 cup plus 1 tablespoon (125 g) sugar
1 tablespoon vanilla sugar, page 18
3 tablespoons brandy
Scant 2 cups (450 ml) whipping cream
2 teaspoons chopped pistachio nuts
12 sugar Easter eggs

To make pastry, sift flour into a medium bowl. Add butter, sugar, hazelnuts and egg. Knead with enough water to make a dough. Cover and refrigerate 2 hours.

Preheat oven to 400°F (205°C). On a floured surface, roll out dough to fit a 9-inch (23-cm) flan tin with a removable bottom. Place dough in tin without stretching. Bake blind, page 9, 25 to 30 minutes. Cool on a rack.

To make filling and topping, dissolve coffee in hot water in a small saucepan. Add gelatin; stir over low heat until dissolved. Cool. Beat egg yolks, unflavored sugar and vanilla sugar in a medium bowl until thick. Stir in cooled coffee mixture and brandy. Beat egg whites until stiff. Whip cream until stiff. Fold egg whites and two-thirds of cream into coffee mixture. Pour into pastry shell. Refrigerate until firm. Put remaining whipped cream into a pastry bag fitted with a fluted nozzle. Pipe rosettes of cream onto tart; decorate with pistachios and Easter eggs.

Polish Easter Rings

Yeast Dough:
1/2 cup (120 g) sugar
1 cup (250 ml) warm milk (110°F, 43°C)
2 pkgs. active dry yeast
4 cups (500 g) all-purpose flour
1/2 teaspoon salt
1-1/2 cups (375 g) butter
Grated peel of 1/2 orange
Grated peel of 1/2 lemon
5 eggs
1 cup (150 g) raisins

Frosting:
2 cups (250 g) powdered sugar, sifted
1 tablespoon lemon juice
Scant 1/4 cup (50 ml) hot water
6 candied cherries, halved

To make yeast dough, stir 1 teaspoon sugar into warm milk and sprinkle with yeast. Let stand 5 minutes or until frothy. Stir gently to moisten any dry particles remaining on top. Sift flour and salt into a large bowl. Melt butter; cool slightly. In a medium bowl, mix butter, remaining sugar, orange and lemon peel and eggs. Stir in yeast mixture. Beat into flour mixture to make a smooth batter. Cover and let stand in a warm place 30 minutes. Grease and flour two 7-1/2 cup (1.75-liter) savarin or tube molds. Beat raisins into batter. Divide batter between prepared pans. Cover and let rise in a warm place until batter is 1 inch (2.5 cm) from top of pans. Preheat oven to 400°F (205°C).

Bake cakes 50 minutes or until a skewer inserted in cakes comes out clean. Cover cakes with a little foil during cooking if they are becoming too brown. Cool in pans 20 minutes, then turn out onto racks to cool completely.

To make frosting, combine powdered sugar, lemon juice and water in a small bowl. Pour over cooled cakes; decorate with halved cherries while frosting is soft.

Lombardy Easter Loaf

1/4 cup plus 1 tablespoon (70 g) sugar
1 cup (250 ml) warm milk (110°F, 43°C)
2 pkgs. active dry yeast
4 cups (500 g) all-purpose flour
1/2 teaspoon salt
2 eggs
Generous pinch each of grated nutmeg and ground allspice
Grated peel of 1/2 lemon
1/2 cup (120 g) butter, melted
1/3 cup (50 g) finely chopped candied lemon peel
1 egg yolk, beaten

Stir 1 teaspoon sugar into warm milk and sprinkle with yeast. Let stand 5 minutes or until the surface is frothy. Stir gently to moisten any dry particles remaining on top. Sift flour and salt into a large bowl. In a small bowl, beat 2 eggs, remaining sugar, nutmeg, allspice and lemon peel. Stir in yeast mixture. Pour into flour mixture with butter and candied peel, combining to make a dough. On a floured surface, knead dough until smooth and elastic. Cover and let rise in a warm place 30 minutes. Grease a 9-inch (23-cm) cake pan.

Knead risen dough lightly; divide into 4 equal pieces. Roll each piece into a ball; place balls in a ring in pan. Let stand in a warm place 30 minutes. Preheat oven to 400°F (205°C).

Brush loaf with egg yolk. Bake 30 to 40 minutes or until loaf sounds hollow when tapped on underside. Cool on a rack. Serve with butter.

Greek Easter Bread

3/4 cup plus 2 tablespoons (200 ml) warm milk (110°F, 43°C)
1/4 cup (50 g) sugar
2 pkgs. active dry yeast
8 cups (1 kg) all-purpose flour
Pinch of salt
Grated peel of 1 orange
1 cup (250 ml) warm water (110°F, 43°C)
1/3 cup (30 g) sesame seeds
5 eggs, hard-cooked
Red food coloring
1 egg yolk, beaten

Put warm milk into a medium bowl; stir in 1 teaspoon sugar. Sprinkle yeast over milk mixture. Let stand 5 minutes or until the surface is frothy. Stir gently to moisten any dry particles remaining on top. Sift in 1 cup (125 g) flour and remaining sugar. Stir well. Cover and let stand in a warm place overnight.

Oil a baking sheet. Sift remaining flour and salt into a large bowl. Make a well in the center; add yeast mixture and orange peel. Gradually stir in water; mix to a dough. On a floured surface, knead dough at least 10 minutes until smooth and elastic. Shape two-thirds of dough into a long loaf 2 inches (5 cm) high. Place on oiled baking sheet. Make 2 thin rolls the length of the loaf from remaining dough. Roll in sesame seeds; twist and place around loaf. Brush eggs with red food coloring; let dry. Press dried eggs into loaf in an upright position. Brush loaf with egg yolk; sprinkle with sesame seeds. Cover and let stand in a warm place 1 hour. Preheat oven to 375°F (190°C).

Bake 40 to 50 minutes or until loaf sounds hollow when tapped on underside. Cool on a rack.

Easter Specialties

Easter Nests

1/4 cup (50 g) sugar
1 cup (250 ml) warm milk (110°F, 43°C)
2 pkgs. active dry yeast
4 cups (500 g) all-purpose flour
Pinch of salt
4 tablespoons (50 g) butter
1 egg
1 egg yolk, beaten
18 eggs, boiled 5 minutes

Stir 1 teaspoon sugar into warm milk and sprinkle with yeast. Let stand 5 minutes or until the surface is frothy. Stir gently to moisten any dry particles remaining on top. Sift flour and salt into a large bowl. Melt butter; cool slightly. In a small bowl, lightly beat butter, remaining sugar and 1 egg. Stir in yeast mixture. Work into flour mixture to give a dry dough. Knead dough well on a floured surface. Cover and let rise in a warm place 1 hour. Grease baking sheets.

Divide risen dough into 18 small pieces. With floured hands, form into balls. Roll balls into 20-inch (50-cm) lengths. Twist to make spirals; form into circles and knot ends to make nests, see illustration. Place nests on greased baking sheets. Brush with egg yolk. Place 1 cooked egg, still in its shell, in the center of each nest. Let stand 10 minutes. Preheat oven to 400°F (205°C). Bake 15 to 20 minutes or until nests are a rich golden brown. Cool slightly on racks. Decorate eggs using water colors, colored pencils, or felt-tip pens.

Easter Ducklings

Yeast Dough:
1/4 cup (60 g) sugar
1 cup (250 ml) warm milk (110°F, 43°C)
2 pkgs. active dry yeast
4 cups (500 g) all-purpose flour
Pinch of salt
4 tablespoons (60 g) butter, melted
1 egg
1 egg yolk, beaten
2/3 cup (225 g) strawberry jam

Decoration:
3 tablespoons (20 g) powdered sugar, sifted
1 teaspoon lemon juice
Dried currants
Crystallized flowers, if desired

To make yeast dough, stir 1 teaspoon sugar into milk and sprinkle with yeast. Let stand 5 minutes or until frothy. Stir gently. Sift flour, remaining sugar and salt into a large bowl. Stir butter into yeast mixture. Lightly beat in 1 egg. Pour into flour mixture, combining to make a dough. Knead dough on a floured surface. Cover and let rise in a warm place 1 hour. Grease a baking sheet. On a floured surface, roll out dough 1/4 inch (5 mm) thick. From two-thirds of dough, cut out an even number of circles 3 inches (7.5 cm) in diameter. Brush edges of circles with egg yolk. Put a little jam in the center of half the circles. Join pairs of circles together until all are used. From remaining dough, cut out smaller rounds for heads and ovals for beaks. Attach heads to bodies and beaks to heads with a little egg yolk. Place on greased baking sheet. Let stand in a warm place 15 minutes. Preheat oven to 425°F (220°C). Brush ducklings with egg yolk. Bake 15 minutes or until golden brown.
To make decoration, blend powdered sugar and lemon juice. Drop or pipe blobs of frosting onto heads; add currants for eyes. Decorate ducklings with crystallized flowers if desired.

Sesame Seed Cookies

1/2 cup plus 1 tablespoon (125 g) soft margarine
1 cup plus 2 tablespoons (250 g) sugar
2 eggs, beaten
Generous 3/4 cup (100 g) cracked wheat
2/3 cup (100 g) raisins
2/3 cup (120 g) sesame seeds
3 tablespoons milk
2 cups (225 g) whole-wheat flour
1/2 teaspoon grated nutmeg

Brush a baking sheet with oil. Preheat oven to 375°F (190°C).

In a medium bowl, cream margarine and sugar until pale and fluffy. Stir in eggs. Combine cracked wheat, raisins, sesame seeds and milk; gradually stir into creamed mixture. Add flour and nutmeg; stir well.

Using a teaspoon, place small amounts of mixture on oiled baking sheet; flatten slightly. Bake 10 to 15 minutes or until lightly browned. Remove from baking sheet with a spatula; cool on a rack.

Whole-Wheat Honey Hearts

4 cups (450 g) whole-wheat flour
1/2 teaspoon baking powder
1 teaspoon ground ginger
1/3 cup (50 g) cracked wheat
1/3 cup (100 g) creamed honey or honey spread
Generous 1/3 cup (150 g) light corn syrup
1/2 cup plus 2 tablespoons (150 g) margarine

Combine flour and baking powder in a large bowl. Add ginger and cracked wheat. Warm honey, corn syrup and margarine in a small saucepan over low heat. Stir occasionally until margarine has melted and combined with honey and corn syrup. Let cool; when lukewarm, stir into flour mixture to make a dough. Knead well. Press into a ball and wrap in foil or plastic wrap. Refrigerate 1 hour. Grease baking sheets.

Preheat oven to 350°F (175°C). On a floured surface, roll out dough 1/4 inch (5 mm) thick. Cut out heart shapes; place on baking sheets. Bake 12 to 15 minutes or until lightly browned. Remove from baking sheet with a spatula; cool on a rack.

Cook's Tip

Immediately after cooking, the Whole-Wheat Honey Hearts will be quite hard. They will soften after 1 to 2 days in an airtight container.

Crumb-Crust Fruit Tart

Crumb Crust:
Generous 3 cups (250 g) graham cracker crumbs
2 tablespoons (25 g) sugar
1/2 teaspoon ground cinnamon
6 tablespoons (75 g) butter or margarine, melted

Filling & Topping:
1/4 cup (25 g) cornstarch
2 tablespoons (25 g) sugar
1/2 teaspoon vanilla extract
Scant 2 cups (450 ml) milk
1 (1-lb., 456-g) can gooseberries
1 (8-3/4-oz., 248-g) can peach slices
1-1/2 teaspoons lemon-flavored gelatin

Grease a 9-inch (23-cm) flan tin with a removable bottom.
To make crumb crust, combine graham cracker crumbs, sugar, cinnamon and butter or margarine in a medium bowl. Place crumb mixture in greased tin; press down slightly with the back of a spoon. Refrigerate until firm.
To make filling and topping, blend cornstarch, sugar, vanilla and a little milk in a medium bowl. Heat remaining milk in a medium saucepan; stir into cornstarch mixture. Return to saucepan and bring to a boil, stirring constantly until thickened. Cool, stirring occasionally to prevent a skin forming.

Drain gooseberries and reserve juice. Drain peaches. Spread cooled vanilla sauce over crumb crust; top with drained fruit as illustrated. Prepare lemon-flavored gelatin using reserved gooseberry juice, according to package directions. Cool slightly and pour over tart. Refrigerate tart until firm then remove sides of flan tin and serve.

Date Crumble Cake

2 cups (350 g) fresh dates, pitted
8 tablespoons (100 g) soft margarine
1/2 cup (100 g) sugar
1/4 teaspoon vanilla extract
1-1/2 cups (175 g) whole-wheat flour
1/4 teaspoon salt
Generous 1 cup (100 g) rolled oats

Grease a 9-inch (23-cm) springform cake pan. Preheat oven to 350°F (175°C).

Finely chop dates. Cream margarine, sugar and vanilla in a medium bowl until pale and fluffy. Gradually add flour, salt and oats; mix with fingertips until crumbly.

Spread half the oat mixture over bottom of greased cake pan. Press mixture down into pan, raising sides slightly. Spread dates over oat mixture; crumble remaining mixture over top. Bake 45 to 50 minutes or until lightly browned. Let cool slightly in pan then remove from pan and serve warm.

Walnut & Banana Bread

1/2 cup plus 2 tablespoons (150 g) soft margarine
1/2 cup plus 3 tablespoons (160 g) sugar
3 eggs
3 bananas
1/4 teaspoon vanilla extract
2-1/2 cups (275 g) whole-wheat flour
2 teaspoons baking powder
1/4 teaspoon salt
1 cup (100 g) chopped walnuts
3 tablespoons milk

Grease a 9-1/4x5-1/4-inch (23x13-cm) loaf pan. Preheat oven to 350°F (175°C).

In a medium bowl, cream margarine and sugar until pale and fluffy. Beat in eggs. Peel bananas; mash with a fork, or process in a blender. Stir banana pulp and vanilla into creamed mixture. Combine flour, baking powder, salt and walnuts. Fold into creamed mixture with milk. Turn batter into greased loaf pan; smooth the surface. Bake 1-1/4 hours or until a skewer inserted in center comes out clean. Turn out loaf onto a rack to cool.

Wheat Germ Loaf

1/3 cup (100 g) creamed honey or honey spread
3 cups plus 2 tablespoons (750 ml) warm water (110°F, 43°C)
4 pkgs. active dry yeast
8 cups (900 g) whole-wheat flour
2 teaspoons salt
3 tablespoons oil or melted margarine
1 cup (150 g) wheat germ
Water
Additional flour

Stir 1 tablespoon creamed honey or honey spread into warm water and sprinkle with yeast. Let stand 5 minutes or until the surface is frothy. Stir gently to moisten any dry particles remaining on top. Put half the flour and salt into a large bowl. Stir remaining creamed honey or honey spread and oil or melted margarine into yeast mixture. Beat into flour mixture. Cover and let rise in a warm place 30 minutes.

Stir remaining flour and wheat germ into mixture. On a floured surface, knead mixture well to give a smooth and elastic dough. Add a little more flour if dough is too wet. Cover and let stand in a warm place until doubled in size, about 30 minutes. Grease a baking sheet.

Knead risen dough well. Shape into 2 loaves; place on greased baking sheet; cover loosely and let stand in a warm place 15 minutes. Preheat oven to 400°F (205°C).

Using a sharp knife, lightly cut a cross on the top of each loaf. Brush loaves with water and sprinkle with a little additional flour. Bake 50 minutes or until loaves sound hollow when tapped on underside. Cool on a rack.

Whole-Wheat Breakfast Rolls

1 teaspoon sugar
1 cup (250 ml) warm water (110°F, 43°C)
2 pkgs. active dry yeast
4 cups (500 g) whole-wheat flour
1/2 teaspoon salt
3 tablespoons oil
Additional flour

Stir sugar into warm water and sprinkle with yeast. Let stand 5 minutes or until the surface is frothy. Stir gently to moisten any dry particles remaining on top. Put flour and salt into a large bowl. Stir oil into yeast mixture. Pour into flour mixture, combining to make a dough. On a floured surface, knead dough 5 to 10 minutes until smooth and elastic. Cover and let rise in a warm place 30 minutes. Grease a baking sheet.

Knead risen dough lightly with floured hands; divide dough into 16 equal pieces. Roll each piece into a ball. Sprinkle with a little additional flour; place on baking sheet. Let stand in a warm place 15 minutes. Preheat oven to 450°F (230°C).

Bake 15 to 20 minutes or until rolls sound hollow when tapped on undersides.

Whole-Wheat Bread

Pinch of sugar
2 cups plus 2 tablespoons (500 ml) warm milk (110°F, 43°C)
3 pkgs. active dry yeast
3-1/2 cups (400 g) white bread flour
1 teaspoon salt
3-1/2 cups (400 g) whole-wheat flour
1/2 cup plus 1 tablespoon (150 ml) oil
Additional white flour

Stir sugar into warm milk and sprinkle with yeast. Let stand 5 minutes or until the surface is frothy. Stir gently to moisten any dry particles remaining on top. Sift white flour and salt into a large bowl; add whole-wheat flour. Stir oil into yeast mixture. Pour into flour mixture, combining to make a dough. On a floured surface, knead dough 5 to 10 minutes until smooth and elastic. Cover and let rise in a warm place 30 minutes. Sprinkle a baking sheet with flour.

Lightly knead risen dough. Shape into a loaf; place on floured baking sheet. Cover and let stand in a warm place 30 minutes. Preheat oven to 375°F (190°C).

Sprinkle loaf with a little additional white flour. Bake 50 to 60 minutes or until loaf sounds hollow when tapped on underside.

Rum & Raisin Loaf

2/3 cup (100 g) raisins
3 tablespoons rum
3 tablespoons (40 g) sugar
1 cup (250 ml) warm milk (110°F, 43°C)
2 pkgs. active dry yeast
4 cups (500 g) all-purpose flour
1 teaspoon salt
6 tablespoons (80 g) butter
2 eggs
Grated peel of 1 lemon
1 egg yolk, beaten

Mix raisins and rum in a small bowl. Cover and set aside.

Stir 1 teaspoon sugar into warm milk and sprinkle with yeast.
Let stand 5 minutes or until the surface is frothy. Stir gently to
moisten any dry particles remaining on top. Sift flour and salt
into a large bowl. Melt butter; cool slightly. In a medium bowl,
mix remaining sugar, butter, eggs and lemon peel. Stir in yeast
mixture. Pour into flour mixture, combining to make a soft
dough. On a floured surface, knead dough 5 to 10 minutes until
smooth. Cover and let rise in a warm place until doubled in size,
about 30 minutes. Grease a 12x4-inch (30x10-cm) loaf pan.

Knead raisin and rum mixture into risen dough. Shape into a
loaf; place in greased loaf pan. Let stand in a warm place 30
minutes. Preheat oven to 375°F (190°C).

Brush loaf with egg yolk. Bake 40 to 50 minutes or until loaf
sounds hollow when tapped on underside.

Cook's Tip

**Instead of the raisins soaked in rum, knead 1 cup (100 g) chopped
almonds into the dough and bake as above.**

Savory Bacon Baps

Pinch of sugar
About 3-3/4 cups (900 ml) warm water (110°F, 43°C)
1-1/2 pkgs. active dry yeast
8 cups (1 kg) light rye flour
Double quantity Starter Dough, page 163
8 oz. (225 g) sliced bacon
2 teaspoons salt
4 teaspoons caraway seeds
Water
2 teaspoons sea salt

Stir sugar into warm water and sprinkle with yeast. Let stand 5
minutes or until the surface is frothy. Stir gently to moisten any
dry particles remaining on top. Place half the flour in a large
bowl. Add yeast liquid to flour with starter dough, combining to
make a dough. On a floured surface, knead dough until smooth.
Cover and let rise at room temperature overnight.

Lightly broil bacon. Drain on paper towels; chop very finely.
Cool. Preheat oven to 400°F (205°C). Mix salt, 2 teaspoons
caraway seeds, bacon and remaining flour into dough. Knead
until smooth. Sprinkle baking sheets with flour.

Divide dough into 6 equal pieces. On a floured surface, roll
out dough thinly into flat cakes 10 to 12 inches (25 to 30 cm) in
diameter. Brush tops with water; cut crisscross markings.
Sprinkle with remaining caraway seeds and sea salt. Place on
floured baking sheets. Bake 30 minutes or until brown.

Flowerpot Loaves

2 medium onions
1 clove garlic
4 tablespoons (50 g) butter, melted
2 large eggs, beaten
1/2 teaspoon salt
Pinch of grated nutmeg
1 teaspoon ground aniseed
1/2 teaspoon dried fennel
3 tablespoons dried dill
1/2 teaspoon dried rosemary
Pinch of sugar
3/4 cup (175 ml) warm milk (110°F, 43°C)
2 pkgs. active dry yeast
4 cups (500 g) all-purpose flour
Water
Additional ground aniseed

Peel onions and garlic. Finely chop onions; crush garlic. Mix butter, eggs, salt, nutmeg, aniseed, fennel and dill in a medium bowl. Stir in onion and garlic. Pound rosemary in a mortar; add to onion and egg mixture.

Stir sugar into warm milk and sprinkle with yeast. Let stand 5 minutes or until the surface is frothy. Stir gently to moisten any dry particles remaining on top. Sift flour into a large bowl. Stir yeast mixture into onion and egg mixture. Pour into flour, combining to make a dough. On a floured surface, knead dough until smooth and elastic. Cover and let rise in a warm place until dough has doubled in size, about 30 minutes. Line 2 new 4-inch (10-cm) clay flowerpots with aluminum foil. Grease foil.

Knead risen dough lightly. Put half the dough in each flowerpot. Let stand in a warm place 20 minutes. Preheat oven to 400°F (205°C).

Brush surface of loaves with water and sprinkle lightly with additional aniseed. Bake 35 to 40 minutes or until loaves sound hollow when tapped on undersides.

French Bread

Pinch of sugar
2-1/2 cups (600 ml) warm water (110°F, 43°C)
3 pkgs. active dry yeast
8 cups (1 kg) white bread flour
4 teaspoons salt
Additional lukewarm water

Stir sugar into warm water and sprinkle with yeast. Let stand 5 minutes or until the surface is frothy. Stir gently to moisten any dry particles remaining on top. Sift flour and salt into a large bowl. Pour in yeast liquid, combining to make a dough. On a floured surface, knead dough 5 to 10 minutes until smooth and elastic. Sprinkle dough generously with flour so the surface does not form a crust. Cover and let rise at room temperature 2 to 3 hours. Sprinkle large baking sheets with flour.

Quickly knead risen dough. Divide into 4 pieces. Shape each piece into a long roll; place on floured baking sheets. Cover dough and let stand in a warm place 30 minutes. Preheat oven to 425°F (220°C).

Slash loaves diagonally several times with a fine sharp knife; brush with lukewarm water. Bake 15 minutes then reduce heat to 350°F (175°C) and bake 15 to 20 minutes longer or until loaves are golden brown and crusty.

Northern Wheel

Pinch of sugar
About 3-3/4 cups (900 ml) warm water (110°F, 43°C)
1-1/2 pkgs. active dry yeast
8 cups (1 kg) light rye flour
Double quantity Starter Dough, page 163
2 teaspoons salt
2 teaspoons each caraway seeds, dried fennel and ground aniseed
Milk

Stir sugar into warm water and sprinkle with yeast. Let stand 5 minutes or until the surface is frothy. Stir gently to moisten any dry particles remaining on top. Place half the flour in a large bowl. Add yeast liquid to flour with starter dough, combining to make a dough. On a floured surface, knead dough until smooth. Cover and let rise in a warm place overnight.

Preheat oven to 450°F (230°C). Sprinkle a large baking sheet with flour. Knead salt, 1 teaspoon each of caraway seeds, fennel and aniseed and remaining flour into risen dough. Continue kneading dough until smooth. Shape a third of the dough into a long roll. Roll up like a snail's shell; place in the center of the floured baking sheet. Shape remaining dough into eight 8-inch (20-cm) long ropes. Place around central coil and curl the end of each piece as illustrated. Brush surface of dough with milk; sprinkle with remaining caraway seeds, fennel and aniseed. Bake 25 minutes or until golden brown.

Fresh Herb Bread

Pinch of sugar
1-1/2 cups (350 ml) warm milk (110°F, 43°C)
2 pkgs. active dry yeast
3-1/2 cups (400 g) white bread flour
1 teaspoon salt
1 tablespoon chopped fresh mixed herbs,
  such as dill, chives, thyme, parsley
1 teaspoon coarsely ground black pepper
Additional milk

Stir sugar into warm milk and sprinkle with yeast. Let stand 5 minutes or until the surface is frothy. Stir gently to moisten any dry particles remaining on top. Sift flour and salt into a large bowl. Pour in yeast mixture, combining to make a dough. Cover and let rise in a warm place 1 hour. Grease and flour a 12x4-inch (30x10-cm) loaf pan.

On a floured surface, knead herbs and pepper into risen dough. Place in prepared loaf pan; cut the surface diagonally with a sharp knife. Cover loaf and let rise in a warm place 30 minutes. Preheat oven to 425°F (220°C).

Brush loaf with milk. Bake 35 to 40 minutes or until loaf sounds hollow when tapped on underside. Cover with foil during cooking if the loaf is becoming too brown on top.

Aniseed Marble Bread

Plain Dough:
Pinch of sugar
1/2 cup (125 ml) warm milk
  (110°F, 43°C)
1-1/2 pkgs. active dry yeast
3 cups (350 g) all-purpose flour
1/2 teaspoon salt
4 tablespoons (50 g) butter
2 eggs

Rye Dough:
Pinch of sugar
1/2 cup (125 ml) warm milk
  (110°F, 43°C)
1-1/2 pkgs. active dry yeast
3 cups (350 g) rye flour
1/2 teaspoon salt
4 tablespoons (50 g) butter
2 eggs
1/2 teaspoon ground aniseed
Water
1 tablespoon aniseed

To make plain dough, stir sugar into warm milk and sprinkle with yeast. Let stand 5 minutes or until the surface is frothy. Stir gently to moisten any dry particles remaining on top. Sift flour and salt into a large bowl. Melt butter; cool slightly. Lightly beat butter and eggs into yeast liquid. Pour into flour mixture, combining to make a dough. On a floured surface, knead dough until smooth and elastic. Cover and let rise in a warm place 1 hour.

To make rye dough, use the same method as for plain dough. Add ground aniseed to yeast liquid with butter and eggs. Cover dough and let rise in a warm place 1 hour. Sprinkle a large baking sheet with flour.

Divide plain and rye dough into 2 pieces. On a floured surface, lightly knead a piece of each dough together; shape into a loaf. Repeat with remaining 2 pieces. Place 2 loaves on floured baking sheet. Cover and let stand in a warm place 30 minutes. Preheat oven to 425°F (220°C).

Brush loaves with water and sprinkle with aniseed. Bake 30 to 40 minutes or until loaves sound hollow when tapped on undersides.

Strong Rye Bread

Starter Dough:
1 tablespoon milk
3 tablespoons water
1/2 teaspoon oil
1/2 teaspoon active dry yeast
1 tablespoon warm water (110°F, 43°C)
1/2 teaspoon sugar
1/2 cup (50 g) white bread flour
1 teaspoon salt

Rye Bread Dough:
3 cups plus 2 tablespoons (750 ml) warm water (110°F, 43°C)
6-1/2 cups (750 g) coarse rye flour
2-1/4 cups (250 g) whole-wheat flour
2 teaspoons salt
Additional lukewarm water
Cold water

To make starter dough, put milk, 3 tablespoons water and oil in a small saucepan; bring to a boil. Cool until lukewarm. Blend yeast, 1 tablespoon warm water and sugar in a small bowl; let stand 5 minutes or until the surface is frothy. Sift flour and salt into a medium bowl. Add lukewarm milk mixture to yeast liquid. Stir into flour; mix until blended. Cover and let stand 12 to 18 hours.
To make rye bread dough, combine starter dough and 2 cups plus 2 tablespoons (500 ml) warm water. Warm a large bowl.

Mix rye flour and whole-wheat flour in warmed bowl. Make a well in the center of flour mixture; pour in starter dough. Stir half the flour mixture into starter dough until a thick flowing dough is formed. Cover bowl with a cloth towel and let rise in a warm place overnight.

The next day, add 1 cup (250 ml) warm water and salt to dough. Mix remaining flour into dough. On a floured surface, knead dough until firm. Warm a large bowl and sprinkle lightly with flour. Shape dough into a ball; place in prepared bowl. Cover with a cloth towel and let rise in a warm place 3 hours.

Line a large baking sheet with foil. With floured hands, shape dough into a flat round loaf. Place on prepared baking sheet and let rise at room temperature 1-1/2 to 2 hours. During this time brush top of loaf 3 or 4 times with lukewarm water so no crust forms. Cut crisscross patterns on top of risen loaf with a sharp knife. Preheat oven to 400°F (205°C). Bake 2 hours or until loaf sounds hollow when tapped on underside.

Turn off oven. Remove bread; brush with cold water and return to oven for a few minutes to dry.

Cook's Tip

Bread made from rye flour has a good flavor and will remain fresh longer than ordinary bread.

Hearty Peasant Bread

Pinch of sugar
About 3-3/4 cups (900 ml) warm water (110°F, 43°C)
1-1/2 pkgs. active dry yeast
8 cups (1 kg) rye flour
Double quantity Starter Dough, page 163
8 oz. (225 g) sliced bacon
2 teaspoons salt
1-3/4 cups (200 g) shredded Emmenthal cheese
1 cup (100 g) chopped almonds
3 tablespoons chopped parsley
Water
Additional flour

Stir sugar into warm water and sprinkle with yeast. Let stand 5 minutes or until the surface is frothy. Stir gently to moisten any dry particles remaining on top. Place half the flour in a large bowl. Add yeast liquid to flour with starter dough, combining to make a dough. On a floured surface, knead dough until smooth. Cover and let rise overnight at room temperature.

Lightly broil bacon. Drain on paper towels; chop very finely. Preheat oven to 425°F (220°C). Mix bacon, salt, cheese, almonds, parsley and remaining flour into dough. Knead until smooth. Sprinkle baking sheets with flour.

Shape dough into 2 round loaves; place on floured baking sheets. Brush tops of loaves with water and sprinkle with additional flour. Using a sharp knife, mark tops with a crisscross pattern. Bake 20 to 30 minutes or until loaves sound hollow when tapped on undersides.

French Onion Loaves

Pinch of sugar
About 3-3/4 cups (900 ml) warm water (110°F, 43°C)
1-1/2 pkgs. active dry yeast
8 cups (1 kg) rye flour
Double quantity Starter Dough, page 163
2 teaspoons salt
1/2 teaspoon freshly ground black pepper
Generous pinch of ground cardamom
4 medium onions
2 tablespoons (25 g) butter or margarine
Water
Additional flour

Stir sugar into warm water and sprinkle with yeast. Let stand 5 minutes or until the surface is frothy. Stir gently to moisten any dry particles remaining on top. Put half the flour into a large bowl. Add yeast liquid to flour with starter dough, combining to make a dough. On a floured surface, knead dough until smooth. Cover and let rise in a warm place overnight.

Mix salt, pepper, cardamom and remaining flour into dough. Knead until smooth. Peel and finely chop onions. Melt butter or margarine in a medium skillet. Add half the onions; cook until lightly browned. Drain well; knead cooked onion into dough with remaining raw onion. Sprinkle a baking sheet with flour.

Shape dough into 3 loaves about 14 inches (35 cm) long; place on floured baking sheets. Cover and let stand in a warm place 15 minutes. Preheat oven to 450°F (230°C).

Brush loaves with water and sprinkle with a little additional flour. Using a fine sharp knife, make several diagonal cuts across tops of loaves. Bake 30 minutes or until loaves sound hollow when tapped on undersides.

Spiced Flat Cakes

1 cup (250 ml) warm water (110°F, 43°C)
1/2 cup (125 ml) warm milk (110°F, 43°C)
Pinch of sugar
2 pkgs. active dry yeast
3-1/4 cups (375 g) rye flour
3-1/4 cups (375 g) whole-wheat flour
1 teaspoon salt
2 teaspoons caraway seeds
2 teaspoons crushed coriander seeds
Additional flour

Combine warm water and warm milk in a medium bowl. Stir in sugar and sprinkle with yeast. Let stand 5 minutes or until the surface is frothy. Stir gently to moisten any dry particles remaining on top. Put rye flour and whole-wheat flour into a large bowl. Stir salt, caraway seeds and coriander into yeast liquid. Pour into flour, combining to make a dough. On a floured surface, knead dough until smooth. Cover and let rise in a warm place until doubled in size, about 30 minutes. Brush baking sheets with oil.

Divide dough into 4 equal pieces. On a floured surface, roll out each piece to a large, round flat cake. Place on baking sheets. Sprinkle cakes with a little additional flour. Let stand in a warm place 30 minutes. Preheat oven to 450°F (230°C).

Bake 15 to 20 minutes or until crisp and golden.

Herb Ring Loaf

Pinch of sugar
1 cup (250 ml) warm water (110°F, 43°C)
2 pkgs. active dry yeast
2-3/4 cups (300 g) rye flour
2-3/4 cups (300 g) whole-wheat flour
2 teaspoons salt
4 tablespoons (50 g) butter
1 tablespoon chopped fresh mixed herbs,
   such as marjoram, sage, tarragon, basil
4 tablespoons chopped parsley
Water
Additional flour

Stir sugar into warm water and sprinkle with yeast. Let stand 5 minutes or until the surface is frothy. Stir gently to moisten any dry particles remaining on top. Put rye flour, whole-wheat flour and salt into a large bowl. Melt butter; cool slightly. Stir butter, herbs and parsley into yeast liquid. Pour into flour mixture, combining to make a dough. On a floured surface, knead dough until smooth. Cover and let rise in a warm place 30 minutes. Grease a baking sheet.

Shape risen dough into a round flat loaf. Make a hole in the center of the loaf with a wooden spoon; rotate spoon to make hole larger until you have a ring. Place on greased baking sheet. Cover and let stand in a warm place 30 minutes. Preheat oven to 425°F (220°C).

Brush loaf with water; sprinkle with a little additional flour. Make small slashes in top of loaf with a knife. Bake 30 minutes or until loaf sounds hollow when tapped on underside.

Country Loaves

Savory Veal Loaf

Filling:
1 (1-3/4-lb., 785-g) veal tenderloin
1 teaspoon salt
1 teaspoon paprika
3 tablespoons oil
1 large onion
6 tablespoons chopped green peppercorns
3 tablespoons mustard
Pinch of dried rosemary
Pinch of dried sage

Yeast Dough:
1 (13-3/4-oz., 390-g) pkg. hot roll mix
3/4 cup (185 ml) warm water (110°F, 43°C)
1 egg
1 tablespoon milk

To make filling, season meat with salt and paprika. Heat oil in a skillet; fry meat 15 minutes, turning frequently. Let cool.
Peel onion; chop finely. Finely chop green peppercorns. Preheat oven to 400°F (205°C). Combine mustard, rosemary, sage, onion and peppercorns in a small bowl. Spread mixture over cooled meat. Grease a baking sheet.
To make yeast dough, prepare hot roll mix with warm water and egg according to package instructions. On a floured surface, roll out dough to a rectangle large enough to enclose meat. Place meat on dough and fold dough over carefully to cover it completely. Press edges together firmly to seal. Place loaf seam-side down on greased baking sheet. Brush with milk. Bake 35 minutes or until a rich golden brown. Serve warm or cold.

Savory Chicken Loaves

Yeast Dough:
Pinch of sugar
Scant 2 cups (250 ml) warm water (110°F, 43°C)
1 pkg. active dry yeast
4 cups (500 g) rye flour
1 teaspoon salt
1 quantity Starter Dough, page 163

Filling:
2 tablespoons (20 g) butter
Salt and pepper
4 (6-oz., 175-g) chicken breast portions
4 green onions, finely chopped
3/4 cup (50 g) chopped mushrooms
8 oz. (225 g) bulk pork sausage
1 tablespoon chopped herbs
1 egg yolk
1 tablespoon half-and-half
Pinch each of ground coriander and allspice
1 egg yolk, beaten
Caraway seeds

To make yeast dough, stir sugar into water; sprinkle with yeast. Let stand 5 minutes or until frothy. Stir gently. Put flour and salt into a bowl. Add yeast mixture liquid and starter dough to make a dough. On a floured surface, knead until smooth. Cover and let rise overnight at room temperature.
To make filling, melt butter in a skillet; season chicken and cook gently in butter. Cool. Mix green onions, mushrooms, sausage, herbs, 1 egg yolk, half-and-half, coriander and allspice in a bowl. Preheat oven to 400°F (205°C). Mold sausage mixture around each chicken portion. Flour a baking sheet. Knead dough. Roll out 1/4 inch (5 mm) thick. Cut into 4 rounds; place a chicken portion on each. Fold dough over chicken; press edges together. Place on baking sheet. Brush with egg yolk; sprinkle with caraway seeds. Bake 30 minutes or until golden.

Poppy Seed Rolls

Yeast Dough:
Pinch of sugar
1 cup (250 ml) warm milk (110°F, 43°C)
2 pkgs. active dry yeast
4 cups (500 g) all-purpose flour
1 teaspoon salt
4 tablespoons (50 g) butter or margarine
1 egg
Pinch each of pepper and grated nutmeg

Glaze:
1 egg yolk
1 tablespoon milk
3 tablespoons poppy seeds

To make yeast dough, stir sugar into warm milk and sprinkle with yeast. Let stand 5 minutes or until the surface is frothy. Stir gently to moisten any dry particles remaining on top. Sift flour and salt into a large bowl. Melt butter or margarine; cool slightly. Lightly beat butter or margarine, egg, pepper and nutmeg into yeast mixture. Pour into flour mixture, combining to make a dough. On a floured surface, knead dough until smooth. Cover and let rise until doubled in size. Grease baking sheets.

Lightly knead risen dough. Break off golf-ball size pieces. With floured hands, shape pieces into rounds. Place on greased baking sheets; press down to flatten slightly. Let rise in a warm place 20 minutes. Preheat oven to 450°F (230°C).
To make glaze, beat egg yolk with milk. Brush over rolls and sprinkle with poppy seeds. Cut a cross on the top of each roll. Bake 15 to 20 minutes or until rolls sound hollow when tapped on undersides.

Crusty Rye Rolls

Pinch of sugar
About 2 cups (450 ml) warm water (110°F, 43°C)
1 pkg. active dry yeast
2 cups (300 g) all-purpose flour
1-1/3 cups (200 g) rye flour
1 quantity Starter Dough, page 163
1 teaspoon salt
Water
Additional flour

Stir sugar into warm water and sprinkle with yeast. Let stand 5 minutes or until the surface is frothy. Stir gently to moisten any dry particles remaining on top. Put half the all-purpose and rye flours into a large bowl. Add yeast mixture and starter dough to flour, combining to make a dough. On a floured surface, knead dough until smooth. Cover and let rise overnight in a warm place.

Preheat oven to 450°F (230°C). Grease baking sheets. Work remaining flour and salt into risen dough. Knead dough thoroughly until smooth. Divide dough into 16 pieces; shape into round rolls. Arrange rolls on greased baking sheets. Brush with water and sprinkle with additional flour. Make a cut in each roll with a knife. Bake 20 to 25 minutes or until rolls sound hollow when tapped on undersides.

Dinner Rolls

Pinch of sugar
1 cup (250 ml) warm milk (110°F, 43°C)
2 pkgs. active dry yeast
4 cups (500 g) white bread flour
1 teaspoon salt
1 egg
1 egg yolk, beaten
Sesame seeds and poppy seeds

Stir sugar into warm milk and sprinkle with yeast. Let stand 5 minutes or until the surface is frothy. Stir gently to moisten any dry particles remaining on top. Sift flour and salt into a large bowl. Lightly beat 1 egg into yeast liquid. Pour into flour mixture, combining to make a dough. On a floured surface, knead dough until smooth and elastic. Cover and let rise until doubled in size. Grease baking sheets.

Divide risen dough into small portions; shape into 8-inch (20-cm) long ropes, about 1 inch (2.5 cm) thick. Make ropes into shapes shown in the illustration. Place on greased baking sheets. Cover and let rise in a warm place 20 minutes. Preheat oven to 450°F (230°C).

Brush rolls with egg yolk. Sprinkle some of the rolls with sesame seeds and others with poppy seeds. Bake 10 to 15 minutes or until rolls are golden brown and sound hollow when tapped on undersides.

Milk Crescents

1 teaspoon sugar
1 cup (250 ml) warm milk (110°F, 43°C)
2 pkgs. active dry yeast
4 cups (500 g) all-purpose flour
1/2 teaspoon salt
2 tablespoons (30 g) butter or margarine
1 egg
1 egg yolk, beaten

Stir sugar into warm milk and sprinkle with yeast. Let stand 5 minutes or until the surface is frothy. Stir gently to moisten any dry particles remaining on top. Sift flour and salt into a large bowl. Melt butter or margarine; cool slightly. Lightly beat butter or margarine and 1 egg into yeast mixture. Pour into flour mixture, combining to make a dough. On a floured surface, knead dough until smooth and elastic. Cover and let rise in a warm place until doubled in size.

Divide risen dough into golf-ball size pieces and shape into balls. On a floured surface, roll out each ball into a triangle with sides about 6 inches (15 cm) long. Press point of each triangle firmly onto a baking sheet. Starting at the long side opposite the point, roll up triangles using both hands. Seal points of triangles to rolls with a little egg yolk. Curve each roll into a crescent. Arrange on baking sheet; brush with beaten egg yolk. Cover and let rise in a warm place 15 to 20 minutes. Preheat oven to 450°F (230°C).

Bake crescents 10 to 15 minutes or until golden. Serve hot.

Poppy Seed Braids

Pinch of sugar
1 cup (250 ml) warm water (110°F, 43°C)
2 pkgs. active dry yeast
4 cups (500 g) all-purpose flour
1 teaspoon salt
1 egg
Water
Poppy seeds

Stir sugar into warm water and sprinkle with yeast. Let stand 5 minutes or until the surface is frothy. Stir gently to moisten any dry particles remaining on top. Sift flour and salt into a large bowl. Lightly beat egg into yeast mixture. Pour into flour mixture, combining to make a dough. On a floured surface, knead dough until smooth. Cover and let rise in a warm place until doubled in size, about 30 minutes. Grease a baking sheet.

Divide risen dough into golf-ball size pieces. Make each piece into 3 thin ropes about 6 inches (15 cm) long. Using 3 ropes at a time, weave into small braids. Brush braids with water and sprinkle with poppy seeds. Arrange on greased baking sheet. Cover and let rise in a warm place about 15 minutes. Preheat oven to 450°F (230°C).

Bake 10 to 20 minutes or until braids sound hollow when tapped on undersides. Serve hot.

Croissants

Pinch of sugar
1 cup (250 ml) warm milk (110°F, 43°C)
2 pkgs. active dry yeast
4-1/2 cups (550 g) all-purpose flour
1 teaspoon salt
1 cup (225 g) butter
1 egg
1 egg yolk, beaten

Stir sugar into milk and sprinkle with yeast. Let stand 5 minutes or until frothy. Stir gently to moisten any dry particles remaining on top. Sift 4 cups (500 g) flour and salt into a large bowl. Melt 4 tablespoons (50 g) butter; cool slightly. Lightly beat butter and whole egg into yeast mixture. Pour into flour mixture, combining to make a dough. On a floured surface, knead dough until smooth. Cover and let rise in a warm place 1 hour.

Knead risen dough lightly and roll out to an 14x8-inch (35x20-cm) rectangle. Work the rest of the flour into remaining butter; refrigerate until firm. Divide butter and flour mixture into 3 portions. Mark dough rectangle into 3 sections by drawing lines parallel to short sides. Dot a third of butter mixture over top two-thirds of dough leaving a border around the edge. Fold bottom third of dough over middle third and bring top third down over that. Press edges together. Give dough 1 turn in a clockwise direction. Roll out to original size. Refrigerate 30 minutes. Repeat folding, rolling and refrigerating process twice more with remaining butter mixture. Repeat twice more without butter mixture.

Roll out dough to a 20-inch (50-cm) square. Cut into sixteen 5-inch (12.5-cm) squares. Roll up each square diagonally, going from 1 corner to the opposite corner; curve into crescents. Place on baking sheets. Brush with egg yolk. Let rise in a warm place 30 minutes. Preheat oven to 425°F (220°C).

Bake croissants 5 minutes then reduce heat to 375°F (190°C) and bake 15 minutes longer or until golden.

Brioches

1 teaspoon sugar
1/2 cup (125 ml) warm milk (110°F, 43°C)
2 pkgs. active dry yeast
4 cups (500 g) all-purpose flour
1/2 teaspoon salt
3/4 cup plus 2 tablespoons (200 g) butter
4 eggs
1 egg yolk, beaten

Stir sugar into warm milk and sprinkle with yeast. Let stand 5 minutes or until the surface is frothy. Stir gently to moisten any dry particles remaining on top. Sift flour and salt into a large bowl. Melt butter; cool slightly. Lightly beat butter and 4 eggs into yeast mixture. Pour into flour mixture, combining to make a dough. On a floured surface, knead dough until smooth. Cover and let rise in a warm place 30 minutes. Grease 20 small brioche or muffin pan cups.

Knead risen dough lightly. Take three-fourths of the dough and shape into about 20 small balls. Place in greased pans. Make an equal number of smaller pear-shape pieces from remaining dough. Make a small hollow in dough in pans; place smaller pieces of dough on top with larger end in hollow. Brush brioches with egg yolk. Let rise in a warm place 15 minutes. Preheat oven to 425°F (220°C).

Bake brioches about 15 minutes or until risen and golden brown. Cool on a rack.

Country Plum Strudel

Pastry:
1 tablespoon (15 g) lard
1/2 cup (125 ml) warm water
1 egg
Pinch of salt
2-1/4 cups (250 g) all-purpose flour

Filling:
2 lbs. (1 kg) plums
1/2 cup plus 2 tablespoons (140 g) butter
2 cups (100 g) fresh white breadcrumbs
1/4 cup plus 2 tablespoons (75 g)
  granulated sugar
Additional butter
Powdered sugar
Whipped cream

To make pastry, melt lard and pour into a medium bowl. Add warm water, egg and salt; beat well. Sift flour on top; mix to a smooth dough. Roll dough into a ball; return to bowl. Cover and let stand 1 hour.

On a large floured cloth, roll out dough as thinly as possible. Remove cloth and stretch dough further with your hands, working from the middle outwards until it is paper thin. If dough tears, join it together immediately. Put dough back on cloth. Preheat oven to 400°F (205°C). Grease a baking sheet.

To make filling, wash and quarter plums, removing pits. Melt butter and reserve 2 tablespoons. Combine remaining butter and breadcrumbs in a small bowl. Spread breadcrumb mixture over two-thirds of dough, leaving bottom third uncovered. Arrange plums on top of breadcrumb mixture; sprinkle with granulated sugar. Spread a little additional butter on uncovered third of dough. With the help of the cloth, roll up dough starting from plum and breadcrumb covered side. Place strudel on greased baking sheet. Brush with reserved butter. Bake 40 minutes or until golden brown. Sift powdered sugar over strudel. Serve warm with whipped cream.

Note: To make Apple Strudel, as illustrated, use 1-1/2 lbs. (675 g) cooking apples, peeled, cored and sliced, and 1/3 cup (50 g) raisins instead of plums.

Nut Strudel

2 egg yolks
1/4 cup plus 2 tablespoons (80 g) sugar
4 tablespoons (50 g) butter
1-3/4 cups (200 g) finely chopped or ground walnuts
3/4 cup (75 g) plain cookie crumbs
1/2 teaspoon ground cinnamon
Grated peel of 1/2 lemon
1-1/2 tablespoons rum
1/3 cup (50 g) raisins
2 to 3 tablespoons milk
3/4 (17-1/4-oz., 489-g) pkg. frozen puff pastry, thawed
1 egg yolk, beaten
Whipped cream

Beat egg yolks and sugar in a medium bowl until thick and creamy. Melt butter; combine with walnuts, cookie crumbs, cinnamon, lemon peel, rum and raisins in a medium bowl. Stir into egg yolk mixture. Add just enough milk to make a thick mixture. Sprinkle a baking sheet with water.

On a floured surface, roll out three-fourths of puff pastry dough to a 12x10-inch (30x25-cm) rectangle. Place filling down the center of rectangle. Brush edges with egg yolk; fold dough over filling, pressing edges together to seal. Place seam-side down on dampened baking sheet. Brush with egg yolk. Roll out remaining dough; cut into strips with a pastry cutter. Arrange strips in a lattice pattern on top of strudel; brush with egg yolk. Refrigerate 15 minutes. Preheat oven to 425°F (220°C).

Bake strudel 35 to 45 minutes, covering top with foil if it is becoming too brown. Serve warm with whipped cream.

Apple Fritters

Filling:
1/4 cup plus 2 tablespoons (75 g) sugar
3/4 teaspoon ground cinnamon
3 tablespoons rum
4 large ripe apples

Batter:
1-1/4 cups (125 g) all-purpose flour
1/2 teaspoon baking powder
Pinch of salt
2 eggs, separated
1 tablespoon olive oil
3/4 cup (175 ml) beer
Oil to deep-fry
1/2 cup (100 g) sugar
1 teaspoon ground cinnamon

To make filling, combine sugar, cinnamon and rum in a shallow dish. Peel and core apples; cut into 1/2-inch (1-cm) thick slices. Turn apple slices in sugar mixture. Cover and set aside 30 minutes, turning apple slices once or twice so flavor will be absorbed.

To make batter, sift flour and baking powder together into a medium bowl. Add salt, egg yolks and 1 tablespoon olive oil; beat until smooth. Stir in beer. Beat egg whites until stiff; fold into batter.

Heat oil to 360°F (180°C) in a deep-frying pan. Dip apple slices in batter so they are thoroughly coated. Fry in hot oil 8 to 10 minutes or until golden brown. Turn during cooking with a slotted spoon.

Lift out cooked fritters with slotted spoon; drain on paper towels. Mix sugar and cinnamon; sprinkle over hot fritters. Serve warm.

Sweet Plum Rounds

Yeast Dough:
1/4 cup plus 2 tablespoons (80 g) sugar
1 cup (250 ml) warm milk (110°F, 43°C)
2 pkgs. active dry yeast
4 cups (500 g) all-purpose flour
Pinch of salt
4 tablespoons (50 g) butter
Grated peel of 1/2 lemon
1 egg

Filling:
1 lb. (500 g) cream cheese
4 tablespoons (50 g) butter, softened
1-1/4 cups (280 g) sugar
2 eggs, separated
1 tablespoon cornstarch
1 tablespoon rum
1-1/2 cups (250 g) poppy seeds, ground
1 tablespoon fresh white breadcrumbs
1 cup (250 ml) milk
1 egg yolk, beaten
Generous 1 cup (250 g) drained cooked or canned plums, pureed

To make yeast dough, follow method for Dresden Slices, page 179, adding lemon peel with melted butter.
To make filling, beat cream cheese, butter, 3/4 cup plus 2 tablespoons (200 g) sugar, egg yolks, cornstarch and rum in a large bowl. Beat egg whites until stiff; fold into cream cheese mixture. Combine poppy seeds, remaining sugar, breadcrumbs and milk in a medium saucepan; bring to a boil. Cool.

Divide dough into golf-ball size pieces; shape into 3-1/2-inch (9-cm) rounds. Make a rim; brush with egg yolk. Put 4 small spoonfuls each of cheese mixture and poppy seed mixture alternately into each round. Put a spoonful of plum puree in center. Cover and let rise 10 minutes in a warm place. Preheat oven to 400°F (205°C). Bake rounds 20 to 25 minutes or until golden.

Creamy Raisin Squares

Yeast Dough:
1/4 cup (50 g) sugar
1/2 cup (125 ml) warm milk (110°F, 43°C)
1-1/2 pkgs. active dry yeast
3 cups (350 g) all-purpose flour
Pinch of salt
4 tablespoons (50 g) margarine
2 eggs

Topping:
1-1/4 cups (300 ml) whipping cream
3 eggs, separated
1/4 cup (50 g) sugar
1 tablespoon semolina flour
1/2 cup (75 g) raisins

To make yeast dough, stir a pinch of sugar into warm milk and sprinkle with yeast. Let stand 5 minutes or until the surface is frothy. Stir gently to moisten any dry particles remaining on top. Sift flour, remaining sugar and salt into a large bowl. Melt margarine; cool slightly. Lightly beat margarine and eggs into yeast mixture. Pour into flour mixture, combining to make a dough. On a floured surface, knead dough until smooth and elastic. Cover and let rise in a warm place 1 hour. Grease a 13x9-inch (33x23-cm) cake pan.

Knead risen dough lightly. Roll out to fit bottom of cake pan. Place dough in pan. Preheat oven to 400°F (205°C).
To make topping, mix cream, yolks, sugar and semolina flour in a medium bowl. Beat whites until stiff; fold in raisins. Fold egg white mixture into cream mixture; spread over dough.

Bake 20 to 25 minutes or until filling is golden on top. Cut into squares and serve warm.

Sugar Buns

Yeast Dough:
1/4 cup (50 g) sugar
1 cup (250 ml) warm milk
    (110°F, 43°C)
2 pkgs. active dry yeast
4 cups (500 g) all-purpose flour
1 teaspoon salt
3 tablespoons (40 g) butter
2 eggs
Grated peel of 1/2 lemon

Filling & Glaze:
3/4 cup plus 2 tablespoons (200 g) butter,
    melted
1/2 cup (100 g) sugar
1/2 cup (75 g) raisins
Additional 3 tablespoons (40 g) sugar

To make yeast dough, stir a pinch of sugar into warm milk and sprinkle with yeast. Let stand 5 minutes or until the surface is frothy. Stir gently to moisten any dry particles remaining on top. Sift flour, remaining sugar and salt into a large bowl. Melt butter; cool slightly. Lightly beat butter, eggs and lemon peel into yeast mixture. Pour into flour mixture, combining to make a dough. On a floured surface, knead dough until smooth and elastic. Cover and let rise in a warm place until doubled in size, about 30 minutes.

To fill and glaze buns, divide risen dough into golf-ball size pieces. On a floured surface, roll out pieces of dough to 8x3-inch (20x7.5-cm) strips. Brush with a fourth of the butter; sprinkle with 1/2 cup (100 g) sugar and raisins. Fold over lengthwise and roll up, starting from short side. Pour 5 tablespoons (65 g) of the remaining butter into a round 9-inch (23-cm) cake pan. Place buns in pan rolled-sides up. Cover and let rise in a warm place 15 minutes. Preheat oven to 425°F (220°C).

Brush with remaining butter; sprinkle with additional sugar. Bake 40 to 50 minutes or until a rich golden brown. Serve warm.

Batch Buns

These buns are made using the same dough as above without the filling. Make golf-ball size pieces of the dough into round bun shapes and place in the butter in the cake pan. Let rise then brush with 4 tablespoons (50 g) melted butter. Bake in a preheated 425°F (220°C) oven for 35 minutes.

Buttermilk Waffles

1/2 cup plus 1 tablespoon (125 g) butter, softened
1/4 cup (50 g) sugar
2 tablespoons (25 g) vanilla sugar, page 18
Pinch of salt
4 eggs
2-1/4 cups (250 g) all-purpose flour
1 teaspoon baking powder
About 1 cup (250 ml) buttermilk

In a medium bowl, beat butter, unflavored sugar, vanilla sugar, salt and eggs until creamy. Sift flour with baking powder. Stir into egg mixture alternately with buttermilk. Add enough buttermilk to make a smooth batter.

Heat the waffle iron, brushing the inside well with oil. Pour a little of the mixture carefully into waffle iron, taking care not to overfill it. Cook waffles 4 to 6 minutes or until golden brown.

Cook's Tip

Waffles taste best when eaten almost immediately, having cooled just a little. They are good topped with a spoonful of whipped cream.

Cream-Filled Waffles

Waffle Batter:
1/4 cup (50 g) sugar
2 cups plus 2 tablespoons (500 ml) warm milk (110°F, 43°C)
2 pkgs. active dry yeast
3-1/4 cups (375 g) all-purpose flour
Pinch of salt
1/2 cup plus 1 tablespoon (125 g) butter
4 eggs
Grated peel of 1/2 lemon
Oil

Filling:
1-1/4 cups (300 ml) whipping cream
1/4 cup (25 g) powdered sugar, sifted
Additional powdered sugar, sifted

To make waffle batter, stir a pinch of sugar into warm milk and sprinkle with yeast. Let stand 5 minutes or until the surface is frothy. Stir gently to moisten any dry particles remaining on top. Sift flour, remaining sugar and salt into a large bowl. Melt butter; cool slightly. Lightly beat butter, eggs and lemon peel into yeast mixture. Pour into flour mixture. Beat well until batter begins to bubble. Cover and let rise in a warm place 25 minutes.

Heat the waffle iron, brushing the inside well with oil. Put a little of the batter into waffle iron for each waffle. Cook until golden brown, 5 to 7 minutes, depending on the temperature of the iron. Break up waffles into sections. Cool on a rack.
To make filling, beat cream and 1/4 cup (25 g) powdered sugar until stiff. Put into a pastry bag fitted with a fluted nozzle. Fill pairs of cooled waffles with piped whipped cream mixture. Sprinkle with additional powdered sugar.

Apricot Pastry Pretzels

2-3/4 cups (300 g) all-purpose flour, sifted
1 egg yolk
1/2 cup (100 g) sugar
3/4 cup plus 2 tablespoons (200 g) butter, cut in small pieces
3/4 (17-1/4-oz., 489-g) pkg. frozen puff pastry, thawed
1 egg yolk, beaten
1/2 cup (175 g) apricot jam

In a medium bowl, mix flour, 1 egg yolk, sugar and butter to make a dough. Press dough into a ball and wrap in foil or plastic wrap. Refrigerate 2 hours.

On a floured surface, roll out pastry dough to a 20x14-inch (50x35-cm) rectangle. Roll out refrigerated dough to the same size. Brush refrigerated dough with egg yolk; lay puff pastry dough on top and press firmly. Cut into 3/4-inch (1.5-cm) wide strips. Twist strips into spirals, so puff pastry dough is on the outside. Press ends together firmly; make into pretzel shapes as illustrated. Arrange pretzels on a baking sheet. Refrigerate 15 minutes. Preheat oven to 425°F (220°C).

Bake 15 minutes or until golden. Heat jam and press through a strainer to obtain jelly. Brush jelly over warm pretzels.

Cook's Tip

The pretzels may be frozen, but if you plan to do this, do not brush them with jelly. Pack them while warm and freeze at once. The pretzels can also be glazed with Glacé Frosting, page 14, as illustrated.

Featherlight Cream Sponges

Cake:
4 eggs, separated, plus 1 egg yolk
1/4 cup plus 2 tablespoons (80 g) sugar
1/4 cup plus 2 tablespoons (45 g) all-purpose flour
1/2 teaspoon baking powder
Pinch of salt
3 tablespoons (40 g) butter, melted

Filling:
1-1/4 cups (300 ml) whipping cream
1-1/2 cups (225 g) fruit, raspberries, strawberries or red currants
Powdered sugar, sifted

Line baking sheets with baking parchment or waxed paper. Grease waxed paper lightly. Draw twelve 5-inch (13-cm) circles on baking parchment or waxed paper with a pencil. Preheat oven to 425°F (220°C).

To make cake, beat egg whites until stiff; fold in half the sugar. Beat 5 egg yolks and remaining sugar in a medium bowl set over hot water until thick and creamy. Remove from heat. Sift flour, baking powder and salt together; fold into egg yolk mixture with butter. Fold in beaten egg whites. Put batter into a pastry bag fitted with a plain nozzle. Pipe batter onto circles in a spiral pattern; smooth the surfaces. Bake sponges 10 to 12 minutes or until just firm to the touch.

Invert sponge rounds onto a cloth towel with lining paper still attached. Sprinkle lining paper with cold water and peel it off gently. Fold sponges carefully in half. Cool under cloth towel.

To make filling, beat cream until stiff. Put whipped cream into a pastry bag fitted with a fluted nozzle. Place a little fruit in each cooled sponge shell; fill with piped whipped cream. Sprinkle shells with powdered sugar.

Cream Cheese Crumb Cake

Yeast Dough:
1/4 cup (50 g) sugar
1/2 cup (125 ml) warm milk
 (110°F, 43°C)
1-1/2 pkgs. active dry yeast
3 cups (350 g) all-purpose flour
Pinch of salt
4 tablespoons (50 g) butter
2 eggs

Filling:
3/4 cup (180 g) butter, softened
3/4 cup (180 g) sugar
3 eggs
1-1/4 lbs. (575 g) cream cheese
1/4 cup (25 g) cornstarch
Grated peel of 1 lemon
2/3 cup (100 g) raisins, if desired

Topping:
1-1/2 cups (180 g) all-purpose flour
1/4 cup (50 g) sugar
Pinch of salt
1/4 teaspoon ground cinnamon
6 tablespoons (75 g) butter

To make yeast dough, stir a pinch of sugar into warm milk and sprinkle with yeast. Let stand 5 minutes or until the surface is frothy. Stir gently to moisten any dry particles remaining on top. Sift flour, remaining sugar and salt into a large bowl. Melt butter; cool slightly. Lightly beat butter and eggs into yeast mixture. Pour into flour mixture, combining to make a dough. On a floured surface, knead dough lightly. Cover and let rise in a warm place 1 hour. Grease a 13x9-inch (33x23-cm) cake pan.

To make filling, cream butter and sugar in a medium bowl until light and fluffy. Beat in eggs, cream cheese, cornstarch, lemon peel and raisins, if used.

Knead risen dough; roll out to fit bottom of greased cake pan. Place dough in pan. Spread cream cheese mixture on top.

To make topping, mix flour, sugar, salt and cinnamon in a medium bowl. Melt butter; gradually add to flour mixture using a fork. Mixture should resemble crumbs. Sprinkle crumb topping over cream cheese filling. Let stand 15 minutes. Preheat oven to 400°F (205°C).

Bake 30 to 40 minutes or until topping is golden.

Country Butter Cake

1 cup (225 g) sugar
1 cup (250 ml) warm milk (110°F, 43°C)
3 pkgs. active dry yeast
4 cups (450 g) all-purpose flour
Pinch of salt
1 cup (225 g) butter
1 egg
1 teaspoon ground cinnamon

Stir 1 teaspoon sugar into warm milk and sprinkle with yeast. Let stand 5 minutes or until the surface is frothy. Stir gently to moisten any dry particles remaining on top. Sift flour, 1/4 cup (50 g) sugar and salt into a large bowl. Melt half the butter; cool slightly. Refrigerate remaining butter. Lightly beat melted butter and egg into yeast mixture. Beat into flour mixture to make a dough. On a floured surface, knead dough until smooth and elastic. Cover and let rise in a warm place 1 hour. Grease two 13x9-inch (33x23-cm) cake pans.

Preheat oven to 425°F (220°C). Roll out dough to fit greased pans; place in pans. Make small hollows in the surface of dough. Cut refrigerated butter into small pieces and place in hollows. Mix remaining sugar with cinnamon; sprinkle over cakes. Bake 25 minutes. Cool in pans then cut into slices.

Butter Cream Sandwich Fingers

Yeast Dough:
3/4 cup (175 g) sugar
1 cup (250 ml) warm milk (110°F, 43°C)
1 pkg. active dry yeast
4 cups (500 g) all-purpose flour
7 tablespoons (90 g) butter
1 egg
1/2 teaspoon grated lemon peel
1 cup (100 g) chopped almonds
1 tablespoon cold milk

Filling:
6 tablespoons (75 g) sweet butter, softened
1-1/4 cups (175 g) powdered sugar, sifted
1/2 teaspoon vanilla extract

To make yeast dough, stir a pinch of sugar into warm milk and sprinkle with yeast. Let stand 5 minutes or until the surface is frothy. Stir gently to moisten any dry particles remaining on top. Sift flour and 1/4 cup (50 g) sugar into a large bowl. Melt 4 tablespoons (50 g) butter; cool slightly. Grease a baking sheet. Lightly beat melted butter, egg and lemon peel into yeast mixture. Pour into flour mixture, combining to make a dough. Knead dough on a floured surface. Spread out dough on baking sheet. Cover and let rise in a warm place 1 to 1-1/2 hours.

Preheat oven to 400°F (205°C). Melt remaining butter; mix with remaining sugar and almonds in a small bowl. Stir in cold milk; cool. Spread cooled mixture over risen dough. Bake 40 minutes or until top is a rich golden brown. Cool on baking sheet then cut into fingers.

To make filling, cream butter, powdered sugar and vanilla in a small bowl until light and fluffy. Split each cooled finger in half horizontally. Join fingers together in pairs with butter cream.

Dresden Slices

Yeast Dough:
2 tablespoons (25 g) sugar
1/2 cup (125 ml) warm milk (110°F, 43°C)
1 pkg. active dry yeast
2 cups (225 g) all-purpose flour
Pinch of salt
2 tablespoons (25 g) margarine
1 egg

Filling & Topping:
12 oz. (350 g) cream cheese
1 cup (200 g) sugar
3 eggs
3 tablespoons (20 g) all-purpose flour
Grated peel of 1 lemon
8 tablespoons (100 g) butter, softened
1 cup (100 g) sliced almonds

To make yeast dough, stir a pinch of sugar into milk; sprinkle with yeast. Let stand 5 minutes or until frothy. Stir gently. Sift flour, remaining sugar and salt into a large bowl. Melt margarine; cool slightly. Lightly beat margarine and egg into yeast mixture. Pour into flour mixture, combining to make a dough. On a floured surface, knead dough lightly. Cover and let rise in a warm place 1 hour. Grease a 13x9-inch (33x23-cm) cake pan.
To make filling and topping, beat cream cheese, half the sugar, 1 egg, half the flour and lemon peel in a medium bowl. Preheat oven to 400°F (205°C). Lightly knead dough; roll out to fit pan. Place in pan. Spread filling over dough. Cream butter and remaining sugar until fluffy. Add remaining flour. Beat in 2 eggs one at a time. Spread topping over cream cheese filling. Sprinkle with almonds. Bake 30 to 40 minutes or until golden. Cool slightly in pan. Cut into slices.

Swiss Plum Slice

1/4 cup (50 g) granulated sugar
1/2 cup (125 ml) warm milk (110°F, 43°C)
1-1/2 pkgs. active dry yeast
3 cups (350 g) all-purpose flour
Pinch of salt
4 tablespoons (50 g) butter
2 eggs
2 lbs. (1 kg) plums
About 1/3 cup (50 g) sugar crystals
1/2 teaspoon ground cinnamon

Stir a pinch of granulated sugar into warm milk and sprinkle with yeast. Let stand 5 minutes or until the surface is frothy. Stir gently to moisten any dry particles remaining on top. Sift flour, remaining granulated sugar and salt into a medium bowl. Melt butter; cool slightly. Lightly beat butter and eggs into yeast mixture. Pour into flour mixture, beating to make a dough. On a floured surface, knead dough lightly. Cover and let rise in a warm place 1 hour. Grease a 13x9-inch (33x23-cm) cake pan.

Wash and pit plums; cut lengthwise into fourths. Knead risen dough lightly; roll out to fit cake pan. Place dough in greased pan. Pierce dough all over with a fork. Arrange plums in overlapping rows on dough. Let rise in a warm place 15 minutes. Preheat oven to 400°F (205°C).

Bake 25 to 30 minutes or until plums are wilted and yeast pastry is puffed up and golden between plums. Sprinkle with sugar crystals and cinnamon while still warm. Cool slightly in pan then cut into squares.

Apple Crumb Cake

Yeast Dough:
2 tablespoons (25 g) sugar
1/2 cup (125 ml) warm milk (110°F, 43°C)
1 pkg. active dry yeast
2 cups (225 g) all-purpose flour
Pinch of salt
2 tablespoons (25 g) butter
1 egg
Grated peel of 1 lemon

Topping:
2-1/2 lbs. (1.25 kg) apples, peeled, cored and sliced
3 cups (350 g) all-purpose flour
3/4 cup plus 2 tablespoons (200 g) sugar
2 tablespoons (25 g) vanilla sugar, page 18
3/4 cup plus 2 tablespoons (200 g) butter, cut in small pieces
Generous 1/2 cup (100 g) dried currants

To make yeast dough, stir a pinch of sugar into warm milk and sprinkle with yeast. Let stand 5 minutes or until frothy. Stir gently to moisten any dry particles remaining on top. Sift flour, remaining sugar and salt into a large bowl. Melt butter; cool slightly. Lightly beat butter, egg and lemon peel into yeast mixture. Pour into flour mixture, combining to make a dough. On a floured surface, knead dough lightly. Cover and let rise in a warm place 1 hour. Grease a 15-1/2x10-1/2-inch (39x27-cm) cake pan.

Knead risen dough lightly; roll out to fit cake pan. Place dough in greased pan.
To make topping, place apples in overlapping rows on dough. Let rise in a warm place 15 minutes. Preheat oven to 400°F (205°C). Sift flour, unflavored sugar and vanilla sugar into a large bowl. Cut in butter with a pastry blender or 2 knives until mixture resembles crumbs. Spread crumb topping over apples; sprinkle with currants. Bake 25 to 35 minutes or until apples are soft and crumb topping is golden. Cool slightly in pan then cut into slices.

Hazelnut Stollen

Yeast Dough:
1/4 cup plus 1 tablespoon (70 g) sugar
1 cup (250 ml) warm milk (110°F, 43°C)
2 pkgs. active dry yeast
4 cups (500 g) all-purpose flour
1/2 teaspoon salt
7 tablespoons (100 g) margarine
1 egg, beaten
Grated peel of 1/2 lemon

Filling & Frosting:
1 cup (100 g) ground almonds
1/2 cup (100 g) firmly packed soft brown sugar
1 cup (100 g) ground hazelnuts
2 egg whites, lightly beaten
3 tablespoons rum
1/2 teaspoon ground cinnamon
1 egg yolk, beaten
1 cup (120 g) powdered sugar, sifted
2 to 3 tablespoons lemon juice
1/2 cup (50 g) chopped toasted hazelnuts, page 47

To make yeast dough, stir a pinch of sugar into milk; sprinkle with yeast. Let stand 5 minutes. Stir gently. Sift flour, remaining sugar and salt into a large bowl. Melt margarine; cool slightly. Stir margarine, egg and lemon peel into yeast mixture. Beat into flour mixture to make a dough. On a floured surface, knead dough. Cover and let rise in a warm place 1 hour.
To make filling and frosting, mix almonds, brown sugar, ground hazelnuts, egg whites, rum and cinnamon. Grease a baking sheet. Knead dough; roll out to an 18-inch (45-cm) square. Spread with filling. Brush edges with egg yolk; roll up. Place on baking sheet; brush with egg yolk. Let stand 15 minutes. Preheat oven to 425°F (220°C). Bake 30 to 40 minutes or until golden. Place on a rack. Blend powdered sugar and lemon juice. Spoon frosting over warm stollen; sprinkle with hazelnuts.

Bohemian Braid

1/4 cup (60 g) granulated sugar
1 cup (250 ml) warm milk (110°F, 43°C)
2 pkgs. active dry yeast
4 cups (500 g) all-purpose flour
Pinch of salt
8 tablespoons (100 g) margarine
1/3 cup (50 g) raisins
1 egg yolk, beaten
3 tablespoons sugar crystals

Stir a pinch of granulated sugar into warm milk and sprinkle with yeast. Let stand 5 minutes or until the surface is frothy. Stir gently to moisten any dry particles remaining on top. Sift flour, remaining granulated sugar and salt into a large bowl. Melt margarine; cool slightly. Stir margarine and raisins into yeast mixture. Beat into flour mixture to make a dough. On a floured surface, knead dough lightly. Cover and let rise in a warm place 1 hour. Grease a baking sheet.

Halve dough. Divide 1 half into three 14-inch (35-cm) strips; use to make a braid. Place braid on greased baking sheet. Using two-thirds of remaining dough, make another smaller braid. From remaining dough, make 2 strips and twist together. Brush large braid with egg yolk. Place smaller braid on top; brush with egg yolk. Place twist on top; brush with egg yolk. Sprinkle loaf with sugar crystals. Let rise in a warm place 15 minutes. Preheat oven to 400°F (205°C).

Bake loaf 25 to 30 minutes or until it sounds hollow when tapped on underside. Cool on a rack.

Creamy Rice Flan

Generous 1/2 cup (100 g) short-grain rice
1-1/4 cups (300 ml) milk
1 cup (250 ml) whipping cream
1/4 teaspoon salt
1/4 cup (50 g) granulated sugar
1/2 (17-1/4-oz., 489-g) pkg. frozen puff pastry, thawed
2 eggs plus 2 egg yolks
Scant 1/4 cup (40 g) chopped mixed candied peel
1/4 cup (50 g) chopped red and yellow candied cherries
1/4 cup (25 g) chopped almonds
1/3 cup (50 g) raisins
Powdered sugar, sifted

Put rice, milk, half-and-half, salt and 3 tablespoons (40 g) granulated sugar into a medium saucepan; bring to a boil. Reduce heat; cover pan and simmer 25 to 30 minutes or until rice is tender and has absorbed most of the liquid. Cool. Preheat oven to 400°F (205°C).

On a floured surface, roll out puff pastry dough to fit a 9-inch (23-cm) flan tin with a removable bottom. Place dough in tin without stretching. Bake blind, page 9, 10 minutes.

Beat eggs and 1 egg yolk into cooled rice mixture. Stir in candied peel. Spread half the mixture in pastry shell. Stir candied cherries, almonds and raisins into remaining mixture. Add to flan; smooth the surface. Beat remaining egg yolk and granulated sugar in a small bowl; pour over filling. Bake flan 25 minutes or until top is golden. Cool slightly in tin. Transfer to a rack to cool completely. Sprinkle cooled flan with powdered sugar.

Chelsea Cake

Yeast Dough:
1/4 cup (60 g) sugar
1 cup (250 ml) warm milk (110°F, 43°C)
3 pkgs. active dry yeast
4 cups (500 g) all-purpose flour
7 tablespoons (100 g) margarine

Filling:
Generous 1 cup (200 g) raisins
3 tablespoons rum
1/2 cup (120 g) butter, melted
1/2 cup plus 1 tablespoon (125 g) sugar
1/2 cup (60 g) ground almonds
2 teaspoons ground cinnamon
1/2 cup (80 g) chopped mixed candied peel
1 egg yolk, beaten
3 tablespoons apricot jam, warmed

To make yeast dough, stir a pinch of sugar into warm milk and sprinkle with yeast. Let stand 5 minutes or until frothy. Stir gently. Sift flour and remaining sugar into a large bowl. Melt margarine; cool slightly. Lightly beat margarine into yeast mixture. Pour into flour mixture, combining to make a dough. On a floured surface, knead dough lightly. Cover and let rise in a warm place 1 hour. Grease a 10-inch (25-cm) flan tin with a removable bottom.
To make filling, put raisins into a small bowl and sprinkle with rum. Cover and set aside. Knead risen dough; roll out 1/8 inch (3 mm) thick. Brush dough with all the melted butter; sprinkle with sugar, almonds, cinnamon, rum-soaked raisins and candied peel. Cut dough into 2-inch (5-cm) wide strips. Roll up 1 strip and place in center of greased flan tin. Curve remaining strips of dough around it. Let rise in a warm place 15 minutes. Preheat oven to 425°F (220°C). Brush cake with egg yolk. Bake 35 minutes or until golden. Cool slightly then brush with warmed jam. Cool completely on a rack.

Arabian Honey Cake

Cake:
6 tablespoons (75 g) butter
3 eggs
1/2 cup plus 1 tablespoon (125 g) sugar
Few drops of vanilla extract
1-1/4 cups (150 g) all-purpose flour
1 teaspoon baking powder
3 tablespoons whipping cream

Topping:
8 tablespoons (100 g) butter
1/4 cup plus 2 tablespoons (80 g) sugar
1/4 cup (75 g) creamed honey or honey spread
3 tablespoons whipping cream
1-1/4 cups (150 g) sliced almonds
1/2 teaspoon ground cinnamon
Grated peel of 1/2 orange

Grease a 10-inch (25-cm) springform cake pan. Preheat oven to 400°F (205°C).
To make cake, melt butter; cool slightly. Put eggs, sugar and vanilla into a medium bowl. Beat until pale and creamy, 5 to 10 minutes with an electric mixer. Sift flour and baking powder into mixture; fold in thoroughly. Stir in butter and cream. Turn batter into greased pan; smooth the surface. Bake 15 minutes or until top is just firm. Make topping while cake is cooking. Do not turn off oven. Leave cake in pan.
To make topping, melt butter in a small saucepan; add sugar, creamed honey or honey spread, cream, almonds, cinnamon and orange peel. Stir ingredients well; bring to a boil. Spread mixture over partially cooked cake; return to oven and bake 15 minutes longer or until almonds are browned. Leave cake in pan until topping begins to set. Transfer to a rack to cool.

Frosted Banana Ring

Cake:
1 cup (225 g) margarine or butter, softened
2/3 cup (150 g) sugar
Pinch of salt
5 eggs, separated
1-1/2 tablespoons (15 g) chopped candied ginger
1 cup (75 g) shredded coconut
Grated peel of 1 lemon
1 lb. (500 g) bananas
Scant 1/4 cup (50 ml) lemon juice
1 tablespoon rum
2-1/4 cups (250 g) all-purpose flour
1 teaspoon baking powder

Frosting:
1-2/3 cups (200 g) powdered sugar, sifted
3 to 4 tablespoons lemon juice

Grease a fluted 9-inch (23-cm) tube cake pan. Preheat oven to 400°F (205°C).

To make cake, cream margarine or butter, sugar and salt in a large bowl until light and fluffy. Add egg yolks one at a time with ginger, coconut and lemon peel. Mix well. Peel bananas and put into a medium bowl. Mash bananas and sprinkle with lemon juice and rum. Fold into egg yolk mixture. Sift flour with baking powder; fold into banana mixture. Beat egg whites until stiff; carefully fold into mixture. Turn batter into pan. Bake 1 to 1-1/4 hours or until a wooden pick or skewer inserted in center comes out clean. Turn out cake on a rack to cool.

To make frosting, combine powdered sugar and lemon juice in a small bowl. Spread frosting over cooled cake.

Cinnamon & Almond Flan

Pastry:
2-1/4 cups (250 g) all-purpose flour
Pinch of salt
1/2 cup plus 1 tablespoon (125 g) margarine, cut in small pieces
1/4 cup plus 2 tablespoons (75 g) sugar
1 egg
3 to 5 tablespoons (50 to 75 ml) ice water

Filling:
3 eggs
1/2 cup (125 ml) whipping cream
1/2 cup (125 ml) milk
2/3 cup (150 g) sugar
Pinch of salt
1 teaspoon ground cinnamon
1/2 teaspoon baking powder
1-3/4 cups (200 g) ground almonds
About 1 cup (60 g) plain cookie crumbs
1/3 cup (50 g) finely chopped candied lemon peel

To make pastry, sift flour and salt into a medium bowl. Using a pastry blender or 2 knives, cut in margarine until evenly distributed and mixture resembles breadcrumbs. With a fork, lightly mix in sugar, egg and enough ice water to make a dough. Press dough into a ball and wrap in foil or plastic wrap. Refrigerate 2 hours.

Preheat oven to 400°F (205°C). On a floured surface, roll out dough to fit a 10-inch (23-cm) flan tin with a removable bottom. Place dough in tin without stretching. Bake blind, page 9, 10 minutes. Do not turn off oven.

To make filling, beat eggs, cream, milk, sugar, salt, cinnamon and baking powder in a medium bowl. Stir in almonds, cookie crumbs and candied peel. Spread filling evenly in pastry shell. Bake flan 45 to 50 minutes or until filling is firm. Cool slightly in tin then transfer to a rack to cool completely.

Mizzi's Fruit Cake

2/3 cup (100 g) dried pitted prunes
1/3 cup (50 g) dried apricots
1/3 cup (50 g) raisins
1 cup (100 g) chopped walnuts
1 cup (225 g) soft margarine
1 cup (225 g) granulated sugar
Pinch of salt
Grated peel of 1 lemon
1/2 teaspoon vanilla extract
4 eggs
3 cups (350 g) all-purpose flour
1 teaspoon baking powder
Powdered sugar

Grease an 8-inch (20-cm) fluted oval or round cake pan. Preheat oven to 325°F (165°C).

Cut prunes and apricots into small pieces; mix with raisins and walnuts in a small bowl. Cream margarine, granulated sugar, salt, lemon peel and vanilla in a large bowl until light and fluffy. Beat in eggs one at a time, adding a tablespoon of flour with each egg after the first. Sift remaining flour with baking powder; fold into egg mixture with dried fruit mixture. Turn batter into greased cake pan; smooth the surface.

Bake 1-1/2 to 1-3/4 hours or until a skewer inserted in center comes out clean. Turn out cake onto a rack to cool. Sift powdered sugar over cooled cake.

Date & Fig Flan

Pastry:
1-3/4 cups (200 g) all-purpose flour
Pinch of salt
7 tablespoons (100 g) butter, cut in small pieces
2 tablespoons (30 g) sugar
1 egg yolk
About 3 tablespoons ice water

Filling:
8 tablespoons (120 g) butter, softened
3/4 cup plus 2 tablespoons (200 g) sugar
4 eggs, separated
Grated peel of 1 lemon
1 teaspoon ground cinnamon
1 teaspoon each of ground nutmeg and ground cloves
1/2 teaspoon salt
1 cup (100 g) ground hazelnuts
3/4 cup (75 g) self-rising flour, sifted
3/4 cup (75 g) chopped walnuts
1/2 cup (75 g) finely chopped dried figs
1/2 cup (75 g) finely chopped dates

To make pastry, sift flour and salt into a large bowl. Using a pastry blender or 2 knives, cut in butter evenly. Lightly mix in sugar, egg yolk and enough ice water to make a dough. Press into a ball and wrap in foil or plastic wrap. Refrigerate 2 hours.

Preheat oven to 350°F (175°C). On a floured surface, roll out dough to fit a 9-inch (23-cm) flan tin with a removable bottom. Place dough in tin without stretching.

To make filling, cream butter and sugar in a large bowl until fluffy. Stir in egg yolks, lemon peel, cinnamon, nutmeg, cloves, salt and hazelnuts. Beat egg whites until stiff; fold into egg yolk mixture. Mix flour, walnuts, figs and dates; fold into egg mixture. Spread filling in pastry shell. Bake 55 to 60 minutes or until a wooden pick inserted in center comes out clean. Cool flan slightly in tin then transfer to a rack to cool completely.

Plum Lattice Tart

Pastry:
2-1/2 cups (300 g) all-purpose flour
Pinch of salt
3/4 cup plus 2 tablespoons (200 g) butter, cut in small pieces
1/4 cup plus 3 tablespoons (100 g) sugar
1 egg yolk

Filling:
2 lbs. (1 kg) plums
Water
3 tablespoons (20 g) cornstarch
2/3 cup (150 g) granulated sugar
2 tablespoons (25 g) butter
1/2 cup (50 g) chopped walnuts
Powdered sugar, sifted

To make pastry, sift flour and salt into a large bowl. Add butter, sugar and egg yolk; knead to a dough. Press into a ball and wrap in foil or plastic wrap. Refrigerate 2 hours.
To make filling, wash and pit plums; cut into fourths. Place in a medium saucepan; add a little water and cook over medium heat 5 minutes. Combine cornstarch and about 1/4 cup (50 ml) cold water; stir into plums with granulated sugar. Continue to cook until thickened, stirring constantly. Remove from heat; stir in butter and walnuts. Let cool.
Preheat oven to 400°F (205°C). On a floured surface, roll out three-fourths of the dough to fit a 9-inch (23-cm) flan tin with a removable bottom. Place dough in tin without stretching. Spread plum filling in pastry shell. Roll out reserved dough; cut into thin strips and arrange in a lattice pattern over plum filling. Bake 35 to 45 minutes or until pastry is golden. Cool slightly in tin then sprinkle with powdered sugar. Remove flan from tin and serve warm.

Grape Cream Flan

Pastry:
2-1/2 cups (300 g) all-purpose flour
3/4 cup plus 2 tablespoons (200 g) butter, cut in small pieces
1/4 cup plus 3 tablespoons (100 g) sugar
1 egg

Filling:
2-1/2 cups (600 ml) milk
Scant 1/2 cup (50 g) cornstarch
2 tablespoons (25 g) sugar
2 eggs, separated
1 lb. (500 g) purple grapes, washed and seeded
2/3 cup (150 ml) whipping cream

To make pastry, sift flour into a large bowl. Using a pastry blender or 2 knives, cut in butter until evenly distributed and mixture resembles breadcrumbs. With a fork, lightly mix in sugar and egg to make a dough. Press into a ball and wrap in foil or plastic wrap. Refrigerate 2 hours.
Preheat oven to 375°F (190°C). On a floured surface, roll out dough to fit a 9-inch (23-cm) flan tin with a removable bottom. Place dough in tin without stretching. Bake blind, page 9, 20 minutes or until golden. Cool.
To make filling, combine 1/3 cup (100 ml) milk, cornstarch, sugar and egg yolks in a medium bowl. Bring remaining milk to a boil in a medium saucepan. Stir hot milk into cornstarch mixture. Return to saucepan and bring to a boil, stirring constantly until thickened. Let custard cool, stirring frequently to prevent a skin forming. Beat egg whites until stiff; fold into cooled custard. Place half the filling in prebaked pastry shell. Reserve 12 grapes for decoration; arrange remainder on top of custard filling. Cover evenly with remaining filling. Refrigerate until set then remove from tin.
Whip cream. Put in a pastry bag fitted with a fluted nozzle. Pipe rosettes onto flan; decorate with reserved grapes.

Baked Vanilla Cheesecake

Pastry:
2-1/4 cups (250 g) all-purpose flour
Pinch of salt
1/2 cup plus 1 tablespoon (125 g) butter, cut in small pieces
2 tablespoons (30 g) sugar
1 egg
3 to 5 tablespoons (50 to 75 ml) ice water

Filling:
1-1/2 lbs. (675 g) cream cheese
Scant 1/4 cup (50 ml) oil
1-1/4 cups (275 g) sugar
3 eggs, separated
1/4 cup (50 g) cornstarch
Few drops of vanilla extract
1/2 cup (125 ml) milk

To make pastry, sift flour and salt into a large bowl. Using a pastry blender or 2 knives, cut in butter until evenly distributed and mixture resembles breadcrumbs. With a fork, lightly mix in sugar, egg and enough ice water to make a dough. Press into a ball and wrap in foil or plastic wrap. Refrigerate 2 hours.

Preheat oven to 350°F (175°C). On a floured surface, roll out dough to fit a 10-inch (25-cm) flan tin with a removable bottom. Place dough in tin without stretching.
To make filling, beat cream cheese, oil, sugar, egg yolks, cornstarch, vanilla and milk in a large bowl until smooth. Beat egg whites until stiff; fold into cream cheese mixture. Pour into pastry shell. Bake 50 to 60 minutes or until a wooden pick inserted in center comes out clean. Turn off oven. Let cheesecake cool in oven with door open slightly. Remove cooled cheesecake from tin and serve.

Rich Lemon Cheesecake

Crumb Crust:
2-1/4 cups (175 g) graham cracker crumbs
6 tablespoons (75 g) margarine, melted

Filling:
1-1/4 lbs. (575 g) cream cheese
6 eggs, separated
1/2 cup (100 g) sugar
1/2 cup plus 2 tablespoons (140 ml) dairy sour cream
Grated peel of 1 lemon
1 tablespoon lemon juice
3 tablespoons (20 g) cornstarch
1 teaspoon baking powder

Grease a 10-inch (25-cm) springform cake pan.
To make crumb crust, combine cracker crumbs and margarine in a medium bowl. Press crumb mixture evenly over bottom of greased cake pan. Preheat oven to 325°F (165°C).
To make filling, put cream cheese, egg yolks, sugar, sour cream, lemon peel and juice, cornstarch and baking powder into a large bowl. Beat until smooth. Beat egg whites until stiff; fold into cream cheese mixture. Pour over crumb crust. Bake 1-1/4 to 1-1/2 hours or until a wooden pick inserted in center comes out clean. The cheesecake should be firm to the touch, but still slightly springy. Cover with foil if becoming too brown. Immediately loosen sides of cooked cheesecake with a knife. Turn off oven. Let cheesecake cool in oven with door open slightly. Remove cooled cheesecake from pan and serve.

Classic Sand Cake

3 eggs
3/4 cup (180 g) granulated sugar
1/4 teaspoon vanilla extract
Grated peel of 1/2 lemon
Pinch of salt
1 cup (125 g) self-rising flour
Scant 1 cup (125 g) cornstarch
3/4 cup (180 g) butter, melted
Powdered sugar, sifted

Grease a 12x4-inch (30x10-cm) loaf pan and line with waxed paper; grease paper. Preheat oven to 375°F (190°C).

Put eggs, granulated sugar, vanilla, lemon peel and salt in a medium bowl set over a saucepan of hot water on low heat. Beat until pale and creamy. Do not let mixture become warmer than lukewarm. Remove mixture from heat; beat until cooled. Sift flour with cornstarch; fold into cooled egg mixture. Stir in butter. Turn batter into prepared pan. Bake 40 to 45 minutes or until a skewer inserted in center comes out clean. Cool on a rack. Remove lining paper from cooled cake. Dredge top of cake with powdered sugar.

Chocolate Cherry Cake

Cake:
1/2 cup (100 g) halved candied cherries
3/4 cup plus 2 tablespoons (200 g) butter, softened
1 cup plus 2 tablespoons (250 g) sugar
6 eggs
Pinch of salt
Grated peel of 1 lemon
1/2 teaspoon ground cinnamon
7 oz. (200 g) semisweet chocolate, grated
1 cup (100 g) ground hazelnuts
1 cup (100 g) ground almonds
1-1/4 cups (150 g) all-purpose flour, sifted
1 teaspoon baking powder

Decoration:
3 tablespoons (20 g) powdered sugar
3 tablespoons (20 g) instant chocolate drink powder

Grease a 9-inch (23-cm) springform cake pan; sprinkle with fine breadcrumbs. Preheat oven to 350°F (175°C).
To make cake, wash cherries and pat dry. Cream butter and sugar in a large bowl until light and fluffy. Add eggs, salt, lemon peel, cinnamon, chocolate, hazelnuts and almonds; stir well. Fold in cherries with flour and baking powder. Turn batter into prepared pan; smooth the surface. Bake 1 to 1-1/2 hours or until a wooden pick inserted in center comes out clean. Turn out cake onto a rack to cool.
To decorate, cut center from a paper doily; place it over center of cooled cake and sift powdered sugar over uncovered area. Remove center piece of doily from cake; place rest of doily over cake and sift all over with chocolate powder.

Casanova Slices

Cake:
4 eggs, separated, plus 2 egg yolks
1/2 cup (100 g) sugar
3/4 cup (80 g) all-purpose flour
1 teaspoon baking powder
1 cup (100 g) ground hazelnuts

Filling & Topping:
1/4 cup (25 g) cornstarch
1/4 cup (50 g) granulated sugar
1-1/4 cups (300 ml) milk
1 cup plus 2 tablespoons (250 g) butter
3 tablespoons brandy
2/3 cup (225 g) red currant jelly
3 tablespoons (40 g) brown sugar
12 candied cherries

Line a 11x7-inch (28x18-cm) cake pan with waxed paper; grease paper. Preheat oven to 425°F (220°C).

To make cake, beat 6 yolks and half the sugar in a large bowl until pale and creamy. Beat whites until stiff; fold in remaining sugar. Fold into yolk mixture. Sift flour with baking powder; fold into egg mixture with hazelnuts. Spread batter in pan. Bake 10 to 12 minutes or until a wooden pick inserted in center comes out clean. Turn out cake onto waxed paper. Peel off lining paper. Cool. Cut cooled cake lengthwise into 3 strips.

To make filling and topping, blend cornstarch, granulated sugar and a little milk. Heat remaining milk; stir into cornstarch mixture. Return to heat; bring to a boil, stirring until thickened. Cool, stirring frequently. Beat butter until pale. Gradually beat in cooled cornstarch mixture and brandy. Spread 2 cake strips with jelly and half the butter cream. Place one on top of the other; top with third strip. Spread top and sides of cake thinly with butter cream; sprinkle with brown sugar. Cut into 12 slices; decorate with piped butter cream and cherries.

Chocolate Cake Napoleon

Cake:
6 large eggs, separated
3/4 cup plus 2 tablespoons (200 g) sugar
4 oz. (100 g) semisweet chocolate, melted
1 cup (100 g) all-purpose flour
1 teaspoon baking powder
3/4 cup (80 g) chopped almonds
1/2 teaspoon ground cinnamon
1/4 teaspoon ground cloves
Pinch of salt
3 tablespoons brandy
2 tablespoons (25 g) butter

Frosting:
4 oz. (100 g) semisweet chocolate
1 tablespoon chopped pistachio nuts

Grease a 12-inch (30-cm) long Balmoral pan or a 12x4-inch (30x10-cm) loaf pan; sprinkle with fine breadcrumbs. Preheat oven to 350°F (175°C).

To make cake, put egg yolks and half the sugar into a large bowl. Beat until pale and creamy, 5 to 10 minutes with an electric mixer. Beat egg whites until stiff; fold in remaining sugar. Carefully fold into egg yolk mixture with melted chocolate. Sift flour with baking powder; mix with almonds, cinnamon, cloves and salt. Carefully fold flour mixture into egg mixture with brandy. Melt butter; fold into mixture while warm. Turn batter into prepared pan; smooth the surface. Bake 50 to 60 minutes or until a wooden pick inserted in center comes out clean. Remove from pan; cool on a rack.

To make frosting, melt chocolate in a double boiler over low heat. Spread over cooled cake. Sprinkle pistachios onto chocolate before it sets.

Gâteau Madame Pompadour

Cake:
4 eggs, separated, plus 2 egg yolks
1 tablespoon hot water
1/2 cup (120 g) sugar
1-1/4 cups (150 g) ground almonds
1/2 cup (50 g) all-purpose flour, sifted
Pinch of salt

Filling & Topping:
1/4 cup (25 g) cornstarch
1-1/4 cups (300 ml) milk
1/2 cup (100 g) sugar
1 tablespoon vanilla sugar, page 18
1/2 teaspoon vanilla extract
1 cup plus 2 tablespoons (250 g) butter
1/2 cup (50 g) toasted sliced almonds, page 47

Grease and flour a 9-inch (23-cm) cake pan. Preheat oven to 350°F (175°C).

To make cake, put 6 egg yolks, water and three-fourths of the sugar into a medium bowl. Beat until pale and creamy, 5 to 10 minutes with an electric mixer. Fold in almonds and flour. Beat egg whites and salt until stiff; fold in remaining sugar. Fold into egg yolk mixture. Turn batter into pan. Bake 40 minutes or until a wooden pick inserted in center comes out clean. Cool on a rack. Cut cooled cake horizontally into 3 layers.

To make filling and topping, blend cornstarch, a little milk, unflavored sugar, vanilla sugar and vanilla in a medium bowl. Heat remaining milk in a medium saucepan; stir into cornstarch mixture. Return to heat and bring to a boil, stirring constantly until thickened. Let cool, stirring frequently. Beat butter in a medium bowl until creamy. Gradually beat in cooled cornstarch mixture. Spread half the butter cream over 2 layers of cake; place one on top of the other. Cover top and sides of cake with remaining butter cream; sprinkle with almonds.

Kaiser Franz-Joseph's Cake

Cake:
8 tablespoons (100 g) butter, softened
1 cup plus 2 tablespoons (250 g) sugar
4 eggs, separated, plus 2 egg yolks
Pinch of salt
1 teaspoon ground cinnamon
1-1/2 tablespoons maraschino
1 cup (50 g) fresh white breadcrumbs
2-1/4 cups (250 g) ground almonds
1/3 cup (50 g) finely chopped candied lemon peel
3/4 cup (80 g) self-rising flour, sifted
1/3 cup (100 g) red currant jelly

Frosting:
1-2/3 cups (200 g) powdered sugar, sifted
1 tablespoon lemon juice
1-1/2 tablespoons maraschino

Grease a 9-inch (23-cm) round cake pan. Preheat oven to 375°F (190°C).

To make cake, cream butter and half the sugar in a medium bowl until pale and fluffy. Beat in egg yolks one at a time. Stir in salt, cinnamon, maraschino, breadcrumbs, almonds and candied lemon peel. Fold flour into mixture. Beat egg whites until stiff; beat in remaining sugar until smooth and glossy. Fold into egg yolk mixture. Turn batter into greased pan. Bake 1 hour or until a wooden pick inserted in center comes out clean. Turn out cake onto a rack to cool. Spread top and sides of cooled cake with red currant jelly.

To make frosting, combine powdered sugar, lemon juice and maraschino in a small bowl. Beat frosting until smooth. Pour onto cake, letting frosting run thickly over sides. Smooth the surface with a spatula.

Crisp Fried Cakes

Saffron Braids

4 saffron strands
1 cup (250 ml) hot milk
1/4 cup (50 g) sugar
2 pkgs. active dry yeast
4 cups (500 g) all-purpose flour
1/2 teaspoon salt
8 tablespoons (120 g) margarine
2 eggs
Grated peel of 1/2 lemon
Oil to deep-fry
Additional 1/2 cup (100 g) sugar

Steep saffron in hot milk overnight.

Strain milk and reheat to warm, 110°F (43°C). Pour into a small bowl. Stir in a pinch of sugar and sprinkle with yeast. Let stand 5 minutes or until the surface is frothy. Stir gently to moisten any dry particles remaining on top. Sift flour, remaining scant 1/4 cup (50 g) sugar and salt into a large bowl. Melt margarine; cool slightly. Lightly beat margarine, eggs and lemon peel into yeast liquid. Pour into flour mixture, combining to make a soft dough. On a floured surface, knead dough 5 to 10 minutes until smooth and elastic. Cover and let rise in a warm place 30 minutes.

Knead risen dough lightly. Divide into 4 pieces. Divide each piece into four and roll out to 6- to 8-inch (15- to 20-cm) strips. Use 4 strips at a time to weave braids. Cover and let rise in a warm place 15 to 20 minutes.

Heat oil in a deep-frying pan to 300°F (150°C). Fry braids 10 minutes or until golden, turning at least once during cooking with a slotted spoon.

Lift out cooked braids with slotted spoon; drain on paper towels. Sprinkle with additional sugar while hot.

Sugared Knots

1/2 cup plus 1 tablespoon (125 g) soft margarine
1 cup (225 g) sugar
Pinch of salt
3 eggs
1 tablespoon rum
4 cups (450 g) all-purpose flour
2 teaspoons baking powder
Oil to deep-fry
2 tablespoons (25 g) vanilla sugar, page 18

In a medium bowl, beat margarine, half the unflavored sugar, salt and eggs until smooth. Stir in rum. Sift flour and baking powder together over mixture; fold in thoroughly to make a dough. Knead well. Press dough into a ball and wrap in foil or plastic wrap. Refrigerate 30 minutes.

Heat oil in a deep-frying pan to 360°F (180°C). On a floured surface, roll out dough 1/4 inch (5 mm) thick. Cut dough into 8x3/4-inch (20x1.5-cm) strips. Knot each strip tightly. Fry knots four at a time 5 minutes or until golden. Turn once with a slotted spoon during cooking.

Lift out cooked knots with slotted spoon; drain on paper towels. Mix remaining unflavored sugar and vanilla sugar; sprinkle over warm knots.

Tunisian Honey Rings

Ring Dough:
3 eggs
Scant 1/4 cup (50 ml) oil
Scant 1/4 cup (50 ml) orange juice
Grated peel of 1 large orange
1/4 cup (50 g) sugar
2-3/4 cups (300 g) all-purpose flour
1 teaspoon baking powder

Syrup:
1-1/4 cups (300 ml) cold water
3 tablespoons lemon juice
1-1/4 cups (275 g) sugar
1/3 cup (100 g) creamed honey or honey spread
Oil to deep-fry

To make ring dough, beat eggs, oil, orange juice, 1 teaspoon orange peel and sugar in a medium bowl until frothy. Sift flour with baking powder; add a spoonful at a time to egg mixture. Beat well. Cover and let stand 45 minutes.
To make syrup, heat water, lemon juice and sugar in a small saucepan. Stir constantly until sugar has dissolved. Bring to a boil; reduce heat and simmer 5 minutes. Add creamed honey or honey spread and remaining orange peel; simmer syrup gently another 5 minutes. Keep warm while cooking rings.

Heat oil in a deep-frying pan to 360°F (180°C). Divide dough into 12 pieces. Using floured hands, make each piece into a circle 3 inches (7.5 cm) in diameter. Make a hole in the center of each circle. Enlarge holes using a wooden spoon until they are about 1-1/2 inches (3.5 cm) across. Add 4 rings at a time to hot oil. Fry 5 minutes or until golden, turning once during cooking with a slotted spoon.

Lift out cooked rings with slotted spoon; drain on paper towels. Using a fork, pick up warm rings and hold in syrup a few minutes to let syrup soak in. Serve at once.

Jam Rosettes

3/4 cup (150 g) soft margarine
1/2 cup (100 g) granulated sugar
2 eggs
1/2 cup (50 g) ground almonds
1 teaspoon ground cinnamon
1/2 cup (125 ml) dairy sour cream
4 cups (500 g) all-purpose flour, sifted
Oil to deep-fry
1 egg white, beaten
Powdered sugar, sifted
2/3 cup (225 g) apple jelly

Beat margarine, granulated sugar and eggs in a medium bowl until light. Stir in almonds, cinnamon, sour cream and a little flour; mix until blended. Add remaining flour to make a dough. Press dough into a ball and wrap in foil or plastic wrap. Refrigerate 1 hour.

Heat oil in a deep-frying pan to 360°F (180°C). On a floured surface, roll out dough thinly. Cut out circles using a 2-1/2-inch (6-cm) fluted cookie cutter. Cut notches in edges of circles as illustrated. Brush centers with egg white; stack circles in threes. Using the handle of a wooden spoon, shape a small well in the center of each stack. During cooking, each layer rises to make a rosette shape.

Place 2 or 3 rosettes at a time in hot oil. Fry 4 to 5 minutes or until golden, turning once during cooking with a slotted spoon.

Lift rosettes out of oil with slotted spoon; drain well on paper towels. Sprinkle with powdered sugar. Fill centers of rosettes with apple jelly.

Sweet Poppy Seed Crescents

Yeast Dough:
1 tablespoon sugar
1/2 cup (125 ml) warm milk (110°F, 43°C)
1-1/2 pkgs. active dry yeast
4 cups (450 g) flour
Pinch of salt
8 tablespoons (120 g) butter
1 cup (250 ml) dairy sour cream
1 egg

Filling:
3/4 cup (175 ml) milk
1/2 cup (120 g) sugar
1 tablespoon poppy seeds
1 cup (100 g) finely chopped toasted hazelnuts, page 47
1 cup (175 g) raisins, finely chopped
1/2 cup (175 g) honey
1 egg yolk, beaten

To make yeast dough, stir a pinch of sugar into milk; sprinkle with yeast. Let stand 5 minutes. Stir gently. Sift flour, remaining sugar and salt into a large bowl. Melt butter; cool slightly. Lightly beat butter, sour cream and egg into yeast mixture. Pour into flour mixture, combining to make a dough. On a floured surface, knead dough until smooth. Cover and let rise in a warm place 20 minutes. Grease a baking sheet.
To make filling, heat milk and sugar in a medium saucepan, stirring until sugar dissolves. Stir in poppy seeds, hazelnuts and raisins; boil until thickened. Stir in honey; cool. Preheat oven to 425°F (220°C). Halve dough. On a floured surface, roll out each half to a 15x10-inch (38x25-cm) rectangle. Divide each rectangle into fifteen 5x2-inch (12.5x5-cm) rectangles. Place some filling down the middle of each rectangle. Brush edges with egg yolk; fold dough over. Curve into crescents. Place on baking sheet; brush with egg yolk. Let stand in a warm place 10 minutes. Bake 12 to 15 minutes or until golden.

Fruit & Nut Pumpernickel

3-1/2 cups (450 g) powdered sugar, sifted
5 eggs
3 cups (350 g) chopped almonds
1 cup (100 g) chopped hazelnuts
Pinch of salt
1 teaspoon ground cinnamon
Pinch each of ground cloves and ground cardamom
1/3 cup (50 g) finely chopped candied orange peel
Grated peel of 1/2 orange
Grated peel of 1/2 lemon
4 cups (450 g) all-purpose flour, sifted

Put powdered sugar and eggs into a large bowl. Beat until pale and creamy, 5 to 10 minutes with an electric mixer. Stir in almonds, hazelnuts, salt, cinnamon, cloves and cardamom. Work in candied peel, orange and lemon peel and flour to make a dough. On a floured surface, knead dough lightly. Preheat oven to 375°F (190°C). Grease a baking sheet.

Divide dough in half; shape into 2 loaves. Place on greased baking sheet. Bake 1 hour or until a rich brown. Cut hot bread into thin slices; cool.

Amsterdam Squares

1/2 cup plus 2 tablespoons (150 g) butter, softened
2/3 cup (150 g) sugar
1 egg
Grated peel of 1/2 lemon
Pinch of salt
Pinch of baking powder
2-1/4 cups (250 g) all-purpose flour, sifted
1 egg yolk
Water
1-1/2 cups (175 g) blanched halved almonds, page 124

Cream butter and sugar in a large bowl until light and fluffy. Add egg, lemon peel, salt, baking powder and flour; mix thoroughly to make a dough. Press into a ball and wrap in foil or plastic wrap. Refrigerate 2 hours.

Preheat oven to 400°F (205°C). Grease baking sheets. On a floured surface, roll out dough 1/8 inch (3 mm) thick. Cut into 1-1/2-inch (3.5-cm) squares. Beat egg yolk with a few drops of water; brush over squares. Arrange 4 almond halves on each square. Place cookies on greased baking sheets, leaving room between each one for spreading during cooking.

Bake 10 to 15 minutes or until golden. Let cookies cool slightly on sheets then remove with a spatula to cool on a rack.

Danish Buns

Yeast Dough:
1/2 cup (100 g) sugar
1/2 cup (125 ml) warm milk (110°F, 43°C)
2 pkgs. active dry yeast
4 cups (500 g) all-purpose flour
Pinch of salt
8 tablespoons (100 g) butter
Grated peel of 1/2 lemon
Pinch of ground allspice

Filling:
1/3 cup (50 g) seedless golden raisins
1/3 cup (50 g) dried currants
1/3 cup (50 g) chopped candied lemon peel
1/2 cup (50 g) sliced almonds
2 tablespoons (30 g) butter, melted
Sugar

To make yeast dough, stir a pinch of sugar into warm milk and sprinkle with yeast. Let stand 5 minutes or until frothy. Stir gently to moisten any dry particles remaining on top. Sift flour, remaining sugar and salt into a large bowl. Melt butter; cool slightly. Lightly beat butter, lemon peel and allspice into yeast mixture. Pour into flour mixture, combining to make a dough. On a floured surface, knead dough until smooth. Cover and let rise in a warm place 30 minutes. Grease baking sheets.
To make filling, combine raisins, currants, candied peel, almonds and butter in a medium bowl.

On a floured surface, roll out half the dough to a 12x10-inch (30x25-cm) rectangle. Spread half the fruit mixture over dough rectangle. Roll up from long side; cut into 1-1/4-inch (3-cm) thick slices. Repeat process using remaining dough and filling. Put on baking sheets. Let rise in a warm place 10 to 15 minutes. Preheat oven to 400°F (205°C). Sprinkle buns with sugar. Bake 10 to 15 minutes or until lightly browned.

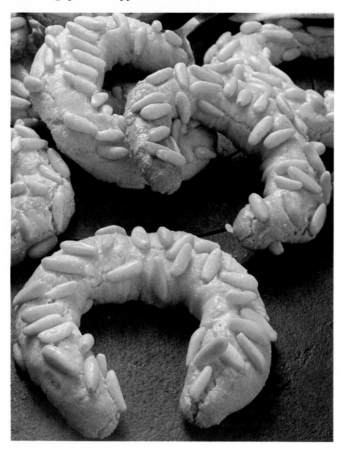

Pine Nut Crescents

Cookie Dough:
2-1/4 cups (250 g) ground almonds
1-1/4 cups plus 2 tablespoons (300 g) sugar
4 egg whites
Grated peel of 1 lemon
1 egg white, beaten
1 cup (100 g) pine nuts or sliced almonds

Glaze:
1/4 cup (50 g) sugar
1 tablespoon water
1 tablespoon rum

To make cookie dough, mix almonds, sugar, 4 egg whites and lemon peel in a double boiler over low heat. Stir constantly 15 minutes. Cool slightly then refrigerate until firm.

Preheat oven to 375°F (190°C). Grease baking sheets. Shape almond dough into a roll; cut into 24 pieces. Make a small crescent shape from each piece; brush with egg white. Sprinkle pine nuts or sliced almonds onto cookies; press nuts into dough so they do not fall off during baking. Place cookies on greased baking sheets. Bake 15 to 20 minutes or until golden.

To make glaze, combine sugar and water in a small saucepan. Simmer over low heat 2 minutes. Remove from heat and stir in rum. Brush cookies with rum glaze 5 minutes before the end of baking time. Remove cookies carefully from baking sheets with a spatula. Cool on a rack.

Orange Almond Cookies

1 cup plus 2 tablespoons (250 g) butter or margarine
1 cup plus 2 tablespoons (250 g) firmly packed soft brown sugar
2 eggs
3 cups (325 g) all-purpose flour
1 teaspoon baking powder
1/2 teaspoon salt
Grated peel of 1 large or 2 small oranges
3/4 cup (75 g) chopped almonds

Cream butter or margarine and sugar in a large bowl until light and fluffy. Beat in eggs one at a time. Sift flour and baking powder with salt; stir a spoonful at a time into creamed mixture. Add orange peel and almonds; mix thoroughly to make a dough. Shape dough into a roll 2-1/2 inches (6 cm) wide at each end. Wrap in foil or plastic wrap. Refrigerate 24 hours.

Preheat oven to 400°F (205°C). Grease baking sheets. Cut thin slices from roll of cookie dough; place slices on greased baking sheets. Bake 8 to 10 minutes or until light brown around the edges. Cool cookies slightly on sheets then transfer to racks to cool completely.

Cook's Tip

Instead of flavoring the cookies with orange, use a mixture of lemon and orange peel and substitute shredded coconut for the almonds.

Macaroon Bars

4 egg whites
1 cup (225 g) sugar
2 cups (225 g) sliced almonds
1/4 teaspoon ground cinnamon
Grated peel of 1 lemon
2 oz. (50 g) semisweet chocolate

Line a 11-1/2x7-1/2-inch (29x19-cm) baking sheet with rice paper. Preheat oven to 230°F (110°C).

Beat egg whites in a large bowl until stiff; gradually beat in half the sugar. Fold in remaining sugar, almonds, cinnamon and lemon peel. Spread mixture over prepared baking sheet. Bake 3 to 4 hours or until just golden. Halfway through cooking time, cut macaroon mixture into fingers. Remove cooked macaroons from baking sheet and cool on a rack.

Melt chocolate in a double boiler over low heat. Dip both ends of cooled macaroons into chocolate. Let set.

Cook's Tip

Place small spoonfuls of the macaroon mixture on the rice paper. When cooked and cooled, join macaroons together in pairs with a little melted chocolate.

Cream Slices

3/4 (17-1/4-oz., 489-g) pkg. frozen puff pastry, thawed
About 2/3 cup (100 g) sugar crystals
Filling:
1-1/4 cups (300 ml) whipping cream
Few drops of vanilla extract
1 tablespoon sugar

On a floured surface, roll out puff pastry dough thinly; cut out ovals about 5 inches (13 cm) long. Rinse a baking sheet with cold water. Arrange dough ovals on dampened baking sheet and sprinkle with sugar crystals. Refrigerate 15 minutes.

Preheat oven to 450°F (230°C). Bake ovals 10 minutes or until puffed and golden. Cool on a rack.

To make filling, whip cream with vanilla and sugar in a medium bowl until stiff. Spread whipped cream mixture over half the cooled pastry ovals on unsugared side; place second oval on top, sugar-side up.

Serve immediately.

Lemon Ring Cookies

Cookie Dough:
1-1/2 cups (150 g) all-purpose flour
1 teaspoon baking powder
Scant 1 cup (100 g) cornstarch
8 tablespoons (100 g) butter
1/2 cup (100 g) sugar
2 egg yolks
Grated peel of 2 lemons

Frosting:
Generous 1 cup (125 g) powdered sugar, sifted
3 tablespoons lemon juice
1/2 cup (50 g) chopped pistachio nuts

To make cookie dough, sift flour, baking powder and cornstarch into a medium bowl. Melt butter; cool slightly in a medium bowl. Stir in sugar, egg yolks and lemon peel. Add to flour mixture; mix to a smooth dough. Cover and refrigerate until firm.

Preheat oven to 400°F (205°C). Grease baking sheets. On a floured surface, roll out dough 1/8 inch (3 mm) thick. Using a 2-1/2-inch (6-cm) fluted cutter, cut out circles from dough. Cut out center of each circle using a 1/2-inch (1-cm) fluted cutter. Roll out centers to make more cookies. Place ring cookies on baking sheets. Bake 10 minutes or until golden. Cool slightly on baking sheets then lift off with a spatula. Cool on a rack.
To make frosting, blend powdered sugar and lemon juice in a small bowl. Spread frosting over cooled cookies. Decorate with pistachio nuts before frosting sets.

Florentines

8 tablespoons (100 g) butter
3/4 cup (150 g) sugar
3 tablespoons (50 g) honey
1/4 cup (70 ml) whipping cream
Pinch of salt
Grated peel of 1/2 lemon
1-3/4 cups (180 g) sliced almonds
3 tablespoons (30 g) finely chopped candied orange peel
4 oz. (100 g) semisweet chocolate
10 candied cherries

Grease baking sheets. Preheat oven to 350°F (175°).

Mix butter, sugar, honey, cream, salt and lemon peel in a medium saucepan. Bring to a boil then reduce heat. Continue to boil gently 4 to 5 minutes, stirring constantly until mixture becomes thick and creamy and leaves sides of pan. Add almonds and candied peel to saucepan; stir well. Remove pan from heat. Place heaped teaspoonfuls of mixture well apart on baking sheets. Flatten mixture slightly with the back of a wet spoon. Bake florentines 10 minutes or until a rich golden brown. Cool on baking sheets a few minutes until firm enough to be lifted onto a rack.

Melt chocolate in a double boiler over low heat. Spread chocolate thickly over undersides of florentines. Mark into ridges with a fork before chocolate sets and place a halved cherry on top of each one.

Almond Tartlets

3/4 (17-1/4-oz., 489-g) pkg. frozen puff pastry, thawed

Filling:
Generous 1 cup (125 g) ground almonds
1/2 cup plus 1 tablespoon (125 g) sugar
1 egg, beaten
Scant 1/4 cup (50 ml) milk
1 tablespoon rum
Grated peel of 1 lemon
12 blanched halved almonds, page 124

On a floured surface, roll out pastry dough 1/8 inch (3 mm) thick. Rinse about 8 small tartlet pans or muffin pan cups with cold water. Cut dough into rounds to fit pans or cups. Place in pans or cups; pierce dough several times with a fork. Refrigerate 15 minutes. Preheat oven to 425°F (220°C).
To make filling, combine almonds, sugar, egg, milk, rum and lemon peel in a small bowl. Fill tartlet shells with mixture; smooth the surfaces. Put 3 almond halves on top of each tartlet. Bake 20 minutes or until filling is just brown around the edges. Cool a few minutes in pans or cups then turn out carefully onto a rack to cool completely.

Swiss Rings

Cream Puff Paste:
4 tablespoons (60 g) butter
1 cup (250 ml) water
Pinch of salt
1 cup (150 g) all-purpose flour, sifted
4 eggs

Frosting:
4 tablespoons (50 g) apricot jam
4 oz. (100 g) semisweet chocolate

Filling:
1/4 cup plus 1 tablespoon (40 g) cornstarch
3/4 cup (180 g) sugar
4 eggs, separated
2 cups plus 2 tablespoons (500 ml) milk
1 teaspoon vanilla extract

Preheat oven to 425°F (220°C). Grease a baking sheet.
To make cream puff paste, put butter and water into a medium saucepan; heat until butter has melted. Add salt and bring to a boil. Add flour all at once and stir vigorously until mixture leaves sides of pan and forms a smooth ball. Cool slightly then beat in eggs one at a time. Using a pastry bag fitted with a fluted nozzle, pipe 16 rings of dough onto baking sheet. Bake 20 minutes or until golden and firm. Make a 1/2-inch (1-cm) slit in each ring after cooking to allow steam to escape; cool on a rack.
To make frosting, warm jam; spread over tops of rings. Melt chocolate in a double boiler over low heat. Spoon over rings.
To make filling, blend cornstarch, sugar, egg yolks and a little milk in a medium bowl. Heat remaining milk in a medium saucepan; stir hot milk and vanilla into cornstarch mixture. Return to heat and bring to a boil, stirring constantly. Boil a few seconds then cool to lukewarm. Beat egg whites until stiff; fold into cornstarch custard which should be just warm. Cool completely. Cut rings in half; fill with cornstarch custard.

Frosted Vanilla Slices

3/4 (17-1/4-oz., 489-g) pkg. frozen puff pastry, thawed

Frosting:
1-2/3 cups (200 g) powdered sugar, sifted
1 tablespoon water
1-1/2 tablespoons lemon juice

Filling:
4 eggs, separated
Generous 1 cup (150 g) powdered sugar, sifted
Scant 1/2 cup (50 g) cornstarch
2 tablespoons (30 g) granulated sugar
1 teaspoon vanilla extract
2 cups plus 2 tablespoons (500 ml) milk

Preheat oven to 425°F (220°C).

On a floured surface, roll out pastry dough to a 24x18-inch (60x45-cm) rectangle. Cut in half lengthwise. Sprinkle a baking sheet with cold water. Place rectangles on baking sheet; pierce dough with a fork. Refrigerate 15 minutes. Bake 12 to 18 minutes or until puffed and golden. Cool on a rack.

To make frosting, combine powdered sugar, water and lemon juice in a small bowl. Spread frosting over one of the cooled pastry pieces.

To make filling, beat egg whites with powdered sugar until stiff and glossy. Blend cornstarch, egg yolks, granulated sugar, vanilla and a little milk in a medium bowl. Bring remaining milk to a boil in a medium saucepan; stir hot milk into cornstarch mixture. Return to saucepan and cook a few minutes, stirring constantly until thickened. Remove from heat; fold in beaten egg white mixture. Cool.

Spread cooled filling thickly over piece of pastry without frosting. Top with frosted pastry. Refrigerate until set then cut into slices.

Toasted Aniseed Cake

5 eggs, separated
2/3 cup (125 g) sugar
Scant 1/4 cup (50 ml) water
1-1/2 cups (175 g) all-purpose flour, sifted
1 tablespoon ground aniseed

Grease two 8-1/2x4-1/2-inch (22x11-cm) loaf pans. Preheat oven to 350°F (175°C).

Put egg yolks, sugar and water into a large bowl. Beat until pale and creamy, 5 to 10 minutes with an electric mixer. Fold flour and aniseed into egg yolk mixture. Beat egg whites until stiff; fold into mixture. Divide batter between 2 greased loaf pans; smooth the surfaces. Bake 40 to 45 minutes or until a wooden pick or skewer inserted in center comes out clean. Turn out cakes onto racks to cool. Cover and let stand 2 days.

Two days later, preheat oven to 400°F (205°C). Cut cakes into 1/2-inch (1-cm) thick slices; arrange on baking sheets. Brown in oven 5 minutes on each side. Alternatively, toast slices under broiler.

Cook's Tip
This Toasted Aniseed Cake tastes best spread with butter and honey.

Hazelnut Buns

Yeast Dough:
1/4 cup (60 g) sugar
1 cup (250 ml) warm milk (110°F, 43°C)
2 pkgs. active dry yeast
4 cups (500 g) all-purpose flour
Pinch of salt
4 tablespoons (60 g) butter
1 egg
Grated peel of 1 lemon

Filling:
1-3/4 cups (200 g) ground hazelnuts
1/4 cup plus 3 tablespoons (100 g) sugar
3 tablespoons rum
2 egg whites
1 egg yolk, beaten

To make yeast dough, stir a pinch of sugar into warm milk and sprinkle with yeast. Let stand 5 minutes or until frothy. Stir gently to moisten any dry particles remaining on top. Sift flour, remaining sugar and salt into a large bowl. Melt butter; cool slightly. Lightly beat butter, egg and lemon peel into yeast mixture. Pour into flour mixture, combining to make a dough. On a floured surface, knead dough until smooth. Cover and let rise in a warm place 15 minutes. Grease baking sheets.
To make filling, combine hazelnuts, sugar, rum and egg whites in a medium bowl.

On a floured surface, roll out risen dough 1/8 to 1/4 inch (3 to 5 mm) thick. Cut out 24 rounds, each 3 inches (7.5 cm) across. Divide filling between half the rounds, leaving edges free. Brush edges with egg yolk; cover with remaining rounds. Press edges together firmly to seal. Brush buns with egg yolk. Cut a cross on top of each bun; place on greased baking sheets. Let rise in a warm place 15 minutes. Preheat oven to 425°F (220°C). Bake buns 15 minutes or until golden brown.

Danish Pastries

Yeast Dough:
Pinch of sugar
1 cup (250 ml) warm milk (110°F, 43°C)
2 pkgs. active dry yeast
4-1/2 cups (500 g) all-purpose flour
1/2 teaspoon salt
1 cup (225 g) butter
1 egg

Filling:
1 cup (100 g) ground almonds
1 tablespoon ground hazelnuts
1 tablespoon liqueur such as arrack or ouzo
1 tablespoon powdered sugar
1 egg, separated

Glaze:
3 tablespoons (20 g) powdered sugar, sifted
1 tablespoon lemon juice

To make yeast dough, follow recipe for Danish Scrolls, page 61, setting aside the extra 1/2 cup (50 g) flour and 3/4 cup (175 g) butter. Work the extra flour into the extra butter. Refrigerate then fold and roll with dough as in recipe. Roll out dough to a 15x12-inch (37.5x30-cm) rectangle. Grease baking sheets.
To make filling, combine almonds, hazelnuts, arrack or ouzo, powdered sugar and egg white in a small bowl.

Cut dough into 9 long triangles measuring 12x3x12 inches (30x7.5x30 cm). Divide filling between triangles, spreading it down the center of each. Roll up dough from bottom edge to point. Place on greased baking sheets. Beat egg yolk; brush over dough. Let stand in a warm place 15 minutes. Preheat oven to 435°F (225°C). Bake 15 to 20 minutes or until lightly browned.
To make glaze, blend powdered sugar and lemon juice in a small bowl. Spoon glaze over warm pastries.

Hazelnut Parcels

3/4 (17-1/4-oz., 489-g) pkg. frozen puff pastry, thawed

Filling:
1 cup (100 g) ground hazelnuts
2 tablespoons (30 g) sugar
Pinch of ground cinnamon
1 tablespoon honey
1 egg, separated

Frosting:
Scant 1 cup (100 g) powdered sugar, sifted
2 to 3 tablespoons hot water

On a floured surface, roll out puff pastry dough to a rectangle about 20x8 inches (50x20 cm). Trim edges. Halve dough lengthwise then cut into 4-inch (10-cm) squares.
To make filling, mix hazelnuts, sugar, cinnamon, honey and egg white in a small bowl. Divide filling between squares, placing it in the center of each one.

Beat egg yolk and brush over edges of squares. Fold all corners in to the middle; press together firmly. Cut small rounds from dough trimmings. Brush rounds with egg yolk and put on top of parcels, pressing to seal. Sprinkle a baking sheet with cold water; place pastries on dampened baking sheet. Refrigerate 15 minutes. Preheat oven to 425°F (220°C).

Bake pastries 15 to 20 minutes or until puffed and golden. Transfer to a rack.
To make frosting, blend powdered sugar and enough hot water to give a coating consistency. Spoon frosting over pastries while they are still warm.

Cherry & Almond Slices

3/4 (17-1/4-oz., 489-g) pkg. frozen puff pastry, thawed

Filling:
3/4 cup (80 g) ground almonds
1 egg, separated
1 tablespoon kirsch
1/4 cup (50 g) sugar
1/4 cup (50 g) candied cherries, chopped

Frosting:
Scant 1/2 cup (50 g) powdered sugar, sifted
1 tablespoon hot water

On a floured surface, roll out puff pastry dough to a 14-inch (35-cm) square. Divide dough into twenty-eight 3x2-inch (7.5x5-cm) rectangles. Sprinkle baking sheets with cold water. Place rectangles on dampened baking sheets.
To make filling, combine almonds, egg white, kirsch, sugar and candied cherries in a small bowl.

Beat egg yolk and brush over edges of dough rectangles. Place a teaspoon of filling in the center of each. Cut thin strips from remaining dough with a pastry cutter; place crosswise over filling. Brush with egg yolk. Refrigerate 15 minutes. Preheat oven to 425°F (220°C).

Bake slices 10 to 15 minutes or until puffed and golden. Cool on a rack.
To make frosting, blend powdered sugar and water in a small bowl. Spread frosting over slices while they are still warm.

Palmiers

About 1/2 cup (100 g) sugar
3/4 (17-1/4-oz., 489-g) pkg. frozen puff pastry, thawed
1 egg yolk, beaten

Sprinkle some sugar over a large piece of waxed paper. Roll out pastry dough on sugared paper to a 14x12-inch (35x30-cm) rectangle. Sprinkle dough with a little sugar and roll up 2 shorter edges of dough towards each other to meet in the center. Brush with egg yolk and turn roll over. Using a sharp knife, cut into slices 1/4 inch (5 mm) thick. Sprinkle baking sheets with cold water. Place slices well apart on baking sheets; brush with egg yolk. Refrigerate 15 minutes. Preheat oven to 400°F (205°C).

Bake 8 to 12 minutes or until puffed and golden.

Cook's Tip

Be careful not to brush the edges of the Palmiers with egg yolk, as this will cause the layers to stick together and prevent the pastry from rising during baking.

Orange Pinwheels

3/4 (17-1/4-oz., 489-g) pkg. frozen puff pastry, thawed

Filling:
1/4 cup (25 g) ground almonds
1 tablespoon orange jelly or marmalade
1 teaspoon orange-flavored liqueur
1 egg yolk, beaten

Frosting:
Scant 1/2 cup (50 g) powdered sugar, sifted
1 tablespoon hot water
Scant 1/4 cup (20 g) chopped pistachio nuts

On a floured surface, roll out puff pastry dough to a 15-inch (37.5-cm) square. Divide into sixteen 3-1/2-inch (8.5-cm) squares, leaving 2 strips of dough for later use. Cut diagonally in from the corners of each square towards the center, leaving dough joined in the center to hold filling.
To make filling, combine almonds, orange jelly or marmalade and orange-flavored liqueur in a small bowl. Place a little filling in the center of each square.

Fold points of 4 cut corners to the center to make pinwheels. Press down firmly and brush with egg yolk. Cut out 16 small rounds from remaining dough and place in the center of each pinwheel. Brush with egg yolk. Sprinkle a baking sheet with cold water. Place pinwheels on dampened baking sheet. Refrigerate 15 minutes. Preheat oven to 425°F (220°C).

Bake pinwheels 10 to 12 minutes or until puffed and golden. Transfer to a rack.
To make frosting, blend powdered sugar and water in a small bowl. Spoon frosting over pinwheels while they are still warm. Sprinkle with chopped pistachios before frosting sets.

Swiss Carrot Cake

Cake:
5 eggs, separated, plus 2 egg yolks
3/4 cup plus 2 tablespoons (200 g) sugar
Pinch each of salt, ground cinnamon and
    ground cloves
1 tablespoon kirsch
1/2 cup (50 g) all-purpose flour, sifted
1 teaspoon baking powder
1-3/4 cups (200 g) finely grated carrots
1 cup (100 g) ground almonds
1 cup (100 g) finely chopped hazelnuts
1 cup (50 g) fresh white breadcrumbs

Frosting:
1-2/3 cups (200 g) powdered sugar, sifted
1-1/2 tablespoons kirsch
1-1/2 tablespoons lemon juice

Decoration:
3 tablespoons apricot jam
1/2 cup (50 g) toasted sliced almonds,
    page 47
Few drops of orange food coloring
4 oz. (100 g) almond paste
Few pistachio nut pieces

Grease a 10-inch (25-cm) springform pan. Preheat oven to 375°F (190°C).
To make cake, put 7 egg yolks, sugar, salt, cinnamon, cloves and kirsch into a large bowl. Beat until thick and creamy, 5 to 10 minutes with an electric mixer. Sift flour with baking powder into a medium bowl. Mix in carrots, almonds, hazelnuts and breadcrumbs. Stir carrot mixture into egg yolk mixture. Beat egg whites until stiff; fold into egg yolk and carrot mixture. Turn cake batter into greased pan; smooth the surface. Bake 45 to 55 minutes or until a wooden pick inserted in center comes out clean. Turn out cake onto a rack to cool. Cover cooled cake and let stand 2 days.
To make frosting, combine powdered sugar, kirsch and lemon juice in a small bowl. Spread frosting over top of cake.
To decorate cake, warm jam and spread over sides of cake. Press on sliced almonds. Knead orange food coloring into almond paste and shape into small carrots. Insert a couple of pistachio nut pieces into top of each carrot to resemble stem. Arrange carrots on top of cake.

Chocolate Gâteau Alice

Cake:
5 oz. (140 g) semisweet chocolate
1/2 cup plus 2 tablespoons (140 g) butter, softened
3/4 cup (160 g) sugar
3 eggs, separated
3/4 cup (80 g) ground almonds
3/4 cup (80 g) rye or whole-wheat flour

Frosting:
4 oz. (100 g) almond paste
6 oz. (175 g) semisweet chocolate
2 tablespoons apricot jam
12 almonds
Sugar crystals

Grease an 8-inch (20-cm) springform cake pan and sprinkle with breadcrumbs. Preheat oven to 350°F (175°C).
To make cake, melt chocolate in a double boiler over low heat. Cream butter and half the sugar in a medium bowl until light and fluffy. Stir in chocolate, egg yolks and almonds. Beat egg whites until stiff; fold in remaining sugar. Fold egg white mixture into chocolate mixture. Fold in flour. Turn batter into prepared pan. Bake 40 to 45 minutes or until a wooden pick inserted in center comes out clean. Cool on a rack.
To make frosting, on a surface sprinkled with powdered sugar, roll out almond paste thinly to a circle large enough to cover top and sides of cake. Melt chocolate in a double boiler over low heat. Spread a thin layer of chocolate over top of cake. Place almond paste over top and sides of cake, pressing lightly. Trim excess almond paste. Spread remaining chocolate evenly over cake. Warm jam. Dip almonds into warm jam and then turn in sugar crystals. Arrange almonds on cake while chocolate is soft.

Charlotte Royal

Jelly Roll:
4 eggs, separated, plus 2 egg yolks
1/2 cup (100 g) sugar
Pinch of salt
Few drops of vanilla extract
3/4 cup (75 g) all-purpose flour
1/2 teaspoon baking powder
1 lb. (450 g) cherry or raspberry jam

Filling:
2 envelopes unflavored gelatin
1 cup (250 ml) white wine
1/2 cup (100 g) sugar
1 tablespoon lemon juice
Pinch of salt
1-1/2 cups (350 ml) whipping cream
Candied cherries

To make jelly roll, follow recipe on page 12, adding salt and vanilla to beaten egg mixture. Turn out cake onto sugared paper; peel off lining paper. Spread warm cake with jam. Trim edges and roll up tightly, using sugared paper to help. Let cool.

Cut cooled jelly roll into 18 slices. Line a 6-1/4-cup (1.5-liter) bowl with 14 jelly-roll slices, pressing well against each other to cover bottom and sides of bowl.
To make filling, dissolve gelatin in 1/3 cup (100 ml) wine over low heat. Transfer to a small bowl. Heat remaining wine, sugar, lemon juice and salt until sugar has dissolved. Stir into gelatin mixture. Cool until just on the point of setting. Whip cream in a medium bowl; reserve a little for piping decoration. Pour wine mixture into whipped cream; fold together carefully. Spoon whipped cream mixture in jelly-roll lined bowl; cover with remaining jelly-roll slices. Refrigerate until set.

Turn out onto a serving dish. Put reserved whipped cream into a pastry bag fitted with a fluted nozzle. Decorate dessert with rosettes of whipped cream and candied cherries.

Viennese Chocolate Cake

Cake:
6 eggs, separated
1 tablespoon vanilla sugar, page 18
Pinch of salt
2/3 cup (150 g) sugar
3-1/2 oz. (100 g) semisweet chocolate, grated
Scant 1-1/2 cups (100 g) plain cookie crumbs
Generous 3/4 cup (100 g) ground hazelnuts

Filling:
Scant 1/4 cup (50 ml) sherry
1 cup (300 g) apricot jam

Frosting:
4 oz. (120 g) semisweet chocolate
1 egg, beaten
1-2/3 cups (200 g) powdered sugar, sifted
4 tablespoons (60 g) butter

Grease the inside bottom of a 10-inch (25-cm) springform cake pan. Preheat oven to 350°F (175°C).
To make cake, put egg yolks, vanilla sugar, salt and unflavored sugar into a medium bowl. Beat until pale and creamy, 5 to 10 minutes with an electric mixer. Stir in grated chocolate. Beat egg whites until stiff; fold carefully into egg yolk mixture. Mix cookie crumbs and hazelnuts; fold into egg mixture. Turn batter into prepared pan; smooth the surface. Bake 50 to 60 minutes or until a wooden pick inserted in center comes out clean. Turn out cake onto a rack to cool overnight so it will be easier to cut into layers.
To fill cake, cut cooled cake horizontally into 3 layers; sprinkle each layer with sherry. Warm jam and spread over 2 layers. Place jam-covered layers one on top of the other; cover with third layer.
To make frosting, melt chocolate in a double boiler over low heat; cool slightly. Stir in egg and powdered sugar. Melt butter. Add butter to chocolate mixture, beating well until frosting is creamy. Spread over top and sides of cake. Use a spatula to swirl frosting. Let frosting set before cutting cake.

Cook's Tip

This cake may also be filled with almond paste. Knead 8 oz. (225 g) almond paste, divide it in half and roll out each half into a thin round the size of the cake. Join the cake layers with the almond paste and apricot jam then frost as in the recipe.

Blueberry Cream Torte

Pastry:
1-1/2 cups (160 g) all-purpose flour
Pinch of salt
6 tablespoons (80 g) butter, cut in small pieces
3 tablespoons (40 g) sugar
1 egg yolk
2 to 3 tablespoons ice water

Topping:
1 lb. (500 g) blueberries
2 to 3 tablespoons orange-flavored liqueur
2 envelopes unflavored gelatin
Scant 1/4 cup (50 ml) water
Scant 2 cups (450 ml) whipping cream
Scant 1/2 cup (50 g) powdered sugar, sifted
3/4 cup (250 g) red currant jelly
1 cup (100 g) toasted sliced almonds, page 47

To make pastry, sift flour and salt into a large bowl. Using a pastry blender or 2 knives, cut in butter evenly. Lightly mix in sugar, egg yolk and enough ice water to make a dough. Press into a ball and wrap in foil or plastic wrap. Refrigerate 1 hour.

Preheat oven to 425°F (220°C). On a floured surface, roll out dough to cover bottom of an 8- or 9-inch (20- or 23-cm) springform cake pan. Place dough in pan; pierce all over with a fork. Bake 15 minutes or until golden. Cool on a rack.

To make topping, wash and dry blueberries. Put into a medium bowl and sprinkle with liqueur; cover and let stand 30 minutes.

Dissolve gelatin in water over low heat. Remove from heat; cool slightly. Whip cream with powdered sugar in a medium bowl until stiff. Fold in cooled gelatin and three-fourths of the blueberries. Return cooled pastry round to cake pan. Arrange blueberry mixture evenly on top of pastry. Cover with remaining blueberries. Warm red currant jelly and pour over fruit. Refrigerate until set.

Remove cake from pan. Sprinkle sides with almonds.

Black Forest Cherry Gâteau

Cake:
4 oz. (100 g) semisweet chocolate
8 tablespoons (100 g) butter, softened
1/2 cup (100 g) sugar
4 eggs
3/4 cup (75 g) ground almonds
3/4 cup (80 g) all-purpose flour
1 teaspoon baking powder

Filling & Topping:
Scant 2 cups (450 ml) whipping cream
2 (1-lb., 456-g) cans pitted cherries, drained
1/2 cup (125 ml) kirsch
12 candied cherries
Chocolate Curls, page 15

Lightly grease three 7-inch (18-cm) layer cake pans. Preheat oven to 350°F (175°C).

To make cake, melt chocolate in a double boiler over low heat; cool. Cream butter and sugar in a medium bowl until light and fluffy. Beat in eggs, almonds and chocolate. Sift flour and baking powder onto creamed mixture; fold in thoroughly. Spread batter evenly in greased layer cake pans. Bake 20 to 25 minutes or until a wooden pick inserted in centers comes out clean. Cool in pans a few minutes then turn out cakes onto racks to cool completely.

To make filling and topping, whip cream until stiff. Dry canned cherries on paper towels. Sprinkle each cake layer with a third of the kirsch. Spread 2 layers with whipped cream, reserving about half. Arrange canned cherries in cream. Place layers on top of each other; cover with third layer. Spread top and sides of cake with two-thirds of remaining whipped cream. Put the rest in a pastry bag fitted with a fluted nozzle. Pipe rosettes of cream onto cake. Decorate with candied cherries. Pile chocolate curls in the center; sprinkle some broken pieces onto sides.

Sachertorte

Cake:
7 eggs, separated
3/4 cup plus 2 tablespoons (200 g) sugar
8 tablespoons (100 g) butter
Scant 1/2 cup (50 g) unsweetened cocoa powder
1 cup (100 g) all-purpose flour
3/4 cup (50 g) plain cookie crumbs

Frosting:
1/2 cup (160 g) apricot jam
8 oz. (225 g) semisweet chocolate
Chocolate sprinkles

Grease two 9-inch (23-cm) layer cake pans and sprinkle with dry breadcrumbs. Preheat oven to 400°F (205°C).
To make cake, put egg yolks and 1/2 cup (100 g) sugar into a large bowl. Beat until pale and creamy, 5 to 10 minutes with an electric mixer. Melt butter; cool slightly. Sift cocoa powder with flour; fold into egg yolk mixture with butter. Beat egg whites until frothy. Add remaining sugar and beat until stiff. Fold egg white mixture and cookie crumbs into egg yolk mixture.

Spoon batter into prepared pans. Bake 30 minutes. Reduce heat to 350°F (175°C) and bake 15 to 20 minutes longer or until a wooden pick inserted in center comes out clean. Cool cake layers in oven 15 minutes with door slightly open. Remove from oven and turn out onto a rack to cool completely.
To make frosting, warm jam and use about a third to join layers. Spread remaining jam thinly over top and sides of cake. Melt chocolate in a double boiler over low heat. Spread chocolate smoothly over cake. Press chocolate sprinkles into soft chocolate around bottom edge of cake.

Chocolate Délice

8 tablespoons (100 g) butter
1/2 cup (100 g) sugar
4 oz. (100 g) semisweet chocolate
6 eggs, separated
1 cup (100 g) ground almonds
3/4 cup (50 g) plain cookie crumbs
3/4 cup (75 g) all-purpose flour, sifted
1/2 cup (50 g) slivered almonds
4 oz. (100 g) semisweet chocolate

Grease and flour a 12-inch (30-cm) long Balmoral pan or a 12x4-inch (30x10-cm) loaf pan. Preheat oven to 350°F (175°C).

Cream butter and sugar in a medium bowl until light and fluffy. Melt 4 oz. (100 g) chocolate in a double boiler over low heat. Add to butter mixture with egg yolks. Beat mixture until very creamy. Stir in ground almonds, cookie crumbs and flour. Beat egg whites until stiff; fold into chocolate mixture. Turn batter into pan. Bake 50 to 60 minutes or until a wooden pick inserted in center comes out clean. Turn out cake onto a rack to cool. Press slivered almonds into cake as illustrated.

Melt 4 oz. (100 g) chocolate in a double boiler over low heat. Cover cooled cake with chocolate.

Raspberry Cream Torte

Shortbread:
7 tablespoons (100 g) butter or margarine, softened
1/4 cup (50 g) sugar
1-1/4 cups (150 g) all-purpose flour, sifted

Cake:
4 eggs, separated, plus 2 egg yolks
1/2 cup (100 g) sugar
3/4 cup (80 g) all-purpose flour
1/2 cup (50 g) unsweetened cocoa powder

Filling:
1/2 lb. (225 g) fresh or frozen raspberries, thawed
1 tablespoon raspberry-flavored liqueur or kirsch
2 envelopes unflavored gelatin
Scant 1/4 cup (50 ml) water
Scant 2 cups (450 ml) whipping cream
Generous 1/2 cup (70 g) powdered sugar, sifted

Decoration:
1 cup (250 ml) whipping cream
1 tablespoon powdered sugar, sifted
1/4 cup (25 g) toasted sliced almonds, page 47

To make shortbread, cream butter and sugar in a medium bowl. Add flour; work into a dough. Press into a ball and wrap in foil or plastic wrap. Refrigerate 2 hours.

Grease a 15-1/2x10-1/2-inch (39x27-cm) cake pan. Line with waxed paper; grease paper. Preheat oven to 425°F (220°C).

To make cake, put 6 egg yolks and half the sugar into a medium bowl. Beat until pale and creamy, 5 to 10 minutes with an electric mixer. Beat whites until stiff; beat in remaining sugar. Fold egg white mixture into egg yolk mixture. Sift flour and cocoa powder onto egg mixture; fold in carefully using a metal spoon. Spread batter evenly in prepared pan. Bake 8 minutes or until a wooden pick inserted in center comes out clean. Do not turn off oven; reduce heat to 375°F (190°C). Sprinkle a sheet of waxed paper with sugar; turn out cooked cake onto it. Peel off lining paper. Cover with a damp cloth towel and roll up with towel on the inside. Cool.

On a lightly floured surface, roll out shortbread dough to fit the bottom of an 10-inch (25-cm) springform cake pan. Place dough round in pan. Bake 15 to 20 minutes or until golden. Cool in pan.

To make filling, drain thawed raspberries. Lightly crush two-thirds of raspberries in a small bowl. Stir in liqueur. Reserve remaining fruit for decoration. Dissolve gelatin in water over low heat. Remove from heat; cool slightly. Whip cream with powdered sugar in a medium bowl until stiff. Fold in cooled dissolved gelatin and crushed raspberry mixture.

Unroll cooled cake and spread evenly with fruit and cream mixture. Cut lengthwise into 6 strips. Roll up one of the strips; stand it upright on the center of the cooled shortbread. Shape the other strips carefully into circles around the central roll, until the whole shortbread base has been covered. Refrigerate cake until filling is firm.

To decorate cake, whip cream with powdered sugar until stiff. Remove cake from pan and place on a serving dish. Spread some whipped cream mixture over top and sides of cake; smooth with a spatula. Place remaining whipped cream mixture in a pastry bag and pipe an attractive design on top of the cake as illustrated. Decorate rosettes of cream with reserved raspberries. Sprinkle almonds over center of cake.

Cherry Cream Layer Gâteau

3/4 (17-1/4-oz., 489-g) pkg. frozen puff pastry, thawed

Filling & Topping:
3 tablespoons (50 g) red currant jelly
Scant 1 cup (100 g) powdered sugar, sifted
1 tablespoon lemon juice
1 (1-lb., 456-g) can pitted cherries
Pinch of ground cinnamon
1 tablespoon cornstarch
Cold water
Scant 2 cups (450 ml) whipping cream
3 tablespoons (40 g) granulated sugar
12 candied cherries

Sprinkle a large baking sheet with cold water. Preheat oven to 400°F (205°C).

Divide puff pastry dough into 3 portions. On a floured surface, roll out each portion to an 8-inch (20-cm) round. Arrange rounds on dampened baking sheet. Refrigerate 15 minutes. Bake 10 to 12 minutes or until lightly browned. Cool pastry rounds on racks.

To make filling and topping, warm red currant jelly and spread over most even pastry round. Combine powdered sugar and lemon juice in a small bowl to make a glaze. Spread glaze over jelly; let cool. Cut glazed pastry layer into 12 slices.

Drain canned cherries, reserving juice. Heat juice with cinnamon in a small saucepan. Blend cornstarch with a little cold water; add to juice mixture. Bring to a boil, stirring constantly until slightly thickened. Stir in canned cherries; let cool. Spread cooled cherry sauce over one of the two uncut pastry layers.

Whip cream with granulated sugar until stiff. Put 6 tablespoons of whipped cream mixture into a pastry bag fitted with a fluted nozzle. Spread some of the remaining cream mixture over cherry sauce; put the last uncovered pastry layer on top. Spread remaining cream thickly over this layer and around sides of gâteau. Arrange glazed pastry slices on top. Decorate each with a rosette of whipped cream mixture and a candied cherry.

Cook's Tip

It is important to cut the glazed pastry layer into slices before placing over the cream filling. If you try to cut it when serving the gâteau, the cream filling will spill out.

Chocolate Hazelnut Meringue

Meringue:
6 egg whites
3/4 cup plus 2 tablespoons (200 g) granulated sugar
Scant 3/4 cup (80 g) powdered sugar
1 tablespoon cornstarch
3/4 cup (80 g) ground hazelnuts

Decoration & Filling:
4 oz. (100 g) semisweet chocolate
1-1/4 cups (300 ml) whipping cream
1 tablespoon powdered sugar
1 teaspoon instant chocolate drink powder

Line baking sheets with baking parchment. Draw five 9-inch (23-cm) circles on baking parchment in pencil. Preheat oven to 250°F (120°C).

To make meringue, beat egg whites in a large bowl until stiff. Add granulated sugar and beat again until stiff. Sift powdered sugar with cornstarch; mix with hazelnuts. Fold powdered sugar mixture into egg white mixture. Spread a fifth of mixture on each circle. Bake 3 to 4 hours or until thoroughly dry. Leave oven door slightly open during baking. Cool on racks.

To make decoration and filling, melt chocolate in a double boiler over low heat. Spread over waxed paper to a 12x9-inch (30x24-cm) rectangle; cool. When cool, divide longest side into 10 equal strips. Cut eight of these strips into 3 equal pieces each, making 24 strips of chocolate. Cut remaining 2 long strips into four each, making 8 strips. Whip cream with powdered sugar until stiff. Spread cooled meringue layers with whipped cream mixture, reserving a fourth for decoration. Stack layers on top of each other. Cover cake with about two-thirds of remaining cream mixture. Put the rest into a pastry bag fitted with a fluted nozzle; pipe rosettes on cake. Sift chocolate powder over cake. Arrange shorter strips of chocolate on the top of the cake and the 24 longer strips overlapping around the sides.

Peach Gâteau Genevieve

1 (8-inch, 20-cm) Chocolate Cake, page 12

Filling & Decoration:
Scant 2 cups (450 ml) whipping cream
Scant 1/2 cup (60 g) powdered sugar, sifted
1/4 cup (30 g) unsweetened cocoa powder, sifted
1 (8-3/4-oz., 248-g) can peach slices
3 tablespoons maraschino

Frosting:
7 oz. (200 g) semisweet chocolate
1-3/4 cups (225 g) powdered sugar, sifted
3 tablespoons water
1 tablespoon (15 g) butter
1 tablespoon chopped pistachio nuts

Make Chocolate Cake, page 12. Cool cooled cake horizontally into 3 layers.

To make filling and decoration, whip cream with half the powdered sugar until stiff; divide into 3 portions. Add remaining powdered sugar and cocoa powder to 1 portion; spread over bottom cake layer. Halve peach slices and arrange all but 2 slices over second cake layer. Mix second portion of whipped cream mixture with maraschino; spread over peaches. Top with third cake layer.

To make frosting, melt chocolate with powdered sugar, water and butter in a double boiler over low heat. Stir until smooth; spread evenly over top and sides of cake. Cool.

Put remaining whipped cream mixture into a pastry bag fitted with a fluted nozzle. Decorate cake with swirls of piped cream, reserved peach slices cut into segments and pistachios.

Dobostorte

6 sponge rounds, see below

Filling:
1-1/4 cups (300 ml) milk
1/4 cup (25 g) cornstarch
1/4 cup (50 g) sugar
1 egg yolk
1 cup plus 2 tablespoons (250 g) butter
1 cup (50 g) marshmallows
2 oz. (50 g) semisweet chocolate

Glaze:
3/4 cup plus 2 tablespoons (200 g) sugar
1 tablespoon (15 g) butter

Prepare and bake the cake layers as in the recipe for Prince Regent Cake, opposite. When cool, fill cake with the following cream mixture.
To make filling, mix a little milk with cornstarch in a medium bowl. Heat remaining milk with sugar in a small saucepan. Stir hot milk mixture into blended cornstarch. Return to saucepan and bring to a boil, stirring constantly until thickened. Stir in egg yolk quickly and thoroughly. Return mixture to bowl; cool. Cream butter until soft, then beat into cooled cornstarch sauce a spoonful at a time. Melt marshmallows and chocolate in a double boiler over low heat. Beat chocolate mixture into cornstarch mixture. Refrigerate until firm enough to spread.

Spread 5 sponge rounds with three-fourths of the chocolate cream; arrange layers on top of each other. Spread remaining chocolate cream around sides of cake.
To make glaze, heat sugar and butter in a small saucepan over medium heat. Stir constantly until sugar has dissolved and butter melted. The mixture should be light brown. Spread caramel glaze over top of cake immediately. While caramel covering is still soft, divide the top into 12 portions with an oiled knife. The caramel cannot be cut after it has hardened.

Prince Regent Cake

Cake:
7 eggs, separated
2/3 cup (150 g) sugar
Pinch of salt
1-1/4 cups (150 g) self-rising flour

Filling & Frosting:
1-1/4 cups (300 ml) milk
1/4 cup (25 g) cornstarch
1/4 cup (50 g) sugar
1 egg yolk
1 cup plus 2 tablespoons (250 g) butter
9 oz. (250 g) semisweet chocolate
Scant 1/2 cup (50 g) unsweetened cocoa powder, sifted

Grease and flour baking sheets. Preheat oven to 425°F (220°C).
To make cake, put egg yolks, half the sugar and salt into a medium bowl. Beat until pale and creamy, 5 to 10 minutes with an electric mixer. Beat egg whites until stiff; beat in remaining sugar. Fold into egg yolk mixture. Sift flour over egg mixture and fold in. Spread batter evenly in six 10-inch (25-cm) rounds on prepared baking sheets. Bake 5 to 7 minutes or until a wooden pick inserted in center comes out clean. Cool on racks.
To make filling and frosting, mix a little milk with cornstarch in a medium bowl. Heat remaining milk with sugar in a small saucepan. Stir hot milk mixture into blended cornstarch. Return to heat and bring to a boil, stirring constantly. Stir in egg yolk quickly and thoroughly. Return mixture to bowl; cool. Cream butter until soft then beat into cooled cornstarch sauce a spoonful at a time. Melt 2 oz. (50 g) chocolate in a double boiler over low heat. Beat into cornstarch mixture with cocoa powder. Spread chocolate cream over cake rounds, placing one on top of the other. Cover top and sides of cake with chocolate cream. Refrigerate until set.

Melt remaining chocolate and spread evenly over cake.

Milanese Almond Cake

Cake:
4 eggs
1/2 cup (100 g) sugar
Grated peel of 1/2 lemon
1/2 cup (50 g) all-purpose flour
1/2 teaspoon baking powder
1/4 cup (25 g) ground almonds
2 tablespoons (25 g) butter, melted
2/3 cup (225 g) raspberry jelly

Topping:
3-1/2 cups (400 g) ground almonds
1/2 cup (100 g) sugar
6 egg yolks
1/3 to 1/2 cup (100 to 125 ml) rum
1 egg white
3/4 cup (80 g) toasted sliced almonds, page 47

Grease and flour an 8-inch (20-cm) springform cake pan. Pre-heat oven to 375°F (190°C).

To make cake, put eggs, sugar and lemon peel into a medium bowl. Beat until pale and creamy, 5 to 10 minutes with an electric mixer. Sift flour and baking powder together; mix with almonds. Fold into egg mixture using a metal spoon. Fold in butter. Turn batter into prepared cake pan. Bake 35 to 45 minutes or until a wooden pick inserted in center comes out clean. Let cake cool overnight on a rack.

Cut cooled cake horizontally into 3 layers. Join layers together using about half the raspberry jelly. Preheat oven to 475°F (245°C).

To make topping, put almonds, sugar and egg yolks into a medium bowl. Add enough rum to give a mixture soft enough to pipe. Put half the almond mixture into a pastry bag fitted with a fluted nozzle. Blend remaining almond mixture with enough egg white to give a spreading consistency. Spread over top and sides of cake. Pipe mixture in pastry bag over cake in a petal design, as illustrated, making a flower pattern.

Bake cake a few minutes or until almond frosting begins to turn light brown. Warm remaining raspberry jelly over low heat. Spoon a little warm jelly into flower petals. Spread the rest of the jelly over sides of cake; press on sliced almonds.

Cook's Tip

Because the cake is already cooked, it need only be put in the oven to brown and slightly crisp the top. Alternatively, the cake could be placed briefly under a hot broiler.

Celebration Nut Cake

Cake:
5 eggs, separated
1/2 cup (100 g) sugar
1 cup (100 g) ground hazelnuts
3 tablespoons (20 g) all-purpose flour, sifted
1/4 teaspoon almond extract

Filling & Frosting:
2 tablespoons (15 g) cornstarch
2 tablespoons (25 g) granulated sugar
2/3 cup (150 ml) milk
2 egg yolks, beaten
1 teaspoon vanilla extract
7 oz. (200 g) almond paste
Scant 1 cup (100 g) powdered sugar, sifted
3 to 5 tablespoons (50 to 75 ml) lemon juice
Walnut halves

Grease an 8-inch (20-cm) springform cake pan. Preheat oven to 375°F (190°C).
To make cake, beat egg yolks and sugar in a large bowl until pale and creamy. Fold in hazelnuts, flour and almond extract. Beat egg whites until stiff; fold into egg yolk mixture. Turn batter into pan. Bake cake 40 minutes or until a wooden pick inserted in center comes out clean. Cool overnight on a rack.
To make filling and frosting, blend cornstarch, granulated sugar, a little milk and egg yolks. Bring remaining milk to a boil. Stir hot milk and vanilla into cornstarch mixture. Return to heat and bring back to a boil. Cook a few seconds, stirring constantly until thickened. Cool, stirring frequently. Cut cake into 2 layers. Spread 1 layer with filling; top with second layer. Knead almond paste to soften. On a surface sprinkled with powdered sugar, roll out almond paste to a round large enough to cover top and sides of cake. Press onto cake. Blend powdered sugar with enough lemon juice to give a coating consistency. Spread over cake. Decorate with walnut halves.

Chocolate Chestnut Gâteau

1 (8-inch, 20-cm) Chocolate Cake, page 12
Filling:
1 (8-3/4-oz., 248-g) can sweetened chestnut puree
1 tablespoon lemon juice
1/3 cup (100 ml) whipping cream

Frosting:
1/4 cup (75 g) apricot jam
8 oz. (225 g) almond paste
6 oz. (175 g) semisweet chocolate

Make Chocolate Cake, page 12. Cut cooled cake horizontally into 3 layers.
To make filling, mix chestnut puree, lemon juice and cream in a medium bowl until smooth. Spread filling over 1 cake layer and top with second layer.
To make frosting, warm apricot jam over low heat and press through a strainer to obtain jelly. Brush warm jelly over top and sides of cake. Reserve about a third of the almond paste. On a surface sprinkled with powdered sugar, roll out remaining almond paste to a thin round large enough to cover top and sides of cake. Place almond paste over cake, pressing lightly. Shape reserved almond paste into small animals as illustrated.

Melt chocolate in a double boiler over low heat. Cover cake with chocolate, smoothing it with a spatula. Decorate with animals before chocolate sets. Let set before serving.

Coffee Cream Cake

1 tablespoon coffee powder
Boiling water
1 (8-inch, 20-cm) coffee sponge cake, see below
1/4 cup (75 g) cherry jam

Frosting & Decoration:
1/4 cup (25 g) cornstarch
1-1/4 cups (300 ml) milk
1/4 cup (50 g) sugar
3 tablespoons instant coffee powder
Boiling water
1 cup plus 2 tablespoons (250 g) butter
3 tablespoons (20 g) powdered sugar, sifted
16 candied coffee beans
16 almonds

Dissolve coffee powder in a little boiling water; cool. Follow the recipe for Beaten Sponge Cake, page 11, adding dissolved coffee powder to eggs and sugar before beating. Cut cooled cake horizontally into 2 layers and fill with jam.

To make frosting and decoration, blend cornstarch with a little milk in a small bowl. Heat remaining milk with sugar in a small saucepan. Stir hot milk mixture into cornstarch mixture. Return to saucepan and bring to a boil, stirring constantly until thickened. Dissolve coffee powder in a little boiling water. Stir into cornstarch mixture. Return mixture to bowl and cool, stirring frequently. Cream butter until soft then beat into cooled cornstarch sauce a spoonful at a time. Mix in powdered sugar.

Spread about half the coffee cream over top and sides of cake. Mark top of cake into 16 portions with a knife. Put remaining coffee cream into a pastry bag fitted with a fluted nozzle. Pipe in a pattern on cake as illustrated. Decorate with candied coffee beans and almonds.

Strawberry Layer Gâteau

Plain Cake:
3 eggs
1/4 cup plus 2 tablespoons (75 g) sugar
1/2 cup (50 g) all-purpose flour
1/2 teaspoon baking powder

Chocolate Cake:
3 eggs
1/4 cup plus 2 tablespoons (75 g) sugar
1/2 cup (50 g) all-purpose flour
1/2 teaspoon baking powder
2 tablespoons (15 g) unsweetened cocoa powder

Filling & Decoration:
Scant 1 cup (100 g) strawberries
1 envelope unflavored gelatin
3 tablespoons water
2-1/2 cups (600 ml) whipping cream
Scant 1/2 cup (50 g) powdered sugar, sifted
16 candied cherries
2 oz. (50 g) Chocolate Curls, page 15
Additional powdered sugar
1/4 cup (25 g) toasted sliced almonds, page 47

Make plain and chocolate sponge cake batters as on pages 11 and 12. Bake in two 8-inch (20-cm) greased and floured pans 30 to 40 minutes. Cut each cooled cake horizontally into 2 layers.

To make filling and decoration, puree strawberries in a blender and place in a medium bowl. Dissolve gelatin in water over low heat; cool. Whip cream; fold in powdered sugar. Fold a third of whipped cream mixture and gelatin into strawberry puree. Spread some of remaining cream mixture over both plain cake layers; put a chocolate layer on top of each. Join pairs of layers with strawberry cream. Cover cake with two-thirds of remaining cream. Decorate cake with piped rosettes of cream. Add cherries and chocolate curls. Sift powdered sugar over chocolate. Press almonds onto sides of cake.

Honey Crunch Cake

Yeast Dough:
2 tablespoons (25 g) sugar
3 tablespoons warm water (110°F, 43°C)
1-1/2 pkgs. active dry yeast
1/2 cup (125 ml) milk
2 tablespoons (25 g) butter
3-1/4 cups (380 g) all-purpose flour
1/4 teaspoon salt
3/4 cup (80 g) sliced almonds
3 tablespoons (25 g) raisins
1 egg, beaten

Filling & Topping:
4 tablespoons (50 g) butter
4 tablespoons (50 g) sugar
1/2 teaspoon ground cinnamon
1/3 cup (100 g) honey
1 cup (100 g) chopped almonds

To make yeast dough, stir a pinch of sugar into water; sprinkle with yeast. Let stand 5 minutes. Boil milk in a small saucepan. Stir in remaining sugar and butter; cool. Sift flour into a large bowl. Add salt, almonds and raisins. Stir yeast mixture and egg into milk mixture. Add to flour, making a dough. On a floured surface, knead dough until smooth. Cover and let rise in a warm place 20 minutes. Grease a 9-inch (23-cm) springform pan. Roll out dough to a 14x12-inch (35x30-cm) rectangle.
To make filling and topping, spread half of butter over dough. Sprinkle with half of sugar and cinnamon. Roll up from shorter side; cut into 1-inch (2.5-cm) slices. Heat remaining butter, honey, remaining sugar and almonds in a small saucepan over low heat. Pour dissolved honey mixture into pan.

Form balls from dough slices; arrange in pan. Let rise in a warm place 25 minutes. Preheat oven to 375°F (190°C). Bake 30 to 40 minutes or until golden. Invert onto a rack to cool.

Frosted Rum Cake

Cake:
1 cup (50 g) pumpernickel breadcrumbs
2 teaspoons rum
8 eggs
2/3 cup (150 g) sugar
1 cup (120 g) ground almonds
2 oz. (50 g) semisweet chocolate, grated
Grated peel of 1/2 lemon
Pinch of ground cloves
1/3 cup (50 g) chopped mixed candied peel

Frosting:
1-2/3 cups (200 g) powdered sugar, sifted
1 tablespoon rum
1-1/2 to 3 tablespoons water
12 candied cherries

Grease a 10-inch (25-cm) springform cake pan. Preheat oven to 400°F (205°C).
To make cake, mix breadcrumbs and rum in a small bowl; set aside. Separate 6 of the eggs. Put 2 whole eggs, 6 egg yolks and sugar into a large bowl. Beat until pale and creamy, 5 to 10 minutes with an electric mixer. Stir in almonds, chocolate, lemon peel, cloves and candied peel; mix well. Beat egg whites until stiff; fold into mixture. Stir in rum-soaked breadcrumbs. Pour batter into greased pan; smooth the surface. Bake cake 45 to 55 minutes or until a wooden pick inserted in center comes out clean. Cover with foil during cooking if cake is becoming too brown. Turn out cake onto a rack to cool.
To make frosting, put powdered sugar into a small bowl. Add rum and enough water to give a coating consistency. Spread frosting over cake. Decorate with candied cherries while frosting is soft.

Linzertorte

3/4 cup plus 2 tablespoons (200 g) butter or margarine, softened
3/4 cup plus 2 tablespoons (200 g) sugar
3 eggs
Pinch each of salt and ground cloves
1/2 teaspoon ground cinnamon
Grated peel of 1/2 lemon
Scant 1 cup (100 g) plain cookie crumbs
1-1/4 cups (150 g) ground almonds
2 cups (225 g) all-purpose flour, sifted
1 cup (350 g) raspberry jam
1 egg yolk, beaten

Grease a 10-inch (25-cm) springform cake pan.

Cream butter or margarine and sugar in a large bowl until
light and fluffy. Add 3 eggs one at a time with salt, cloves, cinnamon and lemon peel. Mix cookie crumbs and almonds; stir
into egg mixture. Fold in flour to make a soft dough. Cover and
refrigerate 2 hours.

Preheat oven to 375°F (190°C). On a floured surface, roll or
pat out two-thirds of the dough to a 10-inch (25-cm) round.
Leave remaining dough in refrigerator. Place round of dough in
greased pan and shape it so it is about 3/4 inch (2 cm) high
around the edges. Spread jam over dough. Roll out remaining
dough about 1/8 inch (3 mm) thick. Cut into 1/2-inch (1.5-cm)
strips with a pastry cutter. Arrange strips in a lattice pattern over
jam. Brush with egg yolk. Bake 35 to 40 minutes or until pastry
is lightly browned. Cool in pan about 30 minutes. Remove to a
rack to cool completely.

Mandorla Almond Cake

Pastry:
3/4 cup plus 2 tablespoons (200 g) all-purpose flour
Pinch of salt
7 tablespoons (100 g) butter, cut in small pieces
3 tablespoons (40 g) sugar
Grated peel of 1/2 lemon
1 egg yolk
About 3 tablespoons ice water
1/4 cup (75 g) apricot jam

Filling:
1 whole egg plus 2 eggs, separated
1/2 cup plus 1 tablespoon (125 g) sugar
Pinch of salt
1/2 teaspoon vanilla extract
1 tablespoon all-purpose flour
1 cup (100 g) ground almonds
4 tablespoons (60 g) butter, melted

Topping:
2 egg whites
1/2 cup (100 g) sugar
1 cup (100 g) ground almonds

To make pastry, sift flour and salt into a large bowl. Using a
pastry blender or 2 knives, cut in butter evenly. Mix in sugar,
lemon peel, egg yolk and enough water to make a dough. Wrap
in foil and refrigerate 2 hours. On a floured surface, roll out
dough to fit a 9-inch (23-cm) springform pan. Place dough in
pan. Spread jam over dough. Preheat oven to 350°F (175°C).
To make filling, mix egg, egg yolks, half the sugar, salt,
vanilla, flour and almonds in a medium bowl. Beat egg whites
with remaining sugar until stiff; fold into mixture. Fold butter
into egg mixture. Pour into pastry shell. Bake 45 minutes.
Remove from oven. Increase temperature to 400°F (205°C).
To make topping, beat egg whites and sugar until stiff. Fold in
almonds. Spread topping over hot cake. Bake 15 minutes.

Feather-Frosted Layer Cake

1 (8-inch, 20-cm) Beaten Sponge Cake, page 11

Filling:
Generous 1/2 cup (70 g) ground almonds
1/4 cup (30 g) powdered sugar, sifted
Scant 1/4 cup (50 ml) rum
2/3 cup (150 ml) orange juice
1 tablespoon lemon juice

Topping:
2/3 cup (250 g) orange marmalade
3-1/2 oz. (100 g) almond paste
Scant 1 cup (100 g) powdered sugar, sifted
1-1/2 to 3 tablespoons hot water
1 teaspoon unsweetened cocoa powder
3/4 cup (75 g) toasted sliced almonds, page 47

Make Beaten Sponge Cake, page 11. Cut into 3 layers.
To make filling, combine almonds, powdered sugar and half
the rum in a small bowl. Spread almond mixture over bottom
cake layer. Place second cake layer on top. Mix orange and
lemon juice with remaining rum; pour over second layer so it
soaks in. Place third cake layer on top.
To make frosting, warm marmalade and press through a
strainer to obtain jelly. Brush warm jelly over top and sides of
cake. On a surface sprinkled with powdered sugar, roll out
almond paste to a round large enough to cover top of cake.
Place on top of cake, pressing down lightly. Blend powdered
sugar and hot water in a small bowl to give a smooth frosting.
Mix 3 tablespoons of frosting with cocoa powder.
   Spread white frosting over almond paste, smoothing it with a
spatula. Put chocolate frosting into a baking parchment pastry
bag, page 16, which has a very small opening. Pipe frosting onto
cake in a spiral starting from the center. Using a knife or
skewer, draw lines outwards from the center of the cake to
make feather pattern. Press almonds onto sides of cake.

Malakoff Cake

Butter Cream:
1/4 cup plus 1 tablespoon (40 g) cornstarch
2 cups plus 2 tablespoons (500 ml) milk
1/4 cup plus 2 tablespoons (70 g) granulated sugar
1 cup plus 2 tablespoons (250 g) butter, softened
3 tablespoons (20 g) powdered sugar, sifted
3 tablespoons rum
32 ladyfingers

Syrup & Decoration:
1 tablespoon sugar
1 tablespoon warm water
Scant 1/4 cup (50 ml) Marsala
1 tablespoon rum
3 tablespoons red currant jelly
1 cup (100 g) toasted sliced almonds, page 47
14 cookies, half-coated with melted chocolate

To make butter cream, blend cornstarch with a little milk and
granulated sugar in a medium bowl. Boil remaining milk in a
medium saucepan. Stir hot milk into cornstarch mixture.
Return to heat and bring to a boil, stirring constantly until
thickened. Return mixture to bowl. Cool, stirring frequently.
Cream butter and powdered sugar until light and fluffy. Gradually beat butter mixture and rum into cooled cornstarch sauce.
   Line the bottom of an 8-inch (20-cm) springform cake pan
with ladyfingers.
To make syrup and decoration, dissolve sugar in water; add
Marsala and rum. Spoon half the syrup over ladyfingers. Warm
jelly; dot half over ladyfingers. Spread with a layer of butter
cream. Repeat layers, ending with butter cream. Reserve
enough butter cream for sides of cake and decoration. Refrigerate cake overnight. Remove cake from pan. Spread two-thirds
of reserved butter cream over sides of cake; sprinkle with
almonds. Use remaining butter cream to pipe 14 rosettes onto
cake. Refrigerate cake. Just before serving, add cookies.

Chocolate Cherry Layer Gâteau

Cake:
4 eggs
1/2 cup (100 g) sugar
Pinch of salt
Pinch of ground cinnamon
1/4 cup (25 g) all-purpose flour
1/2 teaspoon baking powder
2 tablespoons (15 g) unsweetened cocoa powder
1/4 cup (25 g) ground almonds
1 tablespoon rum

Filling & Topping:
1/4 cup (25 g) cornstarch
2 teaspoons unsweetened cocoa powder
1/2 cup (100 g) sugar
2 egg yolks
1-1/4 cups (300 ml) milk
3/4 cup plus 2 tablespoons (200 g) butter
3 tablespoons cherry-flavored liqueur
3 oz. (80 g) semisweet chocolate, finely grated
12 candied cherries
Chocolate Curls, page 15

Grease an 8-inch (20-cm) pan. Preheat oven to 375°F (190°C).
To make cake, beat eggs, sugar, salt and cinnamon until thick. Sift flour, baking powder and cocoa; fold into mixture with almonds and rum. Turn batter into greased pan. Bake 35 to 40 minutes or until a wooden pick inserted in center comes out clean. Cool on a rack. Cut cooled cake into 3 layers.
To make filling and topping, blend cornstarch, cocoa powder, sugar, egg yolks and a little milk. Bring remaining milk to a boil. Stir milk into cornstarch mixture. Return to heat and stir until boiling. Cool, stirring frequently. Beat butter until soft. Gradually beat cornstarch sauce, liqueur and chocolate into butter. Join layers with chocolate cream and spread thinly over top and sides. Decorate with rosettes, cherries and chocolate curls.

Gâteau Saint-Honoré

Pastry:
6 tablespoons (80 g) butter, cut in small pieces
3 tablespoons (40 g) sugar
Pinch of salt
1 egg yolk
1-1/2 cups (160 g) all-purpose flour, sifted

Cream Puff Paste:
4 tablespoons (60 g) butter
1 cup (250 ml) water
Pinch of salt
1 cup (150 g) all-purpose flour, sifted
4 eggs, beaten

Filling & Glaze:
1 quantity Custard Butter Cream, page 13, or
   French Butter Cream, page 14
1/4 cup (75 g) apricot jam

To make pastry, knead butter, sugar, salt, egg yolk and flour to make a dough. Cover and refrigerate 30 minutes. On a floured surface, roll out dough to a 10-inch (25-cm) round. Place on a baking sheet. Preheat oven to 400°F (205°C).
To make cream puff paste, put butter, water and salt into a medium saucepan; melt butter over low heat. Quickly bring to a boil. Remove from heat and beat in flour all at once. Return to heat and cook 1 minute, stirring constantly. Cool slightly. Gradually beat in eggs, making sure they are thoroughly mixed. Put cream puff paste into a pastry bag fitted with a large fluted nozzle. Pipe a thick ring over the edge of the dough round. Pipe 8 to 10 individual puffs separately on baking sheet. Bake 25 to 35 minutes or until firm and golden. Cool on a rack.
To fill and glaze, make Custard Butter Cream, or French Butter Cream and use to fill cooled cream puff ring. Arrange puffs around edge of filling. Warm jam; press through a strainer to obtain jelly. Brush warm jelly over ring and puffs.

Variations from a Package

Cherry Slice

1 (1-lb., 456-g) can pitted cherries
1 (18-1/2-oz., 526-g) pkg. yellow cake mix
Eggs
Water
Oil, if required
1 cup (100 g) ground hazelnuts
1/4 teaspoon ground cinnamon
Powdered sugar, sifted
Whipped cream, if desired

Grease and flour a 13x9-inch (33x23-cm) cake pan. Preheat oven to 350°F (175°C).

Drain cherries, reserving juice. Dry cherries thoroughly with paper towels. Prepare cake mix with eggs, water and oil, if required, according to package instructions, using half cherry juice and half water instead of all water. Fold cherries, hazelnuts and cinnamon into batter. Spread batter evenly in prepared pan. Bake 35 to 40 minutes, following package instructions to test doneness. Cool as indicated on package.

Cut cooled cake into slices and sprinkle with powdered sugar. Serve with whipped cream, if desired.

Mocha Ring Cake

Cake:
1 (18-1/2-oz., 526-g) pkg. yellow cake mix
Eggs
Oil, if required
Water, of which 1 cup (250 ml) is prepared coffee, cooled
6 oz. (170 g) semisweet chocolate, grated or finely chopped

Frosting:
2-1/4 cups (275 g) powdered sugar, sifted
Generous pinch of ground cinnamon
3 to 4 tablespoons hot water

Grease and flour a 10-inch (25-cm) fluted Bundt or tube pan. Preheat oven to 350°F (175°C).

To make cake, prepare cake mix with eggs and oil, if required, according to package instructions, adding prepared coffee with enough water to make up amount specified on package. Fold in half the chocolate. Turn batter into prepared pan. Bake 50 to 60 minutes, following package instructions to test doneness. Cool as indicated on package.

To make frosting, put powdered sugar and cinnamon into a small bowl. Beat in enough hot water to give a coating consistency. Pour frosting over cake. Decorate around bottom edge of cake with remaining chocolate while frosting is soft.

Cook's Tip

This cake is delicious served with a bowl of whipped cream to which a little apple pie spice has been added.

Chocolate Cream Gâteau

Cake:
1 (18-1/2-oz., 526-g) pkg. yellow cake mix
Eggs
Water
Oil, if required
1 cup (100 g) ground hazelnuts

Filling & Topping:
2-1/4 cups (275 g) powdered sugar
3 tablespoons (20 g) unsweetened cocoa powder
3/4 cup plus 2 tablespoons (200 g) butter, softened
1 tablespoon kirsch
Candied coffee beans

Grease and flour two 8-inch (20-cm) layer cake pans. Preheat oven to 350°F (175°C).

To make cake, prepare cake mix with eggs, water and oil, if required, according to package instructions. Fold hazelnuts into batter. Spread batter evenly in prepared pans. Bake 35 to 40 minutes, following package instructions to test doneness. Cool as indicated on package.

To make frosting, sift powdered sugar with cocoa powder. Cream butter in a medium bowl until light. Beat in powdered sugar mixture and kirsch. Place a fourth of the chocolate frosting in a pastry bag fitted with a fluted nozzle. Spread a third of the remaining frosting over 1 cake layer. Place second cake layer on top. Use remaining frosting to cover top and sides of cake. Decorate top with rosettes of piped frosting; top each rosette with a candied coffee bean.

Alicante Gâteau

Cake:
1 (18-1/2-oz., 526-g) pkg. orange cake mix
Eggs
Water
Oil, if required

Frosting:
2 cups (250 g) powdered sugar
3 to 5 tablespoons (50 to 75 ml) hot water or orange juice
Few drops orange food coloring

Decoration:
6 candied orange slices
16 candied cherries
Angelica strips

Grease and flour a petal-patterned or regular 10-inch (25-cm) springform cake pan. Preheat oven to 350°F (175°C).

To make cake, prepare cake mix with eggs, water and oil, if required, according to package instructions. Spread batter evenly in prepared pan. Bake 50 to 60 minutes, following package instructions to test doneness. Cool as indicated on package. Do not cool completely before frosting.

To make frosting, sift powdered sugar into a medium bowl. Heat water or orange juice. Stir enough hot water or hot orange juice into powdered sugar to give a coating consistency. Beat in orange food coloring thoroughly. Spread frosting over top of warm cake.

To decorate cake, arrange candied orange slices, candied cherries and angelica strips on cake while frosting is soft.

Cook's Tip

For a stronger orange flavor, you can add finely grated orange peel to the cake batter.

Index

D - 4.8 4 4 2 3 0 5 4 3 4 2 9